Tomorrow there will be Apricots

an Australian Diplomat in the Arab World

Tomorrow There Will Be Apricots: An Australian Diplomat in the Arab World
© 2022 Bob Bowker.

All rights reserved. No part of this book may be reproduced in any form or by any electronic or mechanical means including information storage and retrieval systems, without permission in writing from the author. The only exception is by a reviewer, who may quote short excerpts in a review.

This is a work of nonfiction. The events and conversations in this book have been set down to the best of the author's ability. Every effort has been made to trace or contact all copyright holders. The publishers will be pleased to make good any omissions or rectify any mistakes brought to their attention at the earliest opportunity.

Printed in Australia
First Printing: October 2022
Images in this book are the copyright of Shawline Publishing Group Pty Ltd
Shawline Publishing Group Pty Ltd
www.shawlinepublishing.com.au

Paperback ISBN 978-1-9228-5042-3
eBook ISBN 978-1-9228-5048-5

 A catalogue record for this work is available from the National Library of Australia

Tomorrow there will be Apricots

an Australian Diplomat in the Arab World

Robert Bowker

*For Jenny, who shared the journey.
And for our children—Karmen, Kim, Sam and Tabitha—
who accepted the challenges of a nomadic lifestyle
and unreasonable parental expectations.*

Tomorrow there will be Apricots:
An Australian Diplomat in the Arab World

بُكرة في المشمش

Meaning something like the English expression 'pigs might fly', the Syrian saying: *bukra fi'l mishmish*[1]—'tomorrow there will be apricots'—gives appropriate weight to the human qualities of the Arab world. It captures an unquenchable, droll optimism which, together with the deep appreciation of culture and hospitality, ranks highly among the virtues that define what it means to be Arab. It also reflects an abiding scepticism toward the pretentions of those in positions of authority.

In short, it captures a distinctive element of Arab culture and society. It is an asset, and a quality, which I believe deserves to be recognised, and applauded.

---

[1] Technically, *'bukra fi al-mishmish'* بُكرة في المشمش

A stylised *tughra*, designed by Hassan al-Zahabi, based on my name and title in Arabic as Australian Ambassador to Syria.

Testimonies

Professor the Hon Gareth Evans AC QC, Australian Foreign Minister 1988-96.

An evocative account by one of Australia's most accomplished diplomats of the highs and lows, rewards and frustrations, delights and stresses of diplomatic life—not least, it seems, in working with their Ministers. But also a deeply thoughtful analysis of the multiple geopolitical challenges the Middle East continues to pose, charting possible ways forward in writing that is often provocative but always stimulating. Two books for the price of one—and both eminently worth the purchase.

Nick Warner AO PSM, former Director of the Office of National Intelligence, Director General of ASIS, Secretary of the Department of Defence, and Australian Ambassador to Iran.

The Middle East matters to Australia, and we have been lucky in recent decades to have a group of exceptional diplomats dedicate their careers to understanding the region. Bob Bowker has been the dean of this group. His important book throws light on the history of our relationship with the Middle East, where we have gone wrong and right, and what we should do now.

Professor the Hon Bob Carr, Australian Foreign Minister 2012-13.

As Foreign Minister I grew to admire the razor-sharp insights of our best diplomats. It was an education and a pleasure to read their cables and savour their briefings. Bob Bowker in his memoirs delivers deep knowledge matched with sound judgement not least in his appraisal of the Arab world and, among other things, its relationship with Israel and the Israeli rule of the 4.5 million Palestinians in the occupied territories. All our best diplomats should write books like this.

Professor Amin Saikal AM FASSA, Founding Director of the Centre for Arab and Islamic Studies, ANU.

Dr Bowker has combined the skills, experiences and nuances of a very seasoned diplomat and academic analyst to produce a fascinating memoir. More than a story of his successful journey through the minefields of Arab politics and society, it is also a very enriching intellectual analysis of various tensions and conflicts that continue to shape the Arab world. The volume is a must read for not only policy and opinion makers, but also for students of the Middle East.

Emeritus Professor William Maley AM.

It is our good fortune that Dr Robert Bowker has now chosen to write about his experiences working as an Australian ambassador, as a UN official, and as a distinguished academic and author of scholarly publications of notable depth and sophistication. This rich and engaging memoir not only chronicles the adventures of the Bowker family; it offers critical insights into the practice—and value—of expert diplomacy in a complex, fascinating and important part of the world.

Contents

Foreword by John McCarthy AO	xi
Disclaimer and Acknowledgements	xv
Preface	xxi
PART I THE CAREER OF A MIDDLE EAST TRAGIC	1
Chapter 1	
How I came to a career in the Middle East	3
Chapter 2	
Jeddah, Saudi Arabia 1974-76 and Canberra	12
Chapter 3	
Damascus and Beirut, Kuala Lumpur and Canberra	24
Chapter 4	
Jordan 1989-92	44
Chapter 5	
The 1990-91 Gulf War	65
Chapter 6	
The Mid-1990s: The Israel Lobby and Policy toward the Arab-Israel Conflict	72
Chapter 7	
1997-98: UNRWA Headquarters Gaza and Jerusalem	94
Chapter 8	
Canberra 1999-2000: the Palestinian Authority, the second Intifada, and the Australian Wheat Board (AWB) Affair	107
Chapter 9	
2001-2004 Centre for Defence and Strategic Studies, and returning to the Australian National University	119
Chapter 10	
Iraq 2003 and its Implications for Australia	122

Chapter 11
2005-2008: Cairo   129
Chapter 12
The 2006 Cairo Bus Crash and other Consular cases   152
Chapter 13
Under the Hangman's Tree: the George Forbes case   160
Chapter 14
Libya: Touring Tobruk by Moonlight   174
Chapter 15
Life after DFAT; ANU and Centamin   182
PART II REFLECTIONS   189
Chapter 16
Issues   193
Chapter 17
The Israeli-Palestinian Conflict   201
Chapter 18
Syria: When a regime outlasts a country   219
Chapter 19
Egypt: where to from here?   238
Chapter 20
The Arab Outlook: on the bridge of the Titanic, smelling ice   244
Chapter 21
The Arab World and the West   254
Chapter 22
The United States, Iran, Israel and the Persian Gulf:
Re-imagining the Middle East   261
Chapter 23
The Lessons of Menzies and Suez   271
Chapter 24
Australia and the Middle East   281
Chapter 25
Australian Archaeologists in the Middle East   288
Chapter 26
On Turning Away   293
Bibliography   304

Foreword by John McCarthy AO[2]

Bob Bowker has given us two books in one. The first is about his career in the Department of Foreign Affairs as a Middle East specialist. The second is a scholarly analysis of the major issues which beset today's Middle East. But the second flows from the first.

Bob was one of Australia's first Middle East experts, nurtured in the seventies. We have continued to develop good Arabists, but somehow since then the Middle East has never been as fashionable in our foreign service. This is a pity. Perhaps this book will stimulate a revival amongst newcomers to diplomacy of the fascination which gripped Bob and his cohort.

My own professional exposure to the Middle East is limited—21 months in the late seventies in Damascus—also covering Jordan and for some of the time Lebanon—and three months on temporary duty in Baghdad in 1980-81 shortly after beginning of the Iran/Iraq war. This was nothing compared to Bob's experience in the region, but those experiences gave me an idea of his world.

Diplomacy has been made technically easier by the communications revolution which began in the latter part of last century. But arguably it has made it less fun and less challenging. Particularly if you were distant from your capital and the issues were not of burning domestic political prominence, you had to manage things using your own wits. I doubt that Bob relied

---

[2] Former Australian ambassador to Vietnam, Mexico, Thailand, the United States of America, Indonesia, Japan and High Commissioner to India.

overly on his capital's views about what he should say to PLO Chairman Yasser Arafat. Those of us in the Middle East in those days did not worry about being instructed in what to say. You were supposed to know.

Middle East work was also an odd mixture of the rough and the smooth, and Bob was adept at both. Look at what he and his colleagues had to confront in the hideously difficult consular issues surrounding the 2006 Cairo bus crash, and the George Forbes case. Then compare the nature of that work with engaging with sophisticated diplomatic interlocutors in the chancelleries of the Middle East, people of the highest professional calibre dealing with existential issues.

Bob preferred his time in the field to headquarters—as I did. But in policy roles in Canberra he had to deal repeatedly with what is the single most politically contentious ongoing Middle East Issue in Australia—voting in international organizations on Israel/Palestine questions.

Until the mid-1990s, when the Australian Labor Party was in power Australia usually voted alongside the major Europeans and other western countries on human rights issues, Jewish settlements in the Occupied Territories, and the key question of Palestinian self-determination. Coalition governments, at least since 1996, have sided with the United States and two or three small countries in supporting Israeli policies on Palestine. Indeed, we almost copied President Trump's decision to move his embassy to Jerusalem.

Bob was in a key role when in 1996, against his advice, Australia under Prime Minister John Howard moved away from the well-established Australian position explicitly supporting Palestinian self-determination and the right to statehood. The approach Bob advocated better served Australian interests.

The second part of the book, addressing policy issues, is written from an Australian perspective but merits international attention—surveying as it does the profound seismic trends in the Middle East of today.

These days we think of the Middle East somewhat differently to my limited time in the area, or to when Bob started out. In the wake of three Arab-Israeli wars, the western focus was mainly on Israel, its immediate neighbours, and the Palestine question. Saudi Arabia, the Gulf states and even Iraq were seen mostly in terms of their oil and the wealth derived therefrom. But the dynamics of the region have altered since then. Alliances and battle lines have changed.

The book deals succinctly with the big issues associated with those changes. The dilemma of Palestine remains very much extant. But there are other huge questions in the region. These derive from the aftereffects of the Iraq and Afghanistan wars; and competition for influence between Israel, Iran, Saudi Arabia and Turkey, with not only the United States but also Russia—and potentially China—as vital external players.

The 2011 Arab Uprisings reflected ongoing tensions in most Arab states between rulers and the ruled. Traditional forms of authority are being challenged. Governments reliant on oil production face uncertain energy markets; others have concerns about food security. And all this is taking place amidst the unmet aspirations of an Arab generation, both male and female, that is younger, better educated, and more aware of global issues.

Bob comes out of these memoirs and reflections as a humanitarian and essentially as an idealist—most obviously in his approach on Palestinian issues and his frustration at the enormous suffering of the Syrian people. He has profound concerns for where the Arab world could be headed, especially if it fails to capture the energy and potential of its youth. He identifies some modest practical steps Australia could take to further Australia's interests as the region shapes its own future.

But he also demonstrates a strong sense of realism. He sees

little prospect of a two-state solution for Israel/Palestine. Controversially, he advocates Palestinian outreach to Israelis in the hope of achieving a more balanced, equitable and durable political outcome for both sides. Equally he sees no solution to the misery of Syria without the West, with certain caveats, engaging again with the Assad regime.

We in Australia need to know more about Bob's region. Quite apart from our involvement there in two World Wars, our deployments in the Gulf War, Iraq, and Afghanistan are fresh in our minds. We now have significant diasporas from the Middle East in Australia. While there has been growing recognition over the last generation of the gap in our awareness of Asian issues, that recognition has yet to extend to the Middle East. It is a region we ignore at our peril, but often misunderstand.

Bob Bowker has done something worthwhile about that shortcoming.

Disclaimer and Acknowledgements

The views I put forward in this book are mine alone. They do not represent the views of the Australian Government or the Department of Foreign Affairs and Trade.

The ravages of time and, for the most part, my failure to keep a personal diary mean that some details of my career, and events I describe, may no longer be entirely accurate: responsibility for any errors in that respect rests with me alone. Unless otherwise indicated, all images are in the public domain, or belong to me. I have sought to avoid including any information acquired during my career that might be regarded as being of a national security nature.

Although there are several references in this book to individuals who played a part in my career, there were many more such people who I have failed to mention in the detail they deserve.

The personal qualities of integrity and perseverance of my late parents, Winsome and Athol Bowker, and late brother Bill, and my father's quiet, good-humoured scepticism regarding authority figures were fundamental influences shaping my outlook. I also owe a great deal to the dedicated teachers at my country high school, Timboon, who discerned in me some raw material worth developing. It was their commitment, together with the love and support of my parents, that provided me with a basis for tertiary study that set me on a career path I never anticipated.

Arriving in Canberra barely out of my teens, I had the privilege of being mentored by some of the finest diplomats I ever knew.

Ron Walker in Canberra, and subsequently John Holloway, John Rowland and Alf Parsons in Kuala Lumpur were my earliest role models, both as practitioners and as managers. No less valuable was the opportunity to work a few years later as the Personal Assistant to the Secretary of the Department of Foreign Affairs, Nick Parkinson. Other wonderful colleagues and impressive operators included Jim Humphreys, Max Hughes, Ted Pocock, Sandy Hollway, Trevor Wilson, Kim Jones, Gillian Bird and Frances Adamson, later to become Secretary of DFAT, who was a trainee in my Section for a while.

I will always be grateful to the guardian angels who guided me in my early years in the Department, including Penny Wensley, and Throsby Zouch; and those such as Bill Paterson, Bill Farmer, Richard Rowe and Greg Urwin who supported me and offered sage advice during difficult periods in Canberra. My close friends Leo Cruise and Bob Tyson, fellow trainees from the 1971 intake of diplomatic cadets, remained my trusted sounding boards amidst the mixed fortunes of our profession.

I had the pleasure of working with Australian colleagues well-versed in the Middle East—especially David Hennessy, Ross Burns, Ian Biggs, Anthony Bubalo, Mike Smith, Ralph King, Victoria Owen, Neil Hawkins, Nick Warner, John Bright, Peter and Libby Lloyd, Tony Billingsley, Robert Newton, Paul Robilliard, Axel Wabenhorst, Bernard Lynch, Peter Rodgers, Ian Parmeter, Ben Scott and Glenn Miles—and many others as well.

I benefitted both professionally and personally throughout my diplomatic career from the friendship and advice of British colleagues who were serious Arabists. Among many others, these included Patrick Wright (Lord Richmond), Dominic Asquith, Richard Dalton, Vincent Feane, Alan Goulty, Peter Hinchcliffe, Henry Hogger, Christopher Long, Derek Plumbly and Tony Reeve. Among my American friends, Ed Abington,

Roger Harrison, Sam Wyman (for whom our son Sam is named) and David Arnold were outstanding colleagues.

Among other counterparts, my Irish colleague Richard O'Brien, Klaus Ebermann, and Canadians Michael Bell and Phil McKinnon will always be especially remembered for their insight, humour and friendship in often extraordinary times. I discovered that my friend and colleague in Cairo, Mikhail Bogdanov (at the time of writing, Russian Presidential Envoy to the Middle East) and I had overlapping experience in dealing with the PLO: his contacts, however, were of a somewhat different order to mine.

My academic career at the Australian National University benefitted enormously from the friendship and support of Amin Saikal, James Piscatori, William Maley and Karima Laachir. France Meyer, Leila Kouatly and Huda Tamimi remained stoic in the face of my Arabic; and Carol Laslett helped me navigate the ANU bureaucracy. Though not a scholar of the Middle East, Hugh White has been a constant source of stimulation when thinking about strategic issues.

Further afield I valued warm connections with Jerry Green, Anoush Ehteshami, Emma Murphy, Abdel Moneim Syed Aly, Mark Heller, Joshua Landis, Yezid Sayigh, Nadim Shehadi, Joel Peters, Rex Brynen, Lex Takkenberg, Hisham Hellyer, Shahram Akbarzadeh, Fethi Mansouri, Salim Tamari, Widad Kawar and many other distinguished scholars and analysts.

I was always especially impressed by the insights of the remarkable Fred Halliday into the foreign policy and internal dynamics of the Middle East. I have long admired the insights of my old friend Rami Khouri, as well as the remarkably astute Hafsa Halawa, Shadi Hamid, Aron Lund, Marc Lynch and Hisham Melhem into the challenges facing the region. I am indebted to my good friend Sami el-Raghy, and his family, for their insights, including into the dynamics of the Egyptian business sector.

I gained, personally and professionally, from working with Jim Molan and Raydon Gates at the Australian Defence College; and, at the Centre for Defence and Strategic Studies, Paul Varsanyi and my colleagues on the directing staff, and visiting faculty including Alan Gropman and Rosemary Hollis.

I will always value the insights of dear friends in the region including Tuma Hazou, Bashar and Rafaa Anabtawi, Abdul Karim Kabariti, Wael Karadsheh, Marwan Kassem, Taroub Khoury, Taher Helmy, Hisham Yusuf, Peter Wirth, Amin Badreddin, Tony Loutfi and Hassan al-Zahabi; and the friendship and wisdom generously shared by Arab ambassadors in Canberra including Mohamed Tawfiq, Hassan al-Laithy, Mohamed Khairat, Tammam Sulaiman and Abdullah Dajani. There are of course many others living in the Arab world, especially in Syria, who it might not be prudent, or in their interests, to identify by name.

In addition to the late Peter Harvey, whose support during the Gulf War I recall in this memoir, I deeply appreciated opportunities over the years to interact with the handful of Australians who have worked as journalists covering the region. Linda Mottram, Geraldine Doogue, Matt Brown, Tony Walker and others were always discreet and well-informed interlocutors, whose advice I valued.

Foremost, however, among those who deserve acknowledgement in this memoir is my wife, Jenny Bowker AO. She made her initial contribution to my career at the expense of her own. She often found herself dealing with situations she would never have anticipated when we first met and married. We each have a deep interest in the Middle East: my interest in the region tends to be mainly on its history and politics, and the forces driving social change; as an artist Jenny is more focused on its culture and artisans, both men and women. But we share a deep appreciation of its complexity, as well as its warmth. We value our friendships with the people with whom we have lived and worked there, and we have been keen, together with other members of our family, to promote understanding of the region to our respective audiences.

I love and owe her more than words can say.

Canberra ACT and Mollymook NSW
August 2022

Jenny Bowker AO 2018

Preface

Some forty years ago, my wife Jenny was in Souk Hamidiyeh in Damascus, standing beside a stall selling women's underwear. Syrian women dressed in conservative black were inspecting garments featuring lace, feathers, devices that played "Jingle Bells," and canaries in the most improbable places. How was this contrast possible, she asked the stall owner?. "Ah," he replied. "When foreigners look, they only see the mountain. Syrians see the volcano underneath."

That advice resonated with me while I spent 37 years with the Australian Department of Foreign Affairs and Trade (DFAT), serving in five Middle East posts (including two years with the United Nations in 1997-98, based in Gaza and Jerusalem) and two postings in Malaysia following the Islamic politics of its Malay community. My career as a diplomat was followed by a further 12 years as an academic at the Australian National University, and for some of that period, as an intelligence analyst with the Office of National Assessments (ONA). For six years I was also a non-executive director of Centamin, an Australian gold mining company operating mainly in Egypt.

In addition to being a frequent commentator on Middle East issues for the ABC, SBS and other media, I wrote articles, provided expert reader comment on draft manuscripts for the Lowy Institute, and RAND; provided book reviews on Middle East issues for the *Australian Journal of Politics and History*;

and published opinion pieces with Lowy Institute *The Observer*, ASPI *The Strategist*, the Australian Institute of International Affairs *Australian Outlook*, the *Middle East Journal*, and *Inside Story*.

In the first half of this book I have outlined my service in the Middle East in an anecdotal and often light-hearted manner at least partly with a serious purpose in mind. I came to realise, over time, that it was impossible to understand and analyse the Arab world in all its variety, and its complex interaction with external forces, without appreciating its human qualities, cultures, values and mythologies. As a practitioner of diplomacy, seeking to achieve specific outcomes, I needed to understand their impact on the choices made (or not made) within it. I wanted to be a man without a story, free from tribal delusions. I was prepared at times to be judgmental. But my key aspiration was to understand and, where necessary, to explain how reality was seen, not only from my own considered perspective, but also from within the region, by others, and to proceed from there to achieve results.

I make no claims to significant achievement as an Australian official. I did not help to forge new international agreements, or to nurture, even indirectly, peace and security in the Middle East. I was not especially skilled at working in the grey space between policy advice and political decision-making in Canberra: indeed I was mostly frustrated by having the misfortune (or ineptitude) to work in an area where foreign policy advice is forever constrained by the realities of political life. My analytical work and other inputs on Middle East issues in DFAT, and subsequently with ONA and as an academic at the Australian National University, were satisfying to me, at least, but they had little discernible policy impact. Readers would be well-advised to look elsewhere if they wish to find paths to success on policy-related fronts.

Nevertheless, during my career the notion grew among portfolio ministers, within the Department of Foreign Affairs, and in other government agencies that I was closer than most Australians to understanding the main issues facing the Arab and Islamic world. While I was no stranger to controversy, there were also some occasions on which, with the benefit of hard-working and talented colleagues, and a great deal of good fortune, some complex matters of an operational nature in which I played a substantial part turned out reasonably well.

It is mostly upon the lessons of my experiences as an Australian diplomat, both positive and negative, and the insights arising from that experience that this book turns. I have outlined some of my thoughts, after 50 years of working in and on the Arab world, on topics including the Israeli-Palestinian conflict, Syria, Egypt, the Arab outlook, the challenges that face the region and its relations with western countries, lessons from the Suez Crisis and Australian policy toward the Middle East.

Those who would rather cut to the analytical chase are most welcome to pass over the background story, but I hope some reflections on my career, and its lessons, and a few stories that illustrate the challenges it entailed may help others to understand the pathway which led me to my views. And I will be content if my story helps others to appreciate the complexity of policy choices regarding the Middle East, as well as the privilege of representing Australia in it.

PART I

THE CAREER OF A MIDDLE EAST TRAGIC

Chapter 1

How I came to a career in the Middle East

A former Australian Prime Minister, John Howard, labelled himself a cricket tragic. I am the Middle East diplomacy equivalent. Being an Australian diplomat in the Arab world was more than a career: it was an adventure. In many ways, it was my life.

I never intended to develop a speciality in the Arab world and Islam. My primary and secondary education was at Timboon, a small school in country Victoria. Among other subjects I studied French by correspondence, with the generous assistance of a local French-speaking Englishwoman. Matriculating in 1966, with a handful of other students, my marks in French were good, but mostly because of my ability to read and write the language, rather than to speak it. I had decided to study economics and political science at Melbourne University. In those days, Melbourne University required Arts students to study a language unit in their first year. Realising that if I continued with French I would be at a disadvantage among students who could speak the language well already, I decided to take Indonesian, in which tuition would begin from scratch.

It proved to be an inspired choice. Unsure whether I could cope with the statistical bent of first year Economics (although I enjoyed a second year honours unit on Economic History, undertaken in my first year), I settled eventually into an Honours degree in Indonesian and Malayan Studies, and Political Science. The politics and international relations units were stimulating — I was deeply impressed by a series of lectures by David Kemp on the origins of the First World War and the mechanics of the descent to that conflict — but my real passion was for Indonesian. I studied Bahasa Indonesia under the redoubtable Peter Sarumpaet (whose Batak accent remains with me still). I wrote my BA honours thesis on Soekarno, forcing myself to read in Indonesian each of his 17 August Indonesian National Day speeches. I was absorbed by a profoundly complex honours course on Javanese mysticism taught by the charming Pak Slamet. Malayan studies in my final year were taught in *Jawi* script, a Malay version of the Arabic alphabet.

In late 1969, I visited Indonesia for the first time. Recently turned 20 years old, but already reasonably competent in Indonesian, I was immersed in the sights, sounds and humidity of urban Indonesian life, and the smell of *kretek* blended with Honda fumes. It fascinated me. After initially staying with the family of an Indonesian friend in the modest suburb of Rawasari in Jakarta, and then travelling around Java, I enjoyed several weeks living at Kuta Beach in Bali. There were no other westerners staying in Kuta at the time. The lady owner of the *warong* where I rented a room sold fried bananas at the cockfights next door. I sat in on *gamelan* orchestra rehearsals. Despite never having ridden a motorcycle before, I made my first ride in the main street of Denpasar. I continued touring around Bali until crashing into an irrigation ditch and winding up with a leg infection. Returning to Jakarta I picked up a smattering of Jakartinese slang to accompany my increasingly fluent, yet formal, Indonesian.

Later, I took a ride on a small freighter out of Tanjung Priok delivering fuel oil to villages around the coast of Sumatra. The ship's captain's love of inordinately smelly durian fruit—which unfortunately he stored in his enclosed cabin—meant I spent as little time as possible in his company. But from the roof of the ship's bridge, to which I retreated as often as courtesy allowed, I would see in the evenings the Bugis crew members from Sulawesi performing their *maghreb* prayers. The combination of the serenity of those moments of quiet contemplation, the beauty of the surroundings during tropical sunsets, and the sheer pleasure of being in a place where I was a welcome guest left an indelible impression on me. Although I remain entirely secular in my outlook, my ongoing interest in Islam arose at that time.

On 13 January 1971 I joined the Department of External Affairs as a trainee diplomat. I was a barely 21-year-old country boy, with a practical, down-to-earth approach to life and the range of bush mechanic skills that farming requires. I had an irreverent sense of humour and, by that stage, fluent Indonesian. I had never thought much about what I was going to do after graduation from university: the possibility of joining the Australian Public Service had not occurred to me until I was told, as I approached graduation, that if I were to do postgraduate level Indonesian studies, I would have to learn Dutch. Having to learn another European language did not appeal to me.

Sam Dimmick, the Warden of International House at Melbourne University, where I was resident in 1968-69, suggested I consider joining External Affairs. He had a word in my favour with the departmental recruitment officer visiting Melbourne, who Sam knew from his days as Cultural Attache in Jakarta. I duly had a conversation with that person, followed by a discussion (mostly about beef cattle) with a government psychiatrist; and endured a day of group torment in Canberra which was the final selection process.

The shortlisted candidates had to write an essay on an international issue (I don't remember the topic); summarise a newspaper article and perform a couple of other tasks including a language aptitude test. Then we were sat in a circle and told to choose a topic and discuss it. That was probably the most cunning and insightful of all the tests, as it required individuals to make decisions on how to proceed—to lead, or to follow or conclude a discussion? To be witty or serious? To appear to take control of the situation or at least to shape the outcomes? There were no correct answers to any of those questions, of course—what the Department was seeking (primarily) was to evaluate our level of situational awareness, as well as our capacity to arrange and articulate our thoughts. There was also the fabled cocktail party—'a drink with a few senior officers so you can relax after a hard day'. Anyone silly enough to assume that was the purpose of the event and relax was certain to be culled.

When I was offered a job the prospect of a career in diplomacy did not seem all that special, nor do I think I was an outstanding candidate from the Department's perspective. I suspect I made the cut for the trainee intake mostly because my Indonesian language ability appealed to the then Deputy Secretary of the Department of External Affairs, K C O (Mick) Shann, who had just returned from Jakarta.

Aged 21, 1971.

Diplomatic trainee, with my mother Winsome Bowker, Canberra 1971.

The training course we undertook for about four months covered the full range of political, economic and legal subjects of which diplomats need to have at least a working knowledge. When it came to instruction in the art of persuasion, however, there was no formal training provided by the Department.

Instead, in the era before officers typed their own work, the toughest school in diplomacy, I soon discovered, resided in the departmental typing pool. You were required to plead your case on a daily basis for having work done in any given time frame. If it was urgent, you had to be more persuasive still. Status counted for nothing. And, in perhaps the most valuable of insights for my career in the Middle East, I found that politeness, persistence, charm and a bit of good humour worked better than reference to duty statements.

My first posting was in August 1971, as Third Secretary in the Australian High Commission, Kuala Lumpur since, despite my fluent Indonesian, there was no vacant position in Jakarta. Although the Department in those days wisely expected diplomats on their first posting to undertake work across a range of embassy functions, not least because on their next posting they might be required to supervise those functions as a temporary head of mission, consular 'training' prior to my departure was a brief discussion with the legendary head of Consular Section, Barney Kaye. According to Barney, the Consular Instructions were being reprinted (which was an in-house joke—I suspect they did not exist in any coherent form). Barney said, 'You only need to remember three things. These are: Never take possession of a corpse. Never take possession of a mad woman. Use your common sense.' That was it.

Whereas my personal interest in Islam began during my student days in Indonesia, my professional interest in the Islamic world and its political complexities, including the relationship between religion and the state, began in Malaysia.

Because of my language competence I was asked to follow Malay politics, under the excellent tutelage of the First Secretary in charge of the Political Section of the High Commission, John Holloway, and the benevolent gaze of High Commissioners John Rowland and Alf Parsons. Apart from the valuable experience of assisting the Deputy High Commissioner, Duncan Campbell, finalising the Five Power Defence Arrangements between Australia, the United Kingdom, New Zealand, Malaysia and Singapore I spent most of my time reporting on the competition between the main Malay party, UMNO and its conservative Islamist rival, PAS. I made several visits to the East Coast states of Peninsular Malaysia where PAS enjoyed a strong following as well as Kedah and Perlis where it also had some supporters. I was the interpreter for Andrew Peacock when, as Minister for External Territories, he visited the Cocos Islands in September 1972 to discuss its future with its Malay community and John Clunies-Ross, the last of that family claiming title to the islands under a charter granted by Queen Victoria. I did the same during a visit by his successor as minister under Labor, Bill Morrison, in April 1973.

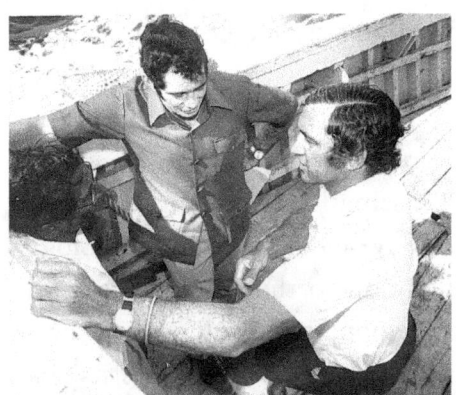

I interpreted for the Minister for External Territories, Andrew Peacock, Cocos Islands, 1972. (Australian Information Service photo)

My career interest in the Arab world was shaped and sustained by an appetite for challenges and, I confess, a youthful taste for adrenalin. From the first time I arrived in the region I realised that compared to the humdrum of other tasks likely to fall to junior diplomats in larger, more important posts—receiving visitors at airports, helping to deliver worthwhile programmes for senior ministers, monitoring media reports, or advocating on minor trade issues and the like—the Middle East was a remarkably interesting, exciting and absorbing place to live and work. There was less tedium, and a great deal more learning to be had, than serving in more glamorous western capitals.

Most importantly, in addition to the pursuit of Australian interests in bilateral dealings with regional governments, for a young man trying to come to grips with the nature of international affairs and diplomacy, the Middle East presented problems and issues of global consequence that I grew to understand were layered in equal measure with contested history and moral ambiguities.

Sustaining my passion for the region, and in some ways an extension of the foregoing comments, was the range of extraordinary people with whom I met or observed first hand. The Middle East seemed to have a disproportionate supply of personalities whose political antics, intellectual acumen, dubious business practices, declamatory styles and capacity for dissembling and guile were quite as extraordinary as the warmth of their friendship. Professional responsibilities aside, I had to be on my guard against allowing fascination, if not empathy, with such personalities, and the collective memories and mythologies that were integral both to them and to the human, historical, and societal character of the region, to interfere with hard-edged analysis of major issues. A dilemma that persists with me to this day is how to pay due heed to the poetic power of mythologies, and memories, real and imagined, without losing critical perspective.

Diplomatic, and later ambassadorial status and frequent travel with Australian ministers, gave me access that few other Australians enjoyed to Arab, Israeli and Iranian leaders and ministers, and political, business and think-tank contacts. The distinguished University of Sydney archaeologist Basil Hennessy as well as many others from that discipline; fellow diplomats, UN officials, spies, bankers and businesspeople; traders in commodities ranging from live sheep to small arms; academics, clergy, artists, comedians, writers, filmmakers and actors all provided perspectives and insights which added to my understanding of, and fascination with, the region.

I was enriched both personally and professionally by the determination of my wife Jenny, an accomplished textile artist and quiltmaker of international standing, not only to support my efforts but to lead a life of her own making beyond the usual circles of embassy contacts. With my gradual accumulation of a reasonable level of mostly colloquial Arabic, Jenny's friends among artisans such as the Tentmakers, the silk spinners and tomb attendants of the City of the Dead in Cairo; the women rug weavers of the Bani Hamida tribe in Jordan and other women in rural Syria, Palestinian embroiderers in Ramallah and the merchants of Damascus enabled me to experience aspects of Arab culture and its many micro societies that deeply impressed and affected me.

What follows is intended to be light-hearted and anecdotal for the most part because after some five decades of working in and on the Middle East I look back at my experiences with few regrets, with fond memories and in some respects, with satisfaction.

There were times when my commitment to being a Middle East specialist was at odds with my prospects for career advancement. But such concerns counted for much less, to me and my family, than the friendships, and the accumulated experiences, both positive and negative, that arose from working in the Arab world over an extended period. From an appreciation of Islamic art to the delights of Syrian cuisine, and much else besides, it has left legacies within my family that I hope will endure.

Chapter 2

Jeddah, Saudi Arabia 1974-76 and Canberra

While in Kuala Lumpur I played cricket for a team of Commonwealth diplomats in a regular competition, and for the Selangor Club Saturday side on the Kuala Lumpur padang. On returning to Canberra in November 1973 I found myself opening the bowling for the Foreign Affairs cricket team in a game against the Canberra press gallery at the Forestry Oval in Yarralumla.

Keeping wicket was Ian Haig, a former Trade Commissioner and an Arabic speaker. One of the more colourful characters one might meet, Ian had just returned from the Middle East sorting out how to avoid Australia being affected by the Organisation of Arab Oil Exporting Countries (OAPEC) embargo on oil exports to western countries supporting Israel in the October 1973 Arab-Israel War.[3] While I was fielding at first slip, Ian said he was going to Jeddah in Saudi Arabia and needed an opener.

---

[3] Ian Haig's solution, with assistance from the Egyptians, who owed him a favour because a couple of years earlier he had arranged for them to purchase Australian wheat on credit while the US was seeking to prevent such deals, was to arrange with the Saudis for Australia not to be on either the Saudi list of those countries to be embargoed, or the list of those with whom oil trade was permitted. He persuaded the Saudis to inform Kuwait orally that the oil trade with Australia could continue. The Kuwaitis, who had already redirected their production destined for Australia, told Qatar it was permissible to supply Australian refineries.

I assumed he meant a post opener. It was only some months later that I realised he meant an opening bowler for the cricket side he planned to create. We became firm friends.

I arrived in Jeddah in January 1974, via a freezing cold Beirut, to help establish the post. It was an unusual place in an unusual time. The city itself was beginning to expand beyond its downtown area, but rather than take a villa in the newer suburbs I chose an apartment overlooking the main square in the city centre. My first impressions were of the cacophony of multiple calls to prayer (*adhan*[4]) made simultaneously by each of the many mosques in the area; Yemeni storekeepers selling all sorts of haberdashery, gold and spices; groups of women shoppers, always veiled, usually accompanied by a male in a spotless white robe (*thobe*); and quiet unpaved alleyways in the oldest area of the city, which somehow remained cool even in the heat and humidity. The wooden window awnings (*mashrabiya*) prevented passers-by from looking into the ancient, multistorey apartment buildings. It was an ideal place from which to get a sense of the pace of the city, its traffic, its events (including public executions) and above all, its people.

Jeddah in 1974 was not an easy place to live as a single male. There were limited entertainment opportunities. I had a few Saudi friends, but in the family-oriented, very private Saudi society invitations to a single male to visit their homes were rare. (One never asked a Saudi 'How is your wife?' but rather, 'How is your family?—to which he would usually reply, 'She is fine, thank you.') Mostly I enjoyed the company of Lebanese, Syrian and Palestinian expatriates, who had a beach house and boat at The Creek, an estuary north of Jeddah. I did a scuba diving course, and spent Fridays diving and water skiing with those friends. My contribution was usually to bring along a cooked chicken, which I would get from a Yemeni-run roadside rotisserie

---

[4] I have used common English transliterations of Arabic terms and names throughout this book. Multiple alternative transliterations are often possible.

along the way. I later realised that when I thought I was asking, in terrible Arabic, for a freshly cooked chicken, I was actually asking for a fresh wife. The stall owner didn't seem to mind.

In the absence of a trade commissioner, I handled the trade work for the first year of the posting as well as my customary political and economic reporting. That included some extraordinary moments, the most memorable of which was my attempt to introduce air freighted chilled lamb into the Saudi market, in the hope of competing with the New Zealand grip on the market for frozen lamb.

I arranged for the despatch to Jeddah of a container of chilled lamb carcasses from Metro Meats at Cootamundra. It was August 1974, and very hot. As the Sudan Air flight with the lamb circled the airport, I asked Ali, the local urger, where was the refrigerated truck he was supposed to organise. He said the driver could not work out how to connect the air brakes. Was there another truck, I asked? He said the only other refrigerated truck in Jeddah was full of fish. I sent Ali off to get any truck he could find.

Meanwhile, the container with the carcasses was unloaded onto the general luggage carousel at the airport—126 carcasses in their stockingette wraps going around the circuit among the suitcases until Ali returned with a truck. Eventually, the lamb was sent off to a cool store. But when I asked a few days later how the meat was going in the market, I was told the chilled meat had been frozen (so the comparative advantage over New Zealand lamb had been lost) because the Ministry of Finance refused to grant the same subsidy for chilled meat that they provided for the frozen product.

Another fond memory was when an initial shipment of Australian live sheep was released onto the wharf at Jeddah port, because the Saudis insisted (unwisely) they did not need fences to control Australian wethers. A happier experience was arranging in 1975 for the first shipment of Australian camels to Saudi Arabia, at the request of then Saudi Crown Prince, later King, Khaled ibn Abdul Aziz who had a camel breeding experimental stud near Riyadh. The camels were provided by the well-named Hump Enterprises from Alice Springs, and they were accompanied by a charming Australian Afghan, Sally (Saleh) Mohamed, who Prince Khaled sent off to perform an umrah as his guest. (The Saudis found the camels were small by their standards, but were good milkers.)

I took every opportunity I could to travel within the Kingdom and around the countries that were covered by the post—the United Arab Emirates, Oman, Kuwait, Bahrain and Qatar. In addition to collecting a diplomatic bag (and loading into it bottles of alcohol for the embassy, wrapped in toilet tissue) I would fly every few months to Beirut, have a pleasant lunch with a glass of wine or two at the St George Hotel (sadly destroyed in the civil war) and fly on that afternoon to Kuwait. I enjoyed visiting Dubai, especially to see the evocative trading dhows up from Zanzibar in East Africa, and from elsewhere in the Persian Gulf; and to see the range of people and races mingled together there. I listened to live music at the Hilton in Abu Dhabi (which was at that time the only major hotel in the city). Oman, its picturesque capital Muscat, and Omanis were delightful. I also visited Cairo in 1976, and went to Tehran, both for familiarisation purposes and, in the latter case, to play cricket against the British embassy.

I was struck by the contrasts everywhere between tradition and modernity. Within a matter of hours I would go from a briefing at the headquarters of Aramco, the oil producer for the Kingdom, with its American-style bungalows and expatriate community, to meeting the fiercely traditional governor of the Eastern Province, Abdul Mohsin bin Abdullah al-Jiluwi, to be served coffee by a young man with a revolver holstered on his hip. There was only one major hotel in Riyadh, the al-Yamama, where one could purchase soft drinks and truly awful cake. The only tourist attraction, of sorts, was the remains of al-Masmak, the fort which featured a spear point in its front door, said to have been embedded there in 1902 by the great Abdulaziz ibn Saud himself, when he returned from Kuwait and overturned a reversal of dynastic fortune at the hands of the rivals of the al-Saud family, the al-Rashid.

In late 1974, I drove the embassy Toyota Landcruiser south from Jeddah as far as the road through the mountains went (Biljurshi) and then went, via tracks, further on to Abha, and down to the coastal plain at Jizan. From there I drove across the border with North Yemen and from village to village (there was no road) to Hodeidah (noting the African/Somali features of the locals—very different to the Yemeni Arabs) and then up to Sanaa. Delayed for a day by a road collapse, I joined other Yemenis (a thoroughly enjoyable bunch) in the local pastime of throwing stones at pillars of rock set up as targets, until the road was made passable once again.

Although invited, I declined to join in the Yemeni passion for *qat* chewing, but was struck by the fact that almost every male Yemeni was enjoying a soporific afternoon with a bulging cheek of the stuff, while sitting around polishing their Kalashnikov machine guns with steel wool. I purchased three matchlock muskets for a few hundred dollars, reflecting on the fact that whereas such smooth bore weapons were inaccurate beyond about 100 feet but created plenty of noise, smoke and excitement to satisfy family honour in disputes, the lethality of the Kalashnikov was going to be fundamentally destructive of the social order. Along with many other factors, that has proved, tragically, to be the case.

I returned to Jeddah via Saada (later the centre of the Houthi rebellion against the central government) crossing back into Saudi Arabia near Najran. The border was marked only by some oil drums, and the customs and immigration offices were near Najran. However, it had rained, and the wadi outside Najran had flooded, cutting off access from the town to the immigration post. After waiting a couple of days, I went to see the local emir, and explained I needed to get back to Jeddah. That night, there was a loud thumping on the side of the Landcruiser. An immigration official had crossed the wadi from Najran through the floodwater. He opened the office with a flourish, and then realised he had forgotten the key to his own desk. He broke open the drawer, stamped the passport, and said 'Welcome to Saudi Arabia.' It was the only time in my posting I ever heard a Saudi say that.

In early April 1975 I drove my Datsun 240z from Jeddah to Beirut via Damascus. I arrived on the day the Lebanese civil war began, entering Beirut's deserted streets. It was an eerie feeling, made worse by the dawning realisation I was not meant to be there. A few days later, I drove north to Turkey, crossing to the west coast and then on a ferry to Chios and Rhodes to catch up with a friend from Beirut. I returned via Syria and Jordan.

The most entertaining period in Jeddah was the visit by the Australian Treasurer, Jim Cairns, and his party following revelations about the Khemlani affair in which the Australian Minister for Minerals and Energy, Rex Connor, had sought funding through an intermediary for the purchase by the Australian Government of foreign-owned mining companies. Cairns was accompanied by his wife; by Junie Morosi, his Chief of Staff and reputedly his mistress; and various senior officials. The Saudis were understandably perplexed at the rather unusual composition of the delegation, but then to cap it all off Morosi's husband, David Ditchburn, arrived unannounced. And he was Jewish—although Saudi Arabia banned the entry of Jews. I assured the Saudis no-one had told us to expect Ditchburn, and that he was, indeed, the husband of Ms Morosi. The Saudis just sighed and said ok. Somehow it all worked.

During 1975 the Saudis were concerned that the United States intended establishing the International Energy Agency (IEA) as a form of oil consumer nation leverage over the Kingdom, and feared (however improbable the notion) that the United States, at the suggestion of Secretary of State Henry Kissinger, was prepared to restrict food supplies to Saudi Arabia as well. I was party to discussions between the Saudis (Abdullah Alireza, Deputy Minister of Petroleum) and Ian Haig about the possibility of Australia being guaranteed oil supply if we were willing to guarantee willingness to supply foodstuffs (i.e. wheat) to the Kingdom. The proposal from the Saudis was reported to Canberra, and went to Cabinet, where the Whitlam government decided it did not wish to pursue the proposal, because of its potential impact on Australia's relations with the United States.

By the end of the posting to Jeddah I had been bitten by the Middle East bug. I enjoyed the fact that it had an excitement about it—assassinations (King Feisal; Bashir Gemayel—and later Yitzhak Rabin); conflict (Lebanon); larger than life characters (mostly British, and some Australian) and issues (especially oil)—that rarely existed in such profusion elsewhere. My Arabic was appallingly, but it worked well enough to get by. I read Wilfred Thesinger, St John Philby, Charles Doughty, Gertrude Bell and other early Arabists and, of course, T.E. Lawrence without understanding the extent to which, in the majority of cases, their views were coloured by an imperial imagination. Observing latter-day British officials, Australians, and others, some of them quite eccentric, who were serving in various capacities in the region, I could see why they became entrenched in the Arab environment.

As I was preparing to leave, I was offered an opportunity to exit the Australian diplomatic service and work for the Sulaiman family enterprise, a major industrial conglomerate based in

Jeddah with close ties to the Saudi royalty (the family patriarch had been the treasurer of Abdul Aziz ibn Saud, once responsible for the chest which literally held the disposable wealth of the Kingdom). In addition to owning the cement factory which was the local landmark of Jeddah the family had a range of commercial interests, including arms dealing. Though tempted, I decided not to take up the offer, although it would probably have been lucrative. A few months after I left, the US citizen who made the offer was killed in a plane crash while pursuing company business in Sweden. I might have been with him.

I returned to Canberra in August 1976, walking to work on a minus 7 degree morning after 40 degrees and almost 100 per cent humidity in Jeddah, and not sure whether to laugh or cry. I was placed for a few months in the Section dealing with the Middle East, working to the gentle and insightful Tonia Shand. It was an enjoyable time, especially in the light of my posting to Jeddah, and by the standards of later postings and placements, not especially demanding.

Its most memorable moment, in a policy sense, came when I prepared a ministerial submission containing an analysis of international moves at that time toward seeking a negotiated solution to the Arab-Israeli conflict. I said, in essence, that in the light of those efforts by the United States, the Soviet Union and the Europeans to find a solution to the conflict, Israel risked being seen as an *apartheid* state, akin to South Africa, if it maintained its uncompromising stance toward the Palestinians. Tonia told me the *apartheid* reference went beyond what advice the political climate could bear, and asked me to put the draft submission away. I did so.

Shifted over to Transport and Resources Section, I spent a few months preparing an analysis of Australia's economic interests in the debate over a New International Economic Order (a popular idea among the developing (G-77) countries at the time).

This was followed by prolonged bureaucratic combat with Trade, Treasury and Prime Minister's Department (PM&C) officials over the question of Australia's policy toward the establishment of the so-called Common Fund—a device supposedly for stabilising commodity prices for developing country exporters.

It was a tough assignment, not least because the Common Fund proposal was both probably unworkable in practice, and most certainly anathema in principle to the free-market philosophy of very senior Treasury officials led by John Stone, and ex-Treasury officials in PM&C. Although I was a relatively junior officer, my Section Head was happy for me to represent the Department in Interdepartmental Committee meetings (IDCs) and in frequent phone discussions of briefing material about the Common Fund and the calls for a 'New International Economic Order' from which it sprang. I would be utterly obdurate, on foreign policy grounds, to the efforts of other departments to reflect their abhorrence of the proposal in formal briefings and cable traffic. I suspect my Treasury colleagues (with whom I got along well at a personal level) were somewhat bemused to find they were dealing with someone from Foreign Affairs who was every bit as uncompromising as themselves.

The issue eventually went to an IDC where I stared down the (ex-Treasury) Deputy Secretary of PM&C, Ed Visbord, so that the issue had to go to Cabinet. There, fortunately, the Prime Minister (Malcolm Fraser) and Foreign Minister (Andrew Peacock) were more concerned with maintaining positive relations with African Commonwealth countries at a forthcoming Commonwealth Heads of Government Meeting in Zambia than they were with outlining the numerous faults in the Common Fund concept. The upshot was that the Foreign Affairs approach to addressing the issue prevailed over Trade, Treasury and PM&C. To general relief, the whole issue of the Common Fund disappeared from the international agenda within a couple of years.

In late 1977, I became the Personal Assistant to the Secretary of the Department, Nick Parkinson. The hours were extraordinary, as the job mostly involved sorting and selecting out the key cables the Secretary needed to see on his arrival each morning, and continuing to do so until he left at night. I was responsible for running the Secretary's office and for liaison with the Minister's office on departmental submissions and correspondence. But it meant I read everything except personnel-related and intelligence material, attended all Division Head meetings and had a unique opportunity to understand how the components of the Departmental machinery worked (and sometimes failed to work). I also could observe Parkinson's deft handling of senior personnel management: he used to say he knew more about superannuation than most people, because it fell to him to persuade ambassadors who were past their professional prime that it was in their best interests to retire. I greatly enjoyed working to him, and to his charming deputy, Peter Henderson.

At the end of 1978, I became Director of Foreign Service Training for the 1979 intake of 26 diplomatic trainees, 12 of whom were from overseas. Mindful of the almost complete absence of formal training in the practices of diplomacy provided to my own intake of recruits in 1971, as well as the mind-numbing content of the majority of lectures we had been given on international law and economics, I built the course mainly around a series of exercises and simulations. With the help of John Gee and Doug Sturkey, whose experience of multilateral diplomacy was much greater than mine, the trainees were presented with tasks and challenges that were not too far removed from the practical dynamics of their working environment.

The course emphasised management as a foreign service skill. It included exercises to foster skills in cross-cultural communication. I urged the trainees to read widely—especially the memoirs of George F. Kennan and others who had encountered, and dealt with situations of policy ambiguity and an absence of clear instructions from capitals. In the case of Kennan, I drew attention to an incident in which, as the officer temporarily in charge of the US embassy in Lisbon during the Second World War, he was instructed to convey a certain message to Portugal; persuaded the Foreign Ministry through dropping hints that it was of such importance and sensitivity that it was appropriate for the Prime Minister to return to Lisbon from 250 miles away, on a weekend, to receive the message; and then, moments before his audience with the Prime Minister, was instructed not to deliver it. Kennan confessed to the Prime Minister what had happened, and proceeded to engage him in a long-overdue discussion of aspects of US-Portuguese relations which left the Prime Minister 'mollified and not wholly displeased, but still very puzzled.'[5]

I also highlighted the importance of diplomats being themselves in representing Australia to others. Of course, it was important to appreciate and observe the established rules and conventions surrounding diplomatic practice. But we also needed to draw upon those aspects of Australian identity and culture that were distinctive (illustrating that advice by recalling I had found my enjoyment of Banjo Paterson poems had been a starting point for conversations and exchanges of poetry about horses with Saudi friends); and to embody and use the reputation of Australians as honest, positive and constructive in dealing with others, as key tools in working toward the identification of solutions to issues.

Creating and delivering an entirely new course was exciting, and engaging with the incoming generation of diplomats was rewarding. Each of the 14 Australian trainees had managed to survive what we referred to in those days as the Dhaka Test: when all manner of tests of intellectual and practical competence and situational awareness had been passed, and the final cut-off had to be made, the selection committee would look at the

---

[5]George F. Kennan, *Memoirs: 1925-1950*, pp. 148-149.

candidates vying for the final place and ask themselves, 'Could you spend a monsoon in Dhaka with this person?'. Selected from several thousand applicants, they were all extraordinarily impressive young Australians with a wide range of talents they could bring to the table, even at that early stage of their careers. As the Duke of Wellington was said to have observed to his staff officers on reviewing his troops before the Battle of Waterloo, 'I don't know what the French think of them; but by God they scare[d] me.'.

Chapter 3

Damascus and Beirut, Kuala Lumpur and Canberra

As my time as Director of Foreign Service Training was ending, I was posted to Damascus. Jenny had entered my life via a meal of Crepes Suzette on a scuba diving weekend in April 1978. She came complete with Karmen and Kim, then aged around 10 and 8, respectively. I was absolutely smitten. We married in October 1978.

In Jordan around 1990, many years after we married, Jenny and I realised there had been a misunderstanding. I had been told by Staffing in late April or early May 1978 that I was likely to be going to Amman to be in permanent charge of the post while the ambassador was resident in Damascus. That proved premature—the Secretary decided he would prefer someone 'with more grey hair' in that position, and so I was sent as the second in charge in Damascus instead. But still under the impression I was heading to Jordan I broke the news to Jenny that I was going to be leaving in a few months. I said I would like her to come with me. Bearing in mind our courtship had only been going for a few weeks she replied, quite sensibly, 'Why don't you wait until you know me properly?' Being hard of hearing, I mis-heard her response, and thought she was saying 'Why don't you ask me properly?' And so I made a more formal proposal of marriage, which Jenny accepted.

With Jenny in Damascus, 1979.

From July 1979 I had a few months of Arabic training in London to rectify some of the linguistic malpractices I had picked up in Jeddah (I had also done some formal Arabic (*fussha*) in Canberra with Professor Tony Johns at the ANU and, as mentioned, I could already read Malay written in Arabic script). We had shipped the family VW Kombivan over from Canberra to London beforehand, so that when there was a free weekend, I could join the rest of the family wherever in the UK they had reached in the van. Then, in September 1979, we drove from London to Damascus.

For Jenny, Karmen and Kim, driving through France has memories of stopping beside streams to enjoy local charcuterie items and peaches or other fruit for lunch. We feasted at a one Michelin star restaurant in Lyon, and when the children couldn't make up their minds about which dessert to choose, the waiters brought them the entire dessert trolley to sample. Kim had her first, perhaps her only meal of snails in France when she said she would only do so if I carried her to the restaurant half mile away. Food and memories are closely related in our family.

We reached Damascus with stomach upsets all round, probably thanks to consuming a gift of unwashed grapes from the police at the Turkish/Syrian border. The morning after arriving, I had to go to Beirut to be in charge of the embassy for several weeks. The ambassador, Neil Truscott, had authorised my counterpart in Beirut, Les Rowe, going on leave—without consulting me. I had to leave Jenny to cope with sick children, in a hotel in an unfamiliar city, without Arabic. The family did not even have anything beyond the contents of the camper van: someone in Canberra had determined our shipment of clothing and household goods should be sent overland from Frankfurt—except that there was no space available on trucks making that journey until six months later.

I was the First Secretary in the Damascus embassy, and second in charge. Neil Truscott was dually accredited (and, most unusually, dually-resident) in Damascus and Beirut. A reserved, unflappable person who I liked greatly (he and his wife Clare were later to become godparents of our youngest daughter, Tabitha), Neil was not particularly active in Syria. He and Clare clearly preferred to spend as much time in Beirut as they could, and Neil was happy leaving me as the Charge d'Affaires *ad interim (a.i.)* in Damascus. With no direction or feedback forthcoming from Canberra, or my ambassador, I was left pretty much to be my own boss.

My work in Damascus was mostly liaison with the Syria-based (mostly independent) members of the Palestine Liberation Organization (PLO) Executive Committee and other senior PLO figures—including Zuhdi Nashashibi, Walid Qamhawi, Khaled Fahoum, Hussam al-Khatib, and Mahmoud Khalidi—to each of whom I enjoyed ongoing access. As I was not the ambassador, the contacts were at a level within the parameters of the official Australian government stance toward the PLO, but neither were they given any public mention, for reasons of domestic political sensitivity and in anticipation of the likely adverse reaction of the Israel lobby. Canberra almost never provided instructions or talking points for such meetings: I routinely affirmed Australia's support for the right of the Palestinians to self-determination, and for a peaceful resolution of the conflict with Israel, as Canberra would have expected; but I was there mainly to run through Palestinian perceptions of the situation as the PLO saw it, and to report back.

I kept my US colleagues and friends, who were precluded by a 1975 US agreement with Israel from dealings with the PLO, informed of the substance of discussions. This was as the PLO officials would have expected (and hence probably explained the ease of my access to them). Our dinner parties with Palestinian guests provided some memorable 'accidental social encounters' for the Americans: on one occasion the wife of a US diplomat, seated beside a PLO official suddenly realised to her horror he was not from Pakistan Airways (PIA) as she had thought: he had joked that if we had asked, he could have arranged for a Qantas flight to land instead of overflying Damascus with our diplomatic pouch on board.

In December 1979, accompanied by Peter Gregg (Charge d'Affaires *a.i.* in Beirut) and Andrew Vincent (an Immigration officer with academic interests posted to Beirut, who arranged the meeting at short notice through a Palestinian academic at the American University of Beirut) I led the first meeting of Australian officials with the Chairman of the PLO, Yasser Arafat. I don't recall whether approval was sought from Canberra beforehand, but given the political sensitivities involved, it should have been.

It was a theatrical performance on the PLO side, which

mostly involved leaving from the Commodore Hotel on multiple late-night drives around Beirut before being ushered through layers of security guards into the meeting. Arafat recited some well-rehearsed lines which were devoid of substance or simply confusing.

The Iranian revolution had just toppled the Shah in Tehran, and Arafat told me this showed 'the Saudi horse has a wooden leg (or 'a leg of clay'—I no longer remember the exact phrase). His office displayed posters extolling Ayatollah Khomeini, which I found faintly amusing, given Arafat and the PLO's secularism. Amidst frantic signalling from Arafat's media manager Mahmoud al-Labadi that the meeting was over, I tried to get some idea of what course Arafat planned to follow in regard to Israel, and how he saw the direction of regional events unfolding. I gleaned nothing of substance in return: clearly, for Arafat and his minders, it was only the fact of the meeting taking place that mattered to their side. Conscious of the domestic political sensitivities involved, I declined an invitation to be photographed with him.

Arafat struck me at the time, and in subsequent encounters, as primarily a politician, and a facile interlocutor, rather than a strategist. His formulaic statements and the dramatic nonsense which preceded the early-morning meeting were aggravating. I had met many more intellectually and personally impressive Palestinians beforehand. Nevertheless, it was interesting to observe a legendary figure at first hand, and to form some impressions, most of which were rather negative, but which were valuable later in my career, both in Canberra and elsewhere, in making professional assessments of Arafat's actions and behaviour.

With no thanks to Arafat, but largely as a result of positive interaction with other Palestinian contacts and friends including Hossam al-Khatib and Zuhdi Nashashibi, I developed substantial sympathy for the Palestinian cause vis-à-vis Israel. I also developed a sceptical view of the 1978 Camp David Accords and subsequent peace treaty between Israel and Egypt, at least so far as how the conclusion of a peace deal between those countries impacted on the prospects for achieving a durable peace with the Palestinians, and with Syria as well. Around Christmas 1980 those conclusions on my part led to a lively exchange of views, by classified cable, with the ambassador in Tel Aviv, David Goss, who was strongly in favour of the Accords and the Israel-Egypt Peace Treaty which followed.

It was a pointless exercise, from a policy perspective, to indulge in cable exchanges with Tel Aviv from Damascus while Canberra was mostly absent, physically and mentally, over Christmas. I also lacked anyone in the embassy with whom I could sound out my views, although I had the good fortune to enjoy a close relationship with the UK ambassador, Patrick Wright, whose judgement I respected and with whom I could discuss my conclusions. The exchange with Tel Aviv helped me to think through and articulate my views and concerns, some of which remained central to my thinking about the region for much of the next two decades.

The bilateral relationship between Australia and Syria was minimal, although I spent a considerable amount of time trying to get Syrian approval for the import of Australian live sheep amidst farcical allegations that the Australian sheep were diseased. One claim advanced by the Syrian side to justify the exclusion of Australian sheep was the threat of brucellosis, a milk-borne disease which was most unlikely to be a threat among shipments of wethers. I later discovered the Syrian agent who had been advising the Australian Meat and Livestock Corporation on this was actually an agent for Bulgarian sheep exporters who were determined of course to preserve their dominant place in the Syrian market.

From time to time I was asked to report on the situation of the

Jewish community in Syria—which in practice meant the remnant of the community in Damascus as only a handful remained in Aleppo. The requests were usually linked to a wider campaign by Israel and its supporters in the United States to enable Jews to emigrate to Israel on the grounds they faced victimisation in Syria. The reality, of course, was complex: Syria did indeed place unfair restrictions on the Jewish community, especially by prohibiting emigration to Israel, although it argued that as the two countries remained technically at war, they were justified in doing so. But I found no evidence in my discussions with them that the Jewish community which remained in Damascus were anxious to depart, except for individuals for whom marriages were proving difficult to arrange within their community. Nor did their non-Jewish counterparts wish them to leave: in fact, their reaction was quite the contrary.

The Jewish area of Damascus adjoined a predominantly Palestinian area in the Old City. So far as security surveillance was concerned, therefore, like the vast majority of ordinary Syrians, both Jews and Palestinians had an ongoing, ubiquitous presence of Syrian security personnel, perhaps slightly more visible than in other parts of the city, but not much different to the norm. So far as I could tell, living conditions in the adjoining areas were also similar. In short, there was no objective difference between the circumstances of families in the Jewish area of the Old City, and those of their Palestinian neighbours, that would justify claims of persecution beyond the levels which applied to the Syrian population at large.

As I was to find elsewhere in the Middle East, there was a very favourable, albeit hazy, image of Australia among many Syrians. There was less connection through migration than with the Lebanese community in Australia, but the impressions were still positive, assisted somewhat surprisingly by a fondness for low-budget Australian television serials. Asked why shows such as

Bellbird were so popular, a Syrian told me that unlike American television dramas which were based around highly artificial scenarios of action and violence, Australian television soaps were mostly focussed on people and personal relationships. Syrians strongly preferred content of that nature, he said, because they could relate to them without difficulty.

The embassy's Syrian staff were absolutely terrific—except for one individual who I sacked because he couldn't type and I needed someone in the public information area who could; and he was running a flower shop from the embassy. His departure opened a can of worms, however. It turned out he was the Syrian secret police (*Mukhabarat*) agent stationed in the mission. Whatever he must have been telling them about our activity was deemed sufficiently important (or entertaining) by the Syrians for a replacement needing to be found immediately. The embassy accountant disappeared for three days and returned, beaten up. A woman staff member was terrorised. Then suddenly, it all stopped—presumably because someone had been found to fit the bill—and life in the embassy returned to normal.

Such incidents aside, I enjoyed dealing with Syrian officials, who were unfailingly polite, sophisticated interlocutors when discussing issues from a Syrian perspective. Devoid of the defensiveness of Saudis and some Egyptians, the Syrians invariably seized the opportunity for some interesting reflections on the regional situation. They were adept at arguing their point of view and highlighting the unacceptability of Israeli occupation of the Golan Heights, without the slightest acknowledgment or recognition on their part of the Syrian contribution to the circumstances under which that occupation had arisen.

While he was still the Opposition leader, Bill Hayden visited Damascus in August 1980, intent among other things upon having a formal discussion with the Syrian government about Syria's human rights record. The Syrian MFA were not going to have a bar of it. Unfortunately for them, however, a press report appeared on the morning of the scheduled meeting with Hayden, mentioning that Australia had discovered a new trove of diamonds in the Kimberley region. Someone in the Presidency must have read the story, and instructed MFA to seek Australian assistance in undertaking similar exploration in the Alawite Mountains along Syria's Mediterranean coast. It was the first thing the Syrian side raised. Hayden seized the moment (several hours, in fact) and insisted there had to be a discussion of human rights before he could possibly discuss diamonds.

The Syrian officials fretted and fumed, but they were stuck between Hayden and the Palace. Eventually, they gave us a lecture about Syria's problems with people displaced by Israel from the Golan Heights and the egregious nature of the Israeli occupation, insisted Syria's own human rights record was impeccable, and for good measure said how disappointed they were with Australia's record in regard to its Aboriginal peoples. We then moved on to Hayden saying he would see what he could do about diamond mining. Both sides could claim a sort of win, but it was almost certainly the first—and quite possibly the last—time the Syrians were cornered into a discussion (however limited) of their human rights approach with a high-level western interlocutor.

Hayden rose still further in my esteem because of his natural empathy with ordinary people he met, a personal quality that stood out when he visited the Commonwealth War Graves Cemetery in Damascus. Cared for by the Mouallem family for many generations, it is a beautiful place, nestled against the irrigated orchards and cactus gardens of the Ghouta, the farmland beside the suburb of Mezzeh where the embassy was located. It has a wonderful display of conifers and Damascus roses surrounding the well-tended graves of Australian soldiers and others, from the First World War and since.

The elderly Mr Mouallem had waited anxiously with Jenny for

several hours for Hayden to arrive, using scissors to fix any minor blemishes in the roses and lawns. Despite a hearing problem, and the need to work with an interpreter, and an official schedule still to be completed, Hayden spent at least 15 minutes with the caretaker discussing and expressing Australia's gratitude for the role he and his family had played in preserving the resting place of family members far from home. It was the sort of effort that both honoured and respected an ordinary Syrian, and it spoke volumes to those Syrians accompanying Hayden about what Australia stood for.

Leader of the Opposition, Bill Hayden, with Sayed Mouallem, Commonwealth War Graves Cemetery, Damascus, 1980.

By 1981, the internal security situation in Syria was deteriorating. A series of attacks, including on Alawite officer cadets in Aleppo and officials elsewhere and vicious retaliation by the regime meant the cycle of violence deepened rapidly. I saw truckloads of bound young men being taken south from Aleppo to an uncertain fate. Visiting Hama, where an Australian was working for UNDP as an advisor to the wool factory, I happened to be standing outside a government or Baath Party office where someone had just been killed. An agitated young soldier emerged, and, seeing me, aimed his Kalashnikov at my chest. I stood absolutely still—anything else would have made the situation worse—but it was a surreal moment.

Almost equally surreal was attending a graduation of an Alawite youth militia squad under the patronage of the brother of the President, the truly awful, shiny-suited thug Rifaat al-Assad who was later responsible for the slaughter of Muslim Brotherhood and other prisoners at Tadmur (Palmyra) prison following an assassination attempt on Hafiz al-Assad. I watched for an hour or so from the dignitaries' tent while the graduates parachuted down nearby, then formed up and jogged around the parade ground, re-assembled and began chanting slogans in support of Assad and the regime—with odd bits of poetry in praise of the president shouted by young women who would burst forward breathlessly from the ranks. Each graduate was presented with a parachute patch and a service pistol. I left eventually via a hole in the rear of the tent.

Another abiding memory of Damascus was the installation of the new patriarch of one of the Eastern Orthodox churches—I think it was the Assyrian Orthodox—in Bab Sharqi, Damascus in the mid-summer of 1980. The new head of the church was installed in the presence of his deceased predecessor, who was strapped in a chair, turning blue. It was hot, and there was a fan blowing him away from us. However, being Damascus in summer, the power kept failing—at which moments an altar boy would rush forward with incense to help address the problem. For all those reasons, colour and noise, and because it was a ceremony dating back perhaps a thousand years or more, it was absolutely riveting.

The children understood that road trips with me were likely to subject them to instruction in the importance of history, especially while wandering around the locations of epic battles.

From the struggle between Ramses II of Egypt and the Hittites at Qadesh in 1274BC, to Saladin's defeat of the Crusader army at the Horns of Hattin in 1187, I tried to bring history to life—and give them some insight into the challenges of leadership. Taking Karmen and Kim, and later Sam and Tabitha to the Aleppo citadel ramparts, I would ask them how they, as emir, would have responded, in 1260, to the news that the Mongols were on their way, after destroying Baghdad in 1258. Negotiate a surrender, pay the Mongols off, and hope they proceed down to Damascus? Fight and risk annihilation? Hold on, and wait for typhoid, or hopefully a dynastic dispute at home to bring an end to the siege?

We loved travelling through the Alawite mountain areas, and visiting small towns such as Dreikish and Safita, seeing silkworm factories, remnants of Roman temples such as Qalaat Sulaiman, Orthodox villages, churches and castles, and noticing blue-eyed children and countless other reminders of the ceaseless passage of people and conquests through Syria's history. The warmth of Syrian hospitality was incredible, even in the smallest towns and villages. Once, arriving at dusk, we found the only hotel in the main square of Dreikish was closed for winter, and the heating was off, but the owners immediately insisted we stay anyway, the owner's mother sharing her bed for the night with Jenny's somewhat startled mother.

We enjoyed wandering through the ruins of Palmyra and Apamea. We experienced the generosity and hospitality of a farmer and his family near Apamea, our children joining his children in tucking into watermelons washed in the microbe-rich irrigation channel beside the crop. Eating lunch beside the ancient water wheels of Hama, drinking glasses of goat milk mixed with honey (which the children were adept at palming off to me) in the fruit orchards surrounding Damascus, and frequent visits to the Krak des Chevaliers and the amazing souqs of Damascus and Aleppo embedded positive memories of Syria and the Middle East in the minds of all our children. We enjoyed shopping trips to the Bekaa Valley in Lebanon when food and other supplies in Damascus ran low, sometimes eating at a delightful trout restaurant in the small town of Anjar with its beautiful arches dating from the Ommayad period.

During a period of relative calm I also took Jenny, Karmen and Kim to Beirut to enable them to see the damage done by war to the city, and thereby to give the children some idea of the horrors people are capable of inflicting on one another. Having taken to heart my dire warnings about watching and doing exactly what the people around her were doing in the event of a security situation arising, Jenny saw customers at a nearby fruit stall bending over and moving away: so she immediately lay down in the gutter to shelter from what was possibly an impending bomb blast, only to find that the customers at the stall were helping its owner to retrieve a bagful of dropped oranges. But not all her experiences were as dramatic. Whenever we would go camping at Easter we were in the habit of distributing chocolate Easter eggs for our children to hunt. When walking through Apamea with the children, munching on a chocolate egg, Jenny found an exquisite piece of Roman glass; but, as she continued walking, she absent-mindedly bit into the glass instead of the egg.

Syrians displayed the personal idiosyncrasies of much of the remainder of the Arab world. They had a dry, sophisticated sense of humour. Damascenes delighted in joking about or poking fun at their fellow citizens, especially those from Homs. There was long-standing mutual rivalry bordering on disdain between Damascenes and people from Aleppo, where historic and commercial connections to Mosul in northern Iraq were once at least as strong as the ties of northern Syria to Damascus. I once enjoyed teasing a dear Damascene friend, Hassan al-Zahabi, that the economic situation in Aleppo, from which I had just returned, seemed to be rather better than in Damascus, despite the fact that being the centre of government should have given businessmen in Damascus a head start. 'Ah', Hassan replied (and when a Syrian begins a sentence with 'Ah', it is usually the prelude to a clever witticism) 'in Damascus we are honest. Ten plus ten equals twenty. But in Haleb (Aleppo) ten plus ten equals fifteen plus five'.

Visiting after the Gulf war, I found Syrians liked to joke about the liberation of Kuwait from its occupation by Iraq, after Hafez al-Assad sent Syrian forces to be part of the Coalition assembled in Saudi Arabia before the battle began. According to the story, Norman Schwarzkopf, the commanding US General, had so many Arab allies he had problems deciding how best to deploy them. Accordingly, he devised an intelligence test. He turned to the Saudi, and asked, 'What's two plus two?' The Saudi replied that he needed a Jordanian or Palestinian to advise him. He asked the same question to an Egyptian, who replied, 'Anything you would like it to be, Sir,' In frustration Schwarzkopf turned to the Syrian and asked him the question. The Syrian replied, 'Are we buying or selling?' Other Arabs, of course, gave as good as they got from the Syrians when it came to jokes at their expense. One well-known quip was that 'Saudi Arabia exports oil; Iraq exports dates; Egypt exports jokes, and Syria exports trouble.'

We remember with great sadness and frustration those good Syrian friends of ours who died or disappeared because of the conflict. But our memories of Damascus are also inseparable from picnics in the orchards of stone fruit and mulberries in the Ghouta and in nearby hills (Zebdani); of *sfiheh* eaten on the run from a bakery window in the Street Called Straight, or less hurriedly from the el-Ezz restaurant in Souk Hamidiyeh overlooking the spectacular Omayyad Mosque; and of *shwarma* from a small café opposite the Hotel Sultan. Alongside its citadel and souks, Aleppo is framed in my memory by eating rotisserie chicken with our artist friends Wendy Sharpe and Bernard Ollis in a tiny local restaurant off the main square. The restaurant in a small hotel beside the Krak des Chevaliers, run by a charming, flamboyantly gay individual, served the best lemon chicken I have ever eaten. Among the northern Syrian culinary contributions to civilisation—the dip made of ground walnut in red spices (*muhammara*) remains a family favourite, alongside several others from Palestine as well. So too was *hummous bi lahmeh*—*hummous* with ground lamb meat, truly a gift from the gods.

With Jenny, Karmen and Kim in Damascus, 1979.

We left Syria in 1981 with enormous affection for the country, its people, history, culture, food and amazing hospitality. I was to return frequently to Syria from Amman from 1989 to 1992, and accompanying Gareth Evans as Foreign Minister and while working with the UN Relief and Works Agency for Palestine Refugees in the Near East (UNRWA). I met Hafez al-Assad when accompanying visitors—his smile was like moonlight on a tombstone—and witnessed his penchant for delivering historical lectures, and his awe-inspiring bladder control. I never met Bashar al-Assad, although I still have friends close to the Assad family.

We continued to make frequent visits, especially from Amman during my posting to Jordan. The economic situation in Syria became markedly worse a decade later, especially as a result of an extended drought, and the corruption associated with the emergence of the younger generation of the Assad family and its grasping maternal cousins, the Makhloufs. We also saw signs of impending problems as rural communities began to move to the fringes of urban areas such as Homs in search of better opportunities for their children and jobs. It was distressing occasionally to witness the exploitation of those highly vulnerable communities, and especially their children, by local tourism operators offering 'entertainment' to Arab visitors from the Gulf.

Back in Canberra, years after our posting, I had to give the Syrians the sad news that Australia had decided to close the embassy in Damascus as a cost-cutting measure. The Syrians simply could not believe that we would be so unsophisticated in our understanding of the region as to close the post at the heart of the Arab world, and to do so merely for financial reasons, rather than over (at a minimum) some monumental dispute between our governments. They were fully justified in their disbelief: the decision was taken within the parameters of a budget negotiation of which those of us who had immediate responsibility for the Middle East were not aware, let alone invited to comment. But, in a remarkable stroke of personal good fortune, the Syrians also told me (in somewhat of a huff) that in future diplomatic accreditation would have to be from a major Arab capital (i.e. not Amman or Beirut); and so it was a great pleasure later to be accredited to Damascus when I was ambassador to Egypt.

From November 1981 until January 1982 I was the Acting

High Commissioner in Apia, Western Samoa. Jenny, Karmen and Kim joined me in December, and we enjoyed the novelty of a very brief exposure to a different climate and values, and pace of work. I supervised and directed an administrative overhaul of the post, notably in the property and security areas, and undertook a review of policy toward Western Samoa in the light of a major request for development assistance. It was an entertaining interlude, not least because of the charm of the Samoans we met, their somewhat carefree attitude to questions of fiscal rectitude, and their amazing capacity to sing spontaneously in three part harmony on any occasion.

I was then placed in charge of Parliamentary liaison in Canberra—which meant mostly being responsible for identifying and assembling at short notice briefing from around the Department to assist my boss, Kim Jones, briefing the Foreign Minister (Tony Street) and his representative in the Senate (John Carrick) on possible parliamentary questions. The job also involved liaison with Members of Parliament planning travel abroad—and often informing them, to their evident disappointment, that they could not expect to be given free use of embassy vehicles for themselves and their wives on their trips unless it was for official purposes. I enjoyed the cut and thrust of Question Time, and the antics of elected members of Parliament in the House of Representatives and the Senate.

Those assignments were followed by my second posting to Kuala Lumpur where, as Counsellor in charge of the Political Section, I was responsible for coordination for the visit of then Prime Minister Malcolm Fraser in August 1982. It was a visit remarkable mainly for an incendiary clash between Fraser and the Malaysian Prime Minister, Dr Mahathir, who chose the occasion of the official dinner he was hosting to launch a blistering attack on Australia. To his great credit Fraser set aside his prepared speech and gave a dignified and effective reply, followed up by a visit to Mahathir the following day to demand an apology for what was a blatant attempt to embarrass Fraser before the Australian media. Mahathir held a press conference to say he had been misunderstood.

I resumed my interest in intra-Malay politics, striking up a friendship with Anwar Ibrahim, then a key figure in the Islamic youth movement, ABIM. I also revisited Aceh and Jakarta to examine the contrasts between the respective Islamist movements of Indonesia and Malaysia. There were several visits to Sungai Golok in Kelantan on the Thai-Malaysian border where an Australian aid project was being undertaken in an area with a lingering communist insurgency, and liaison was necessary with the Malaysian and Thai security authorities. I took a special interest in the pre-Islamic Orang Asli, whose traditional religious practices were regarded with scepticism by the orthodox Malay community.

Sam was six weeks old when we arrived, and Tabitha was born in Kuala Lumpur. Both spoke Cantonese, courtesy of our beloved *amah*, Ah Lin, before they spoke English. We loved family expeditions to Pulau Carey, where there was an Orang Asli village, and a wonderful chilli crab restaurant overlooking the slow-flowing muddy river. Overall, however, compared to the Middle East, working in Malaysia was rather mundane, and I looked forward to getting back to the Arab world.

Our family in Kuala Lumpur, 1984.

Returning to Canberra in 1985, I was assigned to the Economic Relations Branch of the Department which, inevitably, also saw me addressing incidentally the issues arising from the debt owed by Egypt to Australia for the purchase of Australian wheat. Rescheduling of the wheat debt was forced upon Australia by the United States through the Paris Club, a standing committee in Paris of major creditor countries, when, following the 1978 Camp David Accords, the United States agreed that Egyptian debt burdens could be eased.

Then, from May 1987 to September 1988 I was head of the Middle East Section, spending a considerable amount of time acting as the Assistant Secretary, Middle East and Africa Branch. The Iran-Iraq War was drawing to a close, but concern about Iran and its regional role occupied a great deal of my time. Mindful of the possibility that the Iranian Supreme Leader, Ayatollah Khomeini might die on my watch—and assuming that if he had a choice in the matter, he would probably prefer to die at a moment of maximum inconvenience to the West, such as Christmas—I kept a draft Australian statement for the occasion handy. He died in June 1989.

At the request of the Secretary of the Department, Stuart Harris, I visited Tehran to reinforce certain messages of an administrative nature. As it was the era of *perestroika* and *glasnost*, I also went to meet the Russian ambassador at his embassy, which was also the location of a major meeting between Stalin, Roosevelt and Churchill in 1943. I have enormous admiration for the insight, experience and professionalism of Russia's Middle East specialists, and for me it was a valuable discussion. However, its most memorable moment was when, on arrival at the entrance to the embassy chancery, the ambassador flung open my car door, saying, 'Welcome, welcome. Come inside immediately. The food is ready and the women are waiting.'

That night, the Iraqis managed to land some missiles

on downtown Tehran. As the embassy Residence in north Tehran was further up the mountainside overlooking the city, the closest impact points were at least a kilometre away, and although Iranians claimed rocket attacks caused over 10,000 casualties during the course of the war, the Iraqi missiles striking Tehran carried limited amounts of explosive because of the disproportionate amount of rocket fuel required to travel to Tehran from the Iraqi border area. (Iranian rockets launched against Baghdad from within Iranian territory had a much shorter distance to travel, and correspondingly larger payloads).

Nevertheless, an anti-aircraft battery located immediately behind the ambassador's Residence blazed away all night at targets, real or imagined, and the noise was incredible. The ambassador, Mike Landale, and I spent the night in the stairwell of the Residence since in the absence of a cellar or bomb shelter, the stairwell was the most secure place in the building. Unflappable as always, Mike's main response—apart from moving the embassy operations away from downtown—was to delay for a while the implementation of the Department's prohibition on smoking in embassies. I managed to leave Tehran by commercial aircraft the next morning.

Chapter 4

Jordan 1989-92

In late 1988 I accompanied the Foreign Minister, Bill Hayden and the Secretary of DFAT, Stuart Harris around the Middle East, including Yemen, Jordan and Israel. Hayden was the first Australian foreign minister to visit Yemen, despite its strategic location and its value as a long-standing market for Australian wheat. Although somewhat puzzled why I had insisted on the minister making the visit—as the plane came to a halt at Sanaa Airport, Hayden asked me, 'Please remind me; why am I here?'— he thoroughly enjoyed his discussions. He heard the Yemenis give vent to their frustrations with the Saudis, one of the most vexed and complex relationships in the region. Like other visitors, he was impressed by the remarkable historical architecture of Sanaa with its early mosque and its ancient architecture.[6]

The official discussions in Israel and elsewhere were unremarkable, as they usually are, but the first Palestinian intifada had begun in December 1987 and we had a rock bounce off the roof of the car in Gaza, which added a touch of local colour to the visit.

---

[6]Ten years later, the Yemeni ambassador (based in Jakarta) asked me informally whether Yemen (of which Aden was a former British Protectorate) might have Australia's support if it decided to apply for membership of the Commonwealth. I ducked the question, mainly because if Yemen were to succeed with such a bid, I saw it would raise interesting but awkward problems if a future state of Palestine, and other Arab countries which had also once been under the British, were to follow the Yemeni lead.

While in Israel, I had a phone call from my good friend Bob Tyson, then the DFAT officer seconded to the Victorian State Government to head their External Relations unit, saying that although I had not enquired or applied, the job with the Victorians was mine if I wanted it. I was sorely tempted, and therefore in a quandary. I told Stuart Harris I had received the offer. He asked what I would rather do. I said my preference was to be ambassador to Jordan, at which point Stuart went to see Hayden, and returned to tell me I would be given the Jordan appointment. I later learned that my former boss in Economic Division, Jim Humphreys, who was among the travelling party, had also had a quiet word in my favour with Hayden.

Amman was preceded by around four months of intensive colloquial Arabic at the RAF Language School at Beaconsfield, UK. I commuted from London by rail an hour each day against the flow of traffic, while Jenny arranged for our younger children, Sam and Tabitha, to attend kindergarten. Most of the Arabic class members were UK SAS members on their way to Middle East deployments. Perhaps because my colloquial Arabic was reasonable to begin with, I topped the class. I did not mind that the content of the course was colloquial and heavily slanted toward military subjects and usage rather than formal Arabic. It was especially valuable in conversing with Jordanian beduin, most of whom served in the military.

Although the embassy was small (four Australian staff, and around a dozen Jordanians) Amman was a great posting. It was also a challenging one, because of the 1990 Gulf crisis and war, discussed below. We made friends with a wide range of Jordanians, probably more from East Bank than Palestinian backgrounds, although the upper echelons of Amman society were largely Palestinians who had arrived as refugees from 1947 onwards. It was fascinating to immerse myself in Jordanian history; and to understand the complexity of relations between the Hashemite Palace, the East Bankers, and the Palestinians from both the 1948 generation and the generation which arrived in Jordan in 1967 as a result of the Israeli occupation of the West Bank and East Jerusalem.

We found Jordanians, both of East Bank and Palestinian origin, extraordinarily hospitable and welcoming. At the government level, there were some important complementarities in the relationship, especially with regard to sharing Australian expertise in dryland farming, and a long history of cooperation in archaeology. We were on very cordial terms with Crown Prince Hassan, who was especially interested in both those areas, and those around him.

There was an overwhelmingly positive image of Australia and Australians among almost all Jordanians I met, although I found it was wise to avoid too much discussion of recent history: when I called on the newly appointed Minister of Agriculture, who was from the city of Salt, near Amman, I mentioned Australian soldiers had liberated the city from the Turks during World War I. 'Yes,' he said with a gentle smile. The British had held his grandfather prisoner as a result of the final stages of the campaign. Another Jordanian friend, also originally from Salt, recalled how the Australians had arrived, but failed to secure the town on their first attempt. Every family that had welcomed them had had to flee when the Australians pulled back—and when they returned, their houses had been looted of anything of value.

I also found that ordinary Jordanians took no offence at the fact Australia had committed naval forces to the liberation of Kuwait (although they were overwhelmingly sympathetic to Saddam) because they were sure we were doing so at the direction of the United States—something with which, they said unhappily, Jordanians were all too familiar.

Whereas I never heard any Arab other than Palestinians having anything positive to say about Yasser Arafat, the East Bank Jordanians were especially contemptuous of him. A former Prime Minister, Zaid al-Rifai, recounted to me in glee how Arafat had visited the President of Tunisia, Habib Bourguiba, before he made his famous address to the UN General Assembly in 1974. According to al-Rifai, Arafat told Bourguiba he intended to say (in accordance with a speech drafted for him by Edward Said and Mahmoud Darwish) that he was carrying a freedom fighter's gun in one hand, and an olive branch in the other. Bourguiba responded that Arafat should leave his gun at home, and carry two olive branches instead.

Other senior Jordanians claimed Arafat was eating breakfast in Salt, near Amman, during the battle against an Israeli military incursion at Karameh in the Jordan Valley in 1968. They also insisted (with justification) that it was Jordanian artillery support that saved the day for the Palestinians, despite Arafat's efforts to present the outcome as a notable PLO victory. Most of all, they were deeply resentful that the Palestinians subsequently sought to establish a state within a state in Jordan, leading to King Hussein launching the assault against them in September 1970 that eventually saw the PLO displaced to Lebanon, and later still to Tunisia.

The antagonism toward the Palestinians among the beduin, including our friends, was still palpable: it would have been almost impossible for Hussein to retain the loyalty of his East Bank support base, and therefore his throne, if he had not gone to war against the PLO when he did. For the beduin, in addition to the fundamental issue of the Palestinian challenge to Jordanian sovereignty, Arafat and his militias were guilty of offending against the hospitality which the King had extended to them.

Despite Australia being of no significance to Jordan at least so far as the political issues of the region were concerned, I found senior figures in the Palace and in the Jordanian government were credible and engaging interlocutors. They were challenged by pressures of history and collective memories of Arab defeat and dispossession at the hands of Israel; but they were perceptive and talented at surviving, and attracting external support, amidst the turmoil of regional developments.

The Palace trod a fine line in dealings with the United States, the Iraqi regime, Egypt and Saudi Arabia, and they didn't always get it right, especially where Iraq was concerned. Servicing the Iraqi economy and drawing on Iraqi finance for infrastructure development was important to the Jordanian economy, especially for the port at Aqaba and the highways leading to it. But when Saddam allegedly began exploring the potential fault lines within the Hashemite family; and also reportedly started throwing money in the direction of certain people around the monarch, King Hussein drew back from Saddam's embrace.

Jordanian sensitivity to relations with Syria remained strong. In 1970, at the height of the conflict between the Palestinians and Jordan, the Baathist regime in Syria, under its then civilian leadership, attempted a military intervention in support of the Palestinians. The armoured column was beaten back by the Jordanian Air Force (and, according to some versions, lost its way as well) after threatening to capture the northern Jordanian city of Irbid. Hafiz al-Assad deposed the civilian wing of the Baath Party leadership of Syria shortly afterwards. In 1980, while we were in Damascus, tensions between Syria and Jordan surfaced again, as a result of alleged Jordanian assistance to the Muslim Brotherhood which was mobilising, with Iraqi support, against the Syrian government. Assad despatched additional armour to the Jordanian border and positioned it prominently as a warning to Amman. Overnight, to the embarrassment of the Palace, Syrian flags supposedly appeared on the streets of Irbid.

Amman was an opportunity for me to reflect, together with

other posts, on the dilemmas, including for Australian policy, posed by the growth of Islamic fundamentalism across the region.

I was later to refine my appreciation of the phenomenon of political Islam to some extent, and the character of political Islam evolved as well, reflecting the effects of generational change, political circumstances and other factors. However, my analytical starting point, in 1992, was that in practice and even in theory, political Islam as it was emerging from Saudi Arabia and the Gulf under Wahhabi and more recent radical Islamist influence was a backward-looking, bigoted, intolerant, nihilistic movement utilised by some, and believed in by many.

The Jordanian version of the Muslim Brotherhood was somewhat exceptional in that it arose in the West Bank and had traditionally been disposed to accommodate itself to the Hashemites. But elsewhere, including in Gaza, Islamists exploited the institutions of societies which they fundamentally despised and were seeking to change.

The ideological character of the movement, however, was of less concern to me than its potency, at least in relative terms, in the political and social arena. The Islamists were skilled and highly committed political organisers. Their movement was not simply a transient phenomenon brought about by frustration among a younger generation of Muslims over Palestine, or the West, although both subjects provided convenient targets to attack—and political theatre was alive and well in the movement. Nor was the phenomenon merely a reflection of diminishing economic prospects. There was ample evidence in Jordan of determination and capacity among Islamists to infiltrate and manipulate outcomes to their political advantage among government agencies, professional associations and even the education facilities of UNRWA (where I saw Brotherhood people distributing veils to schoolchildren after the opening of an

UNRWA school by Princess Sarvath, the determinedly unveiled wife of Crown Prince Hassan, insisting the hijab was a gift from the Princess). Their potency had everything to do with superior political talent and commitment, which gave the movement a clear head start over their self-serving, faction-ridden opponents.

In my view, the unfortunate reality was that the secular forces in Middle Eastern countries facing the Islamist challenge were more than willing, in most cases, to rely on the approach least likely to help them survive in the long run—repression—while continuing to pursue irrational economic policies. They exhibited a strong aversion to more arduous but sophisticated responses involving sacrifices on their own part—including the establishment of credible grassroots political organizations motivated, and equipped, to engage the Islamicists in direct debate and struggle for genuine popular support. They preferred to believe, in too many cases, that someone (the military? the King?) somehow, would save them if a crunch should come; or that economic growth would cause the Islamist problem to disappear. It was, after all, far easier to blame the West for failing to resolve the Palestinian problem, and even to warn western interlocutors of the dangers posed by the Islamic movement, than to tackle it at home.

On the question of how Australia should respond to the phenomenon, I argued it was neither consistent with Australia's concern for raising international standards of human rights, nor in the interests of the governments and societies involved, for Australia to endorse in any way abuses of human rights in the name of suppressing Islamic fundamentalism. Our interest lay in remaining an effective and credible interlocutor on human rights issues. We could only damage that interest by abandoning our consistency. (Years later, my Tunisian colleague in Cairo, who was a former Minister of the Interior, responded to that argument by saying with the hint of a smile that 'sometimes, my friend, there are higher values than consistency.')

I suggested that in responding to appeals for understanding of the problems they faced, we could reasonably ask what steps those governments had taken to develop a genuine secular alternative to the Islamists' undeniable popular appeal. Had they permitted the growth of democratic institutions, including political parties, to give expression to grassroots concerns within a meaningful framework of constitutional guarantees and personal security? Had secular interests been prepared to create the sort of grassroots organizations that could undertake the political activity performed so well by the Islamists, such as organized pre-registration of voters, bussing, scrutineering and so forth; and had they been willing to set aside factional differences to ensure a coherent challenge to their opponents? Had they insisted on recruitment on merit to fill government positions, and acted against those—of any political persuasion— who abused their positions for political purposes?

I also suggested it would also be appropriate to ask whether Arab governments had taken steps to limit the capacity of Islamists to utilise Islamic symbolism to intimidate the uncommitted, for example by imposing bans on veils and headscarves in public institutions, schools and government offices? In Tunisia, the government had forced people to choose between such symbolism and more material benefits such as job security and education— and the result had been the virtual disappearance of one of the most potent political weapons at the Islamists' disposal, and a great deal of popular relief, at the time, for secular Tunisians from the Islamists' brow-beating tactics. And finally, one could ask whether governments had been willing, despite the political costs in the short term, to adopt the economic adjustment programmes on which their capacity to meet popular aspirations might ultimately depend?

If the answers to those questions were negative, as I believed in most instances would be the case, it would seem those governments had settled in practice for repression as their policy approach, or had no policy at all. Sympathy for their predicament would seem misplaced.

We loved learning about the archaeology of Jordan, especially the Australian dig at Pella in the northern Jordan Valley and the convivial and impressive Australians working there, who always made the whole family welcome. Good friends of ours were also excavating and reconstructing the Roman hippodrome at Jerash. We took great delight in exploring Petra and the surrounding areas. Our main recreation however was camping in the northern part of Wadi Rum in the south of Jordan, exploring sites of flint scatters from the Neolithic period, seeing ancient Safaitic and other inscriptions and getting to know the beduin from that area—especially my great friend Sheikh Awad al-Zuweideh and his family.

With Sheikh Awad al-Zuweideh and his brother Abu Yusuf (rear) at Duweiseh, Wadi Rum, 1992.

Sheikh Awad and his brother Abu Yusuf, the imam of the local mosque at Duweiseh, near Diseh in Wadi Rum were wonderful people: hospitable, irreverent, and delighting in smuggling across the Saudi border both for income and as a pastime. Awad's father had been an extra during the filming of *Lawrence of Arabia* and Awad would take us to locations which were easily recognised when viewing the movie—including the sand dune on which Peter O'Toole was filmed trying on Arab dress. Naturally the children proceeded to roll down it. Awad was also a guide to some of the remarkable, enigmatic rock art of the area.

In all the years I knew him, including long after my time as ambassador, Awad never asked me for a favour. All I could do was provide, through a fund established by Princess Basma bint Talal, some funding through my ambassadorial Discretionary Aid Program for a community hall facility that was built at Duweiseh. I was also able, again with the use of discretionary funds, to assist the wonderful Australian nurse Aileen Coleman and her colleagues from the tuberculosis hospital in Mafraq to establish a tuberculosis and eye disease clinic in a disused government rest house at Ras al Naqb, on the heights overlooking Wadi Rum, a facility which would have been of benefit to his community.

It saddened me to see the way Awad's fellow beduin, members of the Howeitat tribal grouping, were denied access to jobs, water and grazing, in areas irrigated by irreplaceable fossil water reserves, by the Rum Agricultural Company, which was owned by the Palestinian al-Masri family. Adding to that insult was the fact that the company received US aid funding. (When I asked why the Jordanian government was willing to see its fossil water used for subsidised agriculture of no benefit to the local community the answer was that al-Masri also had a major investment in irrigated agriculture on the Saudi side of the same aquifer, so Jordan was simply going to extract whatever it could from the Jordanian side!).

As I became reasonably familiar with the tribal structure and frictions of East Bank Jordan, Jenny and I had the pleasure of travelling for several days among various encampments of the Abu Tayeh faction of the Howeitat in the company of Akef Abu Tayeh, a grandson of Audeh Abu Tayeh, the legendary beduin warrior (portrayed by Anthony Quinn in *Lawrence of Arabia*) who lent his support to the British-backed Arab uprising against the Ottomans during the First World War. We travelled from the wells at al-Bayir (now part of the tribal area of the rival Bani Saqr) 70kms north of al-Jafr and to Wadi Rum, with Akef receiving respect and requests from the various heads of families in the areas he traversed.

With the assistance of Akef and Awad, and as my fluency in Arabic developed, I became more familiar with the nuances of beduin culture. One never approached a tent without giving its head (the *sheikh al-khaimah*) time to prepare, including isolating the women folk: a favourite method was to halt a few hundred metres away and have some target practice with a Beretta submachine gun belonging to Akef's escort, usually Captain Saleh from the Border Guard, until eventually someone went to check if a visit was convenient. When offered, accepting the hospitality of the host honoured him. To decline his offer was therefore to risk being deeply offensive—but given the poverty of the hosts Akef also had to be careful not to allow too much celebration in his honour either. At times Akef's companions would have to physically restrain the host from killing a goat for that purpose.

It was absolutely obligatory to drink beduin coffee, ground and served (often by a son of the host) with a ritual of hospitality that also demonstrated respect for both guest and host. No matters of consequence could be raised until both coffee and tea had been served. Accepting two serves of coffee did honour to the host, but a slight shake of the coffee cup after at least one serve indicated that you had had sufficient. If the guest intended to ask a favour, it was good form to give the host forewarning by holding onto one's tea glass rather than placing it on the ground. At night, as other tribesmen would arrive to take part in a meeting (*majlis*) with Akef, the host would sit beside him, and requests would be quietly conveyed through the host to Akef. Jenny would join the women in a separate part of the tent, learning about everything from daily work (women, not men, put up the huge goat-hair tents) to popular methods of birth control.

The Jordanian national dish, *mansaf*, was always the centrepiece of beduin hospitality. It was usually a young sheep or lamb, and sometimes in poorer families a goat, cooked in a yoghurt (*labneh*) broth made from dried balls of yoghurt (*jameed*) which were soaked and crumbled into a huge saucepan. The cooked meat was served on a bed of rice on a large tray, around which we would sit while the host ensured the choicest pieces of the meat were given to his principal guests. The head of the sheep was usually placed on top of the meat, its whiskers glistening, as the guests washed their hands in a bowl of water and then tucked in, using their hands to roll portions of rice and meat from the part of the tray directly in front of them into balls, and flicking them into their mouth. It was delicious, quite hygienic and very convivial eating.

Eating *mansaf* was more than a dining pleasure. In a society where honour is all-important (the classic qualities of an Arab gentleman were summarised by an Arab poet as 'my sword, my guest and my pen') sharing *mansaf* was also much more important than eating. It was a ritual of honouring both the host who extended the hospitality, and the guests who accepted it. One never over-ate, because others would be looking forward to eating from the same dish after you. When the host offered you the choicest pieces of meat at a *mansaf*—usually the liver, rather than the sheep eyes of popular fiction, although the eyes were indeed regarded as a delicacy— it was good form for you to insist that the most senior person near you should have it instead: the said portion would then be pushed around amid protestations, thanks and blessings until, colder, greasier and somewhat less appetising, it would inevitably wind up again with you. Sometimes, instead of *mansaf*, our friends would serve a sheep or goat slow-cooked in an earth oven, but the rituals were the same.

I learnt a great deal more than most of my diplomatic colleagues about Arab society and its political dynamics. I took note of the views and attitudes of my friends to outsiders, especially urban, westernised, sometimes Christian, Palestinians, whom the beduin detested for their supercilious airs toward themselves. I was struck by their distaste also for the British, including T.E. Lawrence (known as *Abu Flous*—'father of the small change'—because, according to the Howeitat, he never paid enough). Glubb Pasha, the longstanding British commander of the Arab Legion who was dismissed by King Hussein in 1955, may have acquired legendary status among the British populace and other western audiences longing for post-war heroes and romanticising the British role in the region; but according to Akef, he was mostly remembered among the Howeitat for having targeted the Abu Tayeh home at Al-Jafr for artillery practice. There were occasional glimpses into the intricacies of dealings between the palace and the tribes, including scuttlebutt about the role of King Hussein's cousin, Sharif Jameel bin Nasser (son of Nasser bin Jameel) who, like his father before him, ran the Border Guard, reputedly for a considerable profit.

There were problems, as usual, with Australian live sheep exports, to the extent that I insisted on getting prior warning on when sheep shipments were due to take place, in order to be prepared. Often the problems related to the Australian sheep arriving, after weeks at sea, heavier than the weight range specified in sales contracts. Sometimes there was a problem with the incidence of scabby mouth, an ailment that did not affect meat quality. In some instances of rejections, it was unclear whether the Jordanian authorities denying entry to shipments were simply following their own protocols; or were satisfied with the health status of the animals but afraid of negative publicity for taking sheep rejected by another country. Some would-be importers claimed officials were being bribed, sequentially, by rival importers to deny them access to the market, if not seeking to ruin them.

I found the sheep trade to be both frustrating and entertaining. On one occasion, a shipload rejected by Egypt was rejected, in turn, by Jordan. After much debate, the Australian sheep departed for the Gulf. Somewhere off Fujairah in the United Arab Emirates, however, they changed nationality, and returned to Aqaba as Bulgarian. I flagged down a truck on the Amman-Aqaba highway with sheep on board, checked the papers and established who was importing them. Nationality aside, there was no doubt they were still the same sheep.

On another occasion, there was an awkward moment when a shipload of Australian sheep was anchored off Aqaba during a commercial dispute. Unfortunately, they were rather close to the King's summer residence—and the wind blew the very distinctive aroma of sheep manure in his direction. A weekend in Petra went to waste amidst phone calls on the subject.

When a trader got into disputes with the local authorities over such things as the cost of supplying the vessel with water, disaster for the animals sometimes followed. But at most other times the trade operated smoothly and I would see the traders having lunch together, in scenes reminiscent of a mafia movie. A good friend in the trade, albeit of questionable standards of business propriety, told me that he wanted us to form a partnership—for the sake of our sons, of course. But he wanted to me to find a third partner, who was not too bright. Why, I asked? Because, he replied, we needed three sets of books. One for the government; one for the partner, and one for us.

On a more positive note, Australia had a small but highly successful aid program with Jordan, in dryland farming, run by the South Australian Government-owned Sagric, as a one-off outcome of a connection made by Prime Minister Bob Hawke with Crown Prince al-Hassan bin Talal. The project, which drew on the comparable farming conditions in South Australia to those of northern Jordan and much of Syria, achieved excellent uptake among Jordanian farmers. It did so through a combination of low-key outreach by Australian experts working with the Jordanian Cooperative Organization (JCO), inputs from the International Centre for Agricultural Research (ICARDA) in Aleppo, Syria (notably collaboration between ICARDA and the Waite Institute in South Australia in the development of vetch fodder) and field days which enabled Jordanian farmers to see the opportunity to make money by adopting the Australian methods. Its main problem arose at the end of the period of the project, when the JCO pleaded, without success, for Sagric to remain because it was feared that the capacity of the JCO to secure the seeds, fertilisers and other inputs required from the Jordanian government would be lost without expatriates supporting their requests.

Sagric also had a consultancy funded by the Kuwait Fund for Arab Economic Development aimed at mitigating the problem of soil erosion in the Zarqa River Basin, just north of Amman. The Zarqa River Basin project provided fascinating insight into the power structure of Jordanian agriculture, and a reminder of the need to understand the key elements of that power system if any worthwhile results were to be achieved.

It became clear that decisions on land cultivation methods were not made by the farmers (who were tenant farmers), nor by the owners who were urban-dwelling and cared for little more than the satisfaction of being able to offer olives and cheese 'from my farm' to family and guests. The critical actors were ploughing contractors, who had once used donkeys and therefore had no choice but to plough around hills on the contour; but who now used diesel-powered tractors and maximised their returns by ploughing in any direction that was fast, despite its environmental consequences. Sagric had to focus their efforts on encouraging the contractors to change that part of the system.

We liked and admired members of the Hashemite family we came to know. King Hussein was impulsive in some areas, including personal relationships, but he was good-humoured, subtle in his politics and courageous. Zaid al-Rifai, the extraordinary former Prime Minister told me of one occasion when the convoy in which he was travelling with the king was attacked by a group of dissatisfied soldiers. Unable to go forward, monarch and prime minister dived into a roadside ditch while the king's bodyguard returned fire. Then Hussein pulled out a pistol and began firing as well, from a prone position and failing to observe the basic infantry rule of shooting and moving. According to his account (and I do not vouch for its veracity) Zaid jumped on Hussein's back and told him to, 'Put the gun away before you get us all killed.'

With King Hussein bin Talal and former Australian Prime Minister Malcolm Fraser, 1992.

Though not without faults, King Hussein clearly met the desirable criteria for rulers stipulated by the second Caliph, Omar ibn al-Khattab (586-684AD)—that, 'He alone is fit to rule who is mild without weakness and strong without harshness'. Above all else, Hussein, and those closest to him, were decent and courageous people who, despite occasional errors of judgement, were recognised to be deserving of the loyalty of traditionally-minded fellow Jordanians.

Hussein probably failed to go far enough in the directions I mentioned earlier to contain the Islamist threat, and as a result Jordan saw the majority of the younger generation of Palestinians lost to the Islamists, together with a significant number of young East Bank Jordanians. But with the support of Crown Prince Hassan, Hussein did introduce changes that made the kingdom able to maintain its existing political and economic course. A badly-needed IMF programme of structural adjustment was begun (but caused days of rioting in the South when fuel prices were raised before taxi drivers were allowed to increase fares). Free elections were held, the results of which saw a surge in support for the Brotherhood that surprised and alarmed the Palace. Free speech was allowed for a while in the press, although discussion of the monarch remained off limits. A rough-and-ready parliament debated and criticised everything the government did, and elevated tensions between East Bank and Palestinian-origin representatives, but the political showmanship enabled enough anger to be vented off to enable the regime to come through the Gulf War and continue the implementation of IMF reforms.

King Hussein's role in the lead-up to the Iraqi invasion of Kuwait and in the immediate situation he confronted when the invasion took place has been widely criticised, especially by the Saudis and the Egyptians. On the one hand, despite Saddam's arrogance, brutality and stupidity, Iraqi funding was valuable for infrastructure development, and Saddam was popular across Jordanian society for his robust rhetoric concerning Israel and Palestine. On the other hand, the relationship with the Iraqi regime had soured, several months before August 1990, as Hussein grew suspicious of Saddam's domineering behaviour and attitudes toward the kingdom.

Like Arafat, King Hussein miscalculated badly the consequences of responding to the invasion of Kuwait, not by immediately condemning the attack, but by calling instead for a negotiated Arab solution. But the motives and calculations of the two leaders were very different.

Kuwait had long been a supporter of the PLO, and a haven for Palestinians working there. But Arafat was content to ride, unwisely, the waves of Palestinian popular support for Saddam. He also saw public alignment with Saddam as a means of striking back at Assad of Syria for the latter's relentless pressure upon the PLO, and Assad's vindictiveness toward Arafat personally. It was a catastrophic error of political and strategic judgement on Arafat's part, although the isolation of the PLO which followed Saddam's defeat ultimately compelled Arafat to lend support to the Madrid Process launched by the United States in the aftermath of the war.

In contrast to Arafat, and as a measure of the intellectual gap between them, King Hussein genuinely believed that Saddam had triggered a crisis for the Arab world that a military conflagration would deepen, not resolve. Whereas many who were unaware of Hussein's private shift in attitude toward Saddam saw his public stance as a reflection of continuing personal ties to the Iraqi leader, Hussein was in fact risking his reputation, not out of sympathy for Saddam, but with a view to finding a means of resolving the conflict without the open-ended consequences that a US-led military response would bring.

Although one could sympathise with King Hussein's concerns,

after calculating the odds of success, a wiser person might have stood back: with Saddam consolidating his grip on Kuwait, Hussein could neither gain the breathing space in which to seek a political solution, nor if he were to serve as a mediator could he join in the condemnation of Saddam's actions. Moreover, Hussein lacked the influence, and sympathetic understanding in the US Administration of his concerns, that playing such a role successfully would have required.

In the event, despite some initial suggestion that the Saudis might be willing to consider mediation, within a matter of hours, at the urging of the influential Saudi ambassador Bandar bin Sultan, Washington had determined on a military response. Saudi Arabia and the United States embarked on a course which led, ultimately, to the US overthrow of Saddam and the greatest catastrophe the region has seen in modern times. Compared to the consequences which followed, for Iraq, and at later stages for Syria, Lebanon, the Palestinians, Iran and Afghanistan, King Hussein was fortunate not to have paid a higher price than being ostracised in Arab circles for a couple of years.

The fact that, unlike other ambassadors, we gave our beduin guards and their colleagues from nearby residences meals to break their fast during Ramadan was appreciated by the Palace, and mentioned by King Hussein when Jenny and I paid our farewell call on the monarch and Queen Noor. The affection between the monarch and the tribes was evident: watching the beduin guards on ceremonial display when the king was among them was quite riveting. But even on more informal occasions that sense of connection between the Hashemites and the beduin was obvious: our guards would engage in manoeuvres among themselves to be on hand at the Australian Residence, and would ensure their uniforms and equipment were immaculate whenever a member of the royal family was due to visit.

We were especially fond of Crown Prince al-Hassan bin Talal, who gave his brother the king loyal service in supervising the kingdom's economic policies, and representing it with distinction in international political and intellectual circles. (For better or worse, Hussein decided in his final days to back someone with closer ties to the Jordanian armed forces and tribes and, on his deathbed, reinstated his son Abdullah as his designated successor.) Hassan had a dry, wicked sense of humour and a belly laugh which emerged slowly and then resonated around his surroundings. He also loved Jenny's self-saucing chocolate pudding. The king's sister, the delightful Princess Basma, and Jenny were close friends. We also enjoyed the company of the king's affable cousin, Prince Ra'ad bin Zeid and his Swedish-born wife, Princess Magda.

Jenny with Princess Sarvath, wife of Crown Prince Hassan (standing behind Jenny) 1989.

Jenny acquired painting skills under the guidance of our good friend Aziz Ammoura. I drove Sam and Tabbi to school in the mornings, with arithmetic and history quizzes as we went (they came to understand that the three greatest Greeks of all time were Aristotle, Alexander the Great, and the Collingwood player Peter Daicos). Even becoming ill in Amman with suspected typhoid, acquired during a visit to a Palestinian refugee camp with Princess Basma, had its interesting moments, as nurses alternated between praying over me, forgetting to attend to drips, and asking about acquiring visas for Australia. I was deeply touched that beduin friends (from both the Howeitat and Bani Saqr tribes) came to Amman to visit me in hospital as I recovered.

With my good friend Saud, from the Bani Saqr tribe, 1992.

Chapter 5

The 1990-91 Gulf War

We had returned to Australia from Amman on my mid-term leave and consultations when Iraq invaded Kuwait on the 2nd of August 1990. My father had died in March, and I had just said goodbye to my mother, who was ill, at the family farm in Victoria.

I arrived in Canberra on the 2nd of August. The next morning, as news of the invasion filtered through I had a phone call from DFAT telling me to go back immediately to Amman. I grabbed a few clothes and Jenny drove me to the airport, thinking I had to go back to Victoria. It was only on the way to the airport she realised I was going back to Jordan. I left Canberra sitting in the jump seat behind the pilots on an Australian Airlines flight, which linked up with China Airlines and various other carriers to get me back to the embassy.

It was a difficult time. My highest priorities were to provide as much protection as possible for the Australians in Jordan, and those exiting Kuwait and Iraq via Jordan; to ensure the embassy staff were protected; and to do all that could be done to prepare the embassy itself for whatever conflict might occur. Although, as mentioned earlier, there was no obvious animus among

Jordanians toward Australia, the situation could easily change in the event of an invasion of Iraq or large-scale civilian casualties. I fielded media interviews, which usually involved conversations with talkback radio hosts phoning me in the early hours of the morning Amman time, shortly after I had gone to sleep at the end of an 18 hour day. In several cases, roused from deep sleep, I had no idea or memory of what I had just said.

I also had to keep on positive terms with the Australian community and the media teams for whom I was the face of the Australian Government in the Kingdom. For a brief period, I had to suffer the presence of the Australian celebrity journalist Richard Carlton, reporting for *60 Minutes*, and in a flak jacket at that.

We urged Australians in Jordan to leave, in accordance with Australian Government advice. Tourists readily did so (in fact Jordan became even better to visit because the major tourist sites were deserted) but the 400 or so long term Australian residents (many of whom were married to Jordanians) showed little interest in departing. I made the best of it, having regular meetings with Australian community representatives (who we invited to act as wardens for those other Australians they knew) to reinforce the advice from Canberra, and to hear from them about the mood on the streets.

Jordanians were in a high state of anxiety about the possibility Jordan would be the scene of conflict between Israel and Iraq, or hit by missile exchanges, possibly involving chemical weapons. I tended privately to discount such possibilities (the Jordanians were in close contact with the Israelis and according to the British Defence Attaché, nothing untoward was happening on the military front; and Iraqi missiles were likely to be passing over the northern part of Jordan, quite some distance from Amman). Of much greater concern was the unpredictability of the situation on the street if a land war broke out, since there was considerable anger, especially among Palestinians in Jordan, at US threats to force Saddam out of Kuwait.

The welfare of Australians in Iraq was of particular concern, especially as Australian males were being prevented from leaving Baghdad, and Saddam threatened that they might be used as human shields on Iraq's strategic infrastructure. Wives and children were being allowed to leave, but we in Amman had no prior warning of when, or if, they would be arriving on sporadic, unscheduled commercial flights on Iraq Airways. Consequently, my rock-solid Consul, Phillip Kentwell and I had to meet every flight that we heard was on its way from Baghdad, almost always late at night. Richard Branson, to whom I did not warm in the slightest, no doubt seeking publicity for his newly-established Virgin Airlines, had positioned an aircraft at Amman to fly out those distressed and exhausted (mostly British) families who were arriving.

Apart from providing consular assistance, one of my key concerns was to avoid a situation in which Australian wives on arrival would express their frustration with the Iraqi regime—which of course they were perfectly entitled to do—to the likely detriment of efforts to secure the negotiated release of the hostages. With that in mind, and faced with an unyielding and aggressive UK media pack, it was necessary to form a wedge and simply push our way through the ranks of tv cameras and journalists into the comparative safety of embassy vehicles. It was pretty physical at times. But the Australian media teams (whose behaviour throughout was in stark contrast to their absolutely appalling UK tabloid counterparts) were also understandably keen to get footage. It was obvious that reporting any such outbursts and other moments of distress would make for compelling viewing.

The upshot was that I made an agreement with the Australian press, whose most senior figure was the likeable, utterly professional Peter Harvey, whereby I would let the press party know if we believed a flight was going to arrive, and a pool tv team could interview those wives who wished to speak—but only after I had had a chance to brief them (and, of course, to encourage them to be as restrained as they could bear). The Australian media teams respected that agreement, sharing our frustration in trying to establish when flights would arrive, and sometimes having to follow us, fruitlessly, to the military airport instead of the civilian terminal when the planes landed there. The wives chose to say as little as possible, but Peter and his crew eventually managed to get a few minutes of footage.

It was a hectic and challenging period. We began the task of reducing the embassy holdings of classified material by shredding and burning non-essential files. That was a stressful activity, not least for the sense of foreboding the shredding process generated. It was also time-consuming for staff already working very long hours. It became evident that a simpler approach would be to courier files out in diplomatic bags. Jenny was given a Top Secret clearance before she left Canberra, and when she eventually returned to Amman she took several diplomatic bags to the Australian High Commission in Cyprus for onward despatch to Australia. While doing so, she scouted possible places for families being evacuated from posts around the region to stay, settling on a small hotel in Limassol that was filled from December 1990 and for the duration of the conflict by embassy wives and children from Amman, Tel Aviv, Riyadh and elsewhere. With the support and care of the Australian High Commissioner, Eddy Stevens and the Australian Police Contingent (UNFICYP) stationed on the island, the families later watched the drama unfold.

In Canberra, responsibility for managing the response to the crisis in all its dimensions, including administrative, staffing and security arrangements, was taken over by the extraordinarily capable team of Ric Smith and Michael Landale, who was now head of Middle East Branch. The Residence in Amman was reinforced with heavy steel internal doors and other facilities to provide a secure haven for those who were to remain, should the local situation deteriorate. Basement windows were blast proofed and blacked out, and bars were installed on second-floor windows.

Supplies of gas masks, chemical warfare protective suits and antidotes (atropine) were flown in. Staff and wives were shown how to inject themselves if necessary (hit your thigh twice, inject on the third time). The best indicator of poison gas in the air, so we were told, was that birds would fall out of trees in the area. Unfortunately, there are few trees in Amman, and even fewer birds. A radio dish more than a metre wide appeared in our bedroom to give us communications linked to an Atlantic satellite. An internal water cistern was filled and food supplies (if you happen to like dried beans, tinned meat, milk powder and rice) were purchased. Our lovely Filipina cook started singing, 'Rock of Ages, Cleft for Me.'

When the embassy staff was reduced to the barest minimum, Phillip's replacement as Consul (Paul Comfort, another very impressive officer) and I discussed what additional measures we might require in the event the Jordanian guards on the Residence were unable or unwilling to hold back an angry mob. (We had an armoured car with roof-mounted machine gun guarding the embassy, but nothing at our Residence bolt-hole). I decided not to address the issue with Canberra, whose agreement would have been necessary, and who would probably have withdrawn all staff if the risk were deemed to be so high; but Paul and I agreed that, in theory, if the worst came to the worst, in the crowded conditions of the Residence basement, shotguns would be our best option.

It is not often in civilian life one finds oneself having such a discussion.

In September 1990, as part of the annual commemorative service for the Battle of Britain at the Anglican church in Amman, the excellent British ambassador, Tony Reeve, invited me to read the 23rd Psalm (The Lord is my Shepherd etc.). It was a time of considerable tension, and Tony probably assumed the reading would have a reassuring effect. As I proceeded with the reading, however, about the point where I mentioned the Valley of Death, members of the congregation began weeping. As Tony and I lead the way out of the church, he turned to me and said, 'We won't do that again, will we?'

With Jenny and all other dependants shipped out to Cyprus, and almost all expatriates, wives and non-essential staff also having left Amman, the remaining men tended to get together for freezer clearing dinners, and to share information about the situation. I stayed close to the British, not least because their supplies of smoked salmon and other perishable delicacies were much better than mine, and their Defence staff were willing to keep me briefed. I also met some interesting people transiting through, including the legendary Russia spymaster Yevgeny Primakov, and some very fit youngish British men coming in from undisclosed locations along the Iraqi border. I spent a lot of evenings with my neighbour, the charming and astute Egyptian ambassador Mohab Mokbel, who was rather unhappy that his Residence windows were shot out.

When the war to liberate Kuwait began in January, the remaining handful of Australian staff stayed at the Residence for a few days to monitor the street-level reaction. As it was quiet, we returned to the embassy, but kept a low profile and minimised travel around the city. By the end of January, Jenny and other wives in Cyprus were agitating with Canberra to be allowed to return. DFAT asked for my views. I had to advise against permitting the wives to return, at least for the time being, given that the situation was unpredictable and the liberation of

Kuwait could have seen a renewed level of popular anger towards westerners. It was sound advice, but providing it was one of the hardest moments, professionally and personally, of my life.

When Jenny and other wives eventually arrived back in Amman, she found that for several months afterwards her Jordanian friends were hurt and defensive. They were frustrated and disappointed, not only that their western friends had left during the crisis, but also by the dawning realisation that Saddam Hussein never had the means to deliver on his promises. Nor was he genuinely focussed in his ambitions, in any immediate sense, on Israel. Even when we found ourselves on the menu at dinner parties to which we were invited, we were conscious of an unspoken, shared embarrassment, that so many Jordanians had been gullible enough to believe that Saddam would force Israel's hand in regard to the occupation of the West Bank and Gaza.

Chapter 6

The Mid-1990s: The Israel Lobby and Policy toward the Arab-Israel Conflict

The next period of my career was the most difficult from a professional perspective. It affected me deeply at a personal level, and shaped my career direction.

I returned from Amman in 1992 to head the newly-established Post Liaison and Evaluation Section in Executive Branch. My main task was to devise a credible methodology for reviewing and ranking the performance of posts. Among other responsibilities I was also involved in setting up and going on post liaison visits (PLVs) whereby a Deputy Secretary and someone senior from Corporate Management Division would visit those posts which were identified as priority cases for receiving additional support and guidance.

As someone who preferred to be in the field, rather than in Canberra, I had limited interest in corporate policy. I was also somewhat sceptical about the overall value of the post evaluation mechanism. However, I accepted that something along those lines was required if there were to be a reasonably transparent basis for determining performance ratings against agreed targets—with consequences for performance pay for Heads of Mission and other operational issues for the Department. The ranking system I devised and proposed suited the Executive. I also chaired two advisory committees for promotion rounds—always a challenging but fascinating experience—and was involved at the margins of the DFAT recruitment process. On the post liaison visit side, however, I made the mistake of going back to Amman on one of the PLVs. It would have been better in terms of the corporate interest, and for me personally, for someone less directly connected to the post to have gone on the PLV and reached the same unhappy conclusions as I did.

In late 1993 the Secretary of the Department, Michael Costello, said it was probably time for me to 'rebore myself'. He sent me for a year on full salary to the Australian National University (ANU) Centre for Middle East and Central Asian Studies which had just been established by Amin Saikal (and later renamed the Centre for Arab and Islamic Studies).

I wrote an MA thesis on the challenges surrounding the development of cooperative security in the Middle East—later published as *Beyond Peace: the Search for Security in the Middle East* (Lynne Rienner, 1996). The book, which examined the contrasting political and security cultures of the Arab states and Israel, arms control, water and other security concerns, complemented the work that had just been undertaken by the Foreign Minister, Gareth Evans, with Departmental support, on the more general issue of building cooperative security at a global level. It also reflected field work in Israel where I had an enjoyable few days meeting Israeli academics and officials while staying at the Hebrew University of Jerusalem, and discussions in several Arab capitals.

I analysed whether the notion of cooperative security might be applicable outside a United Nations-based context, arguing that if such a concept were to be applied successfully in the Middle East, it would be important to develop supportive mechanisms operating both between states, and within states. Particular attention would need to be paid to the political culture within which security concerns were pursued, including in regard to weapons of mass destruction, water and environment, and the development of civil society in the Arab states.

I also assessed the role which external parties might play in the fostering of cooperative security approaches. And, in briefing Gareth Evans on my research, I suggested there might be scope for Australia to undertake some activity, both in the Middle East and in Australia, to contribute to the consolidation of relations between Israel and its Arab neighbours at both government and popular levels, while also serving Australia's economic and political objectives.

I emphasised that the process of building new security arrangements in the region would require preparedness by leaders both to persuade their audiences to support the political realities of the situation each of them faced, and to extend to those audiences a sense of participation in making historical compromises where those were needed. Changes in the perceptual predispositions of audiences would require time. It would also require a concerted effort by all concerned not to exacerbate the sensitivity of political and other differences.

As the preeminent regional power, Israel would be tempted to seek unilateral solutions to key issues. But as the country whose interests were most affected by the fate of pragmatic Arab leaders, Israel had the strongest interest in responding to the needs of those leaders and in sharing the political and economic burden a cooperative approach to security would require. Israeli approaches to security might continue to take deterrence as their starting point, but they should not end there. It was essential for Israelis to recognise the linkages between cooperative security and notions of equity—including in both the economic and political domains. On the other hand, Arab leaders committed to peace could not hope for Israelis to compromise beyond politically realistic limits, nor could they afford to ignore or misunderstand the political culture within which Israeli decisions were made.

An important conclusion arising from the research was that even if the Israeli-Palestinian part of the Oslo peace process showed little forward movement, Israel's relations with the Arab world were likely to become increasingly regularised. Syria was unlikely to accept normalised relations, but it was conceivable and desirable that the two countries would eventually develop a range of satisfactory dealings on specific issues, including in regard to their defence security. The other Arab states, including (but to a lesser extent) Egypt, showed every indication of willingness to pursue their own agendas with Israel, with little likelihood of much more than lip service to the principle of Arab unity where the Palestinians were concerned. Provided it played its cards carefully, Israel was in a very strong position to promote its interests in regard to Jordan and the Gulf states, Tunisia and Morocco.

On balance, I concluded that the Palestinians looked likely to be the main losers in a gloomy outlook for the Palestinian track of the peace process. We were more likely to see a long, frustrating period of manoeuvring between the two sides, in which the Palestinians would have few cards to play, and in which they would find that Arab states were not prepared to tie their interests to the outcome of the Palestinians' political demands. Even if the Palestinian track sank under the weight of Israeli reactions to terrorist activity, or in response to Israeli provocations in the form of settlement building in and around Jerusalem, and Palestinians rejected the prospect of an inherently unjust and degrading relationship with Israel, Arab leaders and audiences who were not Palestinian might be willing to accept a very different set of priorities and requirements in order to arrive at new relationships with Israel.

Since I was on cordial personal terms with both Helene Teichmann, the Executive Director of the Zionist Federation of Australia and Colin Rubinstein, the Director of the Australia-Israel Jewish Affairs Committee; and enjoyed excellent relations, both personal and professional, with Opher Aviran at the Israeli embassy, I was bemused to find that in November 1994 Helene had expressed strong opposition to my pending appointment as Director of the Middle East and North Africa Section. Although no evidence for making the charge was presented, Helene told the head of Middle East and Africa Branch, Kevin Boreham, that the Zionist Federation of Australia had had 'very unsatisfactory relations' with the Section when I had been head of the Section in the mid-1980s. Somewhat unwisely, she also said she had 'spoken to Allan Gyngell about it' and that Gyngell (then Senior Advisor to Prime Minister Paul Keating) had undertaken to discuss the matter with the Secretary.

The allegation probably arose from the fact that during my earlier appointment (1987-88) I had been prepared to push back against the advice offered by certain Australian officials who I felt were promoting unduly sympathetic interpretations of Israeli policy towards the Palestinians. There may also have been a view—as put to me by the Israeli ambassador in Canberra in the late 1980s—that I was guilty of attributing 'implied moral equivalence' between Israel and the Palestinians (by which the ambassador meant Palestinian terrorists).

Costello brushed the complaint off, adding that Ms Teichmann 'did not get to decide who gets what job in the Department'; and saying, no doubt correctly, that he was sure Allan Gyngell would not want to raise the issue with him. But like the ambassador's diatribe, it was an unfair allegation that offended me both personally and professionally—and it did nothing to lessen my distaste for Israeli behaviour toward Palestinians under occupation.

Notwithstanding the concerns of the Zionist Federation of Australia I returned refreshed to DFAT in March 1995 as Director of Middle East Section. Having had, for the first time, the chance to read in full most of the major documents concerning the Arab-Israeli conflict, and with the benefit of discussions and insights gained from three postings in the Arab world, and the recent field trip to Israel, I felt I was now considerably better informed and attuned to the complexity of Arab-Israel issues, as well as the regional security picture dominated by the issue of dealings with Iran.

After repeated visits to Iran, I brought to my departmental role a view that so far as Australia's interests in Iran were concerned, we had the potential to do well commercially, even if less well than some Australian businesses tended to hope. Australian commercial activities were directed primarily towards infrastructure development opportunities but with limited debt exposure. The record of our dealings with the Iranians in the business arena had been reasonably good.

On the other hand, the likelihood of enlisting Iranian support for our objectives regarding disarmament, nuclear non-proliferation, missile technology, the renewal of the Nuclear Non-Proliferation Treaty, human rights, and the peaceful resolution of the Arab-Israeli conflict seemed remote. But maintaining Iran's international pariah status held out no hope for Australia, or other countries, to develop a worthwhile dialogue with Iran on those issues; nor would it prevent the Iranians pursuing with some success their own objectives in those areas.

We needed to think carefully before taking actions which would damage our commercial interests, in the hope that the overall and long term benefits of self-denial on our part would be worth it. Other factors would of course have to be considered, including our interests in projecting Australia as an effective middle power player, and our alliance considerations, but the bottom line was that some cost to our interests was probably inevitable, whichever way we went.

More positively, with the end of the first *intifada*, the start of what was known as the Madrid Process (whereby, with active diplomatic efforts by the United States, Israel began meeting with the Arab states and, indirectly, with the Palestinians) and then the launch in 1993 of the Oslo Accords, I believed there was growing scope for a modest Australian role in building constructive contact between Israel and the Palestinians. At the government level, Australia's focus was mainly on contributing technical expertise to an Arms Control and Regional Security Working Group, and to a Water Resources Working Group established under the Madrid Process.

Bearing in mind the suggestion I had made to Gareth Evans about the possibility for Australia to contribute to the consolidation of relations between Israel and its Arab neighbours at both government and popular levels I came up with the idea of bringing together Australian, Israeli and Palestinian women artists, using the good offices and facilities of the Australian National University (where Jenny was completing a Bachelor of Fine Arts degree at the time). The concept of the project gradually took shape, and potential problems such as ensuring the artists would have comparable levels of experience and achievement, were worked through. The Israelis were enthusiastic, and the ANU School of Art gave the project strong support. The ANU's wonderful Arthur Boyd facility at Bundanon on the Shoalhaven River, complete with wombats, wallabies and a fabulous art collection was made available as a venue. Palestinian artists based in Jordan were identified and approached.

In the end, however, the project was abandoned, not out of a lack of personal interest on the part of the individual Palestinian artists, but rather because it quickly became evident that they faced isolation and criticism from their professional peers if they were seen to be contributing to a normalisation of relations with Israel without a just resolution beforehand of the Israeli-Palestinian conflict. The Oslo peace process and the 1994 Jordan-Israel peace treaty were not seen among Palestinians as a sufficient basis for proceeding in that direction. Nor could the individuals concerned justify to themselves the likely sacrifices they would have to make, professionally and personally, from participation in a peace-building program.

It was an instructive experience so far as my understanding of the political dynamics and human complexity of peace-building was concerned. But it was also a pointer to a conundrum which Palestinians are yet to address: if the Oslo process was unacceptable to most Palestinians as a basis for pursuit of a Palestinian state, for a range of deeply-held reasons, and if it was also clear that Israel would not disappear, the only pathway to securing a measure of justice for Palestinians would entail active Palestinian outreach to Israelis in the hope of building a foundation of advocacy for Palestinian rights and dignity among Israelis. I continued to believe that, however gratifying and appropriate many Palestinians and their supporters may find the rhetoric of steadfastness, the absence of such outreach worked to the disadvantage of the Palestinian cause.

It would be deeply painful for many Palestinians to look beyond their legitimate sense of historical injustice and the contemporary abuses of their rights under occupation. No Palestinian or Arab leader, then or now, would be willing to advocate firmly for taking such an approach in the absence of progress on key areas of political concern. It was also likely that the Israeli Right would seize upon such signs of 'normalisation' of relations to argue that their activities, which were in fact quite deliberately undermining the possibility of a two-state solution, were both legitimate and sustainable.

Ultimately, however, those political risks could only be countered by Israelis themselves. Doing so effectively would depend upon Palestinians galvanising support, especially beyond the Israeli Left, for a process exposing more Israelis to the possibility of achieving a different and mutually respectful relationship with their Palestinian neighbours.

Working with Gareth Evans

Working while Gareth Evans was Foreign Minister was demanding and exhilarating. It was demanding because Gareth had an inexhaustible desire to master the detail of every issue presented to him. It was not unusual to receive a phone call from him asking me to elaborate on the history of events, or to send him further explanation. One night I had to sketch and fax to him immediately a mud map of the demarcation zones on the Golan Heights to help him understand how the intersection of the borders and zones of separation between Syria, Israel and Jordan operated before and after the 1973 conflict.

With Foreign Minister Gareth Evans, March 1996

Travelling with Gareth, which I did more than most of my colleagues, was character-building, particularly if he was dissatisfied on his first reading of a brief. But his determination to conquer not only the substance but the details of issues was unlike any other minister for whom I worked. It was perhaps no less testing for some of those foreign ministers who Gareth met—on one occasion, on a bus transiting Rome airport on our way to Tunisia, Gareth was studying his brief with his usual intensity when one of his staff suggested he might try to relax a bit, because he almost certainly knew more about the subject matter of the forthcoming meeting than his interlocutor. Gareth looked shocked. 'But surely,' said Gareth, 'he *ought* to know these things.'

As we came to know, and like, each other, I realised the odd explosions from Gareth were likely to be driven by frustration over an issue, or the challenges of grasping its complexity and possible solutions to it. An outburst by Gareth was unfortunate, but not career-threatening. It was never meant to be personal. He liked people, and he especially warmed to those who shared his belief that optimism, courage and persistence were more likely to build a better world than those who struggled to imagine alternatives.

Against that background, Gareth readily supported my arguments that, for all its imperfections, the Oslo Peace Accord and the search for a two-state solution through that mechanism deserved Australia's support. He was mindful of political realities facing the peace process and advocacy regarding it. He accepted there were limits to the politically possible where Australian policy toward Israel and the Palestinians was concerned. However, he was comfortable with the fact that since March 1980 Australia had supported the right of the Palestinian people to self-determination, initially under a Fraser Liberal government, and subsequently under Labor. From October 1982 onward Australia had also supported the right of the Palestinians, if they should so choose, to an independent state alongside Israel. Australia's position on the questions of Palestinian self-determination and the possibility of a Palestinian state reflected a desire to identify, not only with Israel's right to security, but also with what the Labor Government believed to be justified Palestinian aspirations.

My views on Australian policy toward Israel and the Palestinians came under severe pressure with the fall of the Labor government and its replacement by the Liberal Coalition government of Prime Minister John Howard in March 1996.

The issue of Australian policy toward the questions of Palestinian self-determination and the possibility of an independent state was obviously a major professional concern for me for several decades. It would be bound to feature in my memoirs for that reason alone. But the events in 1996 I describe below played a significant part in determining both my sense of what values I stood for, and how far I was prepared to go in defending my views. It was a pivotal point in my career.

I did not challenge the Departmental chain of command without appreciating the risks and likely consequences that were involved from a career perspective if my arguments were accepted. The process was therefore personally stressful. And the result had a major impact on my life, and that of my family, over the decade that followed, including taking leave from DFAT to work for UNRWA in Gaza.

Moreover, the battle that I fought and ultimately lost in 1996 accentuated my frustration with Yasser Arafat over the absence of leadership on his part in the 2000 intifada. I shared the bitterness of those of my friends, including Israelis, who had put a great deal at risk, personally and professionally, to defend the Palestinian position during the Oslo period, only to see Arafat waste those sacrifices that others had made, because he lacked or failed to demonstrate the leadership qualities that the situation demanded.

From a professional perspective I appreciate the need to preserve the confidentiality of discussions between ministers and officials. Accordingly, I have merely outlined the contending arguments within DFAT, which were obviously well documented at the time. Like any other decisions on matters of policy, other than those where national security is involved, that decision-making process and its outcomes some 25 years ago are part of an archival record that I would expect will be open to public access.

The only genuine point of sensitivity in what follows below is a political matter not directly related to dealings between ministers and officials. Howard overruled Downer. That also was documented at the time, and will no doubt appear in due course in the archival record. Moreover, the shouting match described below between Michael Thawley and me at the Zionist Federation of Australia/United Israel Appeal dinner when learning of Howard's instruction was witnessed by those present. It could scarcely be described as a confidential discussion: indeed it was about as public (and inappropriate) as anyone could imagine.

After much reflection, therefore, I have decided that it would be disingenuous and wrong for these memoirs to gloss over what happened in 1996. I hope that decision is the right one, both for the archival record and for such lessons as may be drawn from it; and because I am struggling to see how I can present my memoirs without disclosing what took place.

The Howard Government

In 1996 a newly-appointed head of Middle East and Africa Branch in DFAT was dismissive of the Palestinian case for sovereignty. With an opportunity to brief the incoming government, he argued that since absolute independence for the Palestinians was unlikely to be attainable, and that since the incoming Government's foreign policy platform *A Confident Australia* made a commitment to ensuring Israel's security, but referred only to 'recognition of the need for a just resolution of the question of autonomy for the Palestinian people' and made no mention of 'self-determination' or 'the possibility of their own independent state', a reworking of Australia's public position on those questions was in order.

The Branch Head took the view that Australia had no interest in prescribing the outcome of the negotiations between whatever government was in power in Israel and the Palestinians. Australia was not party to the negotiations, had no special standing with the parties, and could not pre-judge what they might eventually agree. Intermediate steps (confederation, independence in association, autonomy and the like) were possible.

He also argued, reasonably, that there were formidable obstacles to the establishment of any independent Palestinian state in the medium term. Indeed, if Likud were to come to power, an independent Palestinian state would be merely a hypothetical possibility—Australia would instead face a choice between sticking to the principle of upholding the Palestinian right to self-determination; or seeking to define more exactly our position on autonomy versus self-determination. His views were endorsed by the head of the Middle East and Africa Division.

Meanwhile, I continued to insist that the essential concern for Australia was to uphold the Palestinian right to self-determination in principle, even if it was not clear how such an outcome could ultimately be achieved. Backing a two-state approach was a stance that, if political momentum behind the Oslo Accords could be sustained, offered the best prospects for arriving, eventually, at a durable solution.

Our support since 1982 for the right of the Palestinians to an independent state was forward-leaning by western standards. Australia had supported self-determination before the EC had announced in the Venice Declaration of June 1980 that it was also in favour; and it was well ahead of the US position. Our stance enjoyed general Arab support, and it positioned Australia in a way that minimised risks to Australian interests.

Asked if supporting a reference to 'self-determination' rather than statehood would be more intellectually honest, as it was unrealistic to expect a Palestinian state to be established, I argued that while independence might prove to be beyond reach, the reality was that the Palestinians were firmly committed to statehood as the end goal of their political aspirations. It was equally unrealistic to pretend otherwise.

I insisted there would be costs involved in any retreat from Australia's well-established position, including to Australia's reputation among Arab countries for objectivity and balance. The Arab side had an insecure view of the world. Whereas to an outsider it might seem reasonable to argue that Australia was merely taking a position that was consistent with many other western governments, I argued that changes in our language on Palestinian statehood would lead to questioning by both the Arab community and Arab governments as to why we had decided to do so. Arab governments would be concerned about our motives, rather than taking note of the company we were in.

I warned there was a substantial risk of losing votes from Arab states for Australia's Security Council candidacy, a view shared by colleagues in the International Organizations and Legal Division, and by the Australian mission in New York.

There had been no pressure placed on the previous Government to change its policy. The Israelis had not raised objections to the existing wording, although some concerns had been expressed when the position was first presented. And if Israel was not seeking a change in the Australian approach, I felt there was little reason to risk loss of Arab support by changing our position now.

I believed that if the incoming foreign minister, Alexander Downer, wanted a Middle East foreign policy which allowed him to focus on matters of higher priority and importance to the Government he should choose to retain the existing policy position.

I like and greatly respect Alexander Downer. Unswayed by the multilateralist perspectives and inclined to be sceptical of the idealist inclinations of his Labor counterparts, he was conscious, nevertheless, of the importance to Australia's interests of protecting our standing in the multilateral domain. Certainly not someone to whom it was wise to present vague assertions about where history was headed (or not), he was bemused, perceptive, and realistic in his approach to the Middle East.

Above all, Downer was open to hearing policy advice. He clearly enjoyed robust exchanges. He consistently demonstrated a sharp appreciation of the intellectual merit or otherwise of information and arguments on policy issues. And, in contrast to his more conservative colleagues, he understood that, in addition to domestic political considerations, there was a contest of values underlying policy approaches to the key issues confronting the region.

At the end of April, Downer decided the Government should maintain the approach of the previous Government to the question of Palestinian self-determination, and include reference to Australia's support for the right of the Palestinians to their own independent state, if they so wished. At the same time Australia would acknowledge, as did most Western countries, that this question was subject to the permanent status negotiations under the Oslo peace process.

Shortly afterwards, I was asked to prepare a speech for Downer to deliver to the Zionist Federation of Australia/United Israel Appeal Biennial Conference taking place in Melbourne in early July 1996. It was to be the first explicit statement of the Howard Government's position on Middle East matters. Given the setting, it was intended inevitably to provide comfort to the pro-Israel audience, in addition to outlining policy toward the Arab-Israel conflict.

I was not particularly happy with the speech I drafted, but it captured the policy content decided by Downer, including a reaffirmation of Australia's support for a two-state solution, and it was approved by him. As a matter of routine on all matters regarding Israel, a copy of the draft speech was sent to the Department of Prime Minister and Cabinet so that it could be cleared, if necessary, with the Prime Minister. Nothing was heard back.

What I had not understood at the time was the extent to which Howard and Downer, albeit in the context of their generally constructive relationship following Howard's succeeding of Downer as leader of the Liberal Party, and subsequently his election as Prime Minister, were at odds over policy toward the Israeli-Palestinian conflict. I was aware that Howard was strongly sympathetic to Israel, both at a personal level and as a matter of principle where he believed Israel was unfairly criticised. That was especially so in the United Nations context, where Howard felt it necessary to support Israel when resolutions were voted upon in the UN General Assembly that he believed were unbalanced or unsubstantiated by evidence, and even if well-intended, were unlikely to achieve progress toward a two-state solution to the conflict.

But Howard was also determined to differentiate his stance as a conservative from prominent figures among the liberal progressive elements of his party, including Downer. Meaningful support for Israel, including standing against the tide of international opinion where Israel was concerned provided a base on which to do so.

With Prime Minister John Howard and Helene Teichmann at the Zionist Federation of Australia/United Israel Appeal dinner, 1 July 1996. Photo credit: United Israel Appeal.

The evening before Downer was to deliver his speech, the Prime Minister was to address the conference dinner. As I entered the banquet hall, Howard's foreign policy advisor (and friend of mine) Michael Thawley came over and said, 'The PM wants to be sure there is nothing in Downer's speech tomorrow that deviates from the Party platform.' It later transpired that Howard had been personally responsible for that part of the Liberal Party platform which referred to Israel—and which, in contrast to the long-term policy position of the previous Australian Government, made no reference to Palestinian statehood as a matter of right.

With the Prime Minister seated only a few metres away, at the major Zionist event of the year, Michael Thawley and I had a stand-up shouting match. I was having trouble hearing him, so I tended to shout to make sure he heard me. I emphasised that the line taken in the Liberal Party platform was not what Downer had endorsed, and intended to speak about the following day. If the approach in the Party platform were to be the Government's position, I said, it would surely cost Australia the campaign to win Arab support for our candidacy for the UN Security Council.

Helene Teichmann of the Zionist Federation of Australia (ZFA) entered the argument, stressing that there was no desire on the part of the ZFA to alter the language that I had cleared in advance with her—not least because of concern that it would be seized upon and misinterpreted within the Jewish community as an effective endorsement of the Likud approach. (By this she was referring to the fact that since Likud leader Menachem Begin's term as Prime Minister, Likud had insisted that Palestinian rights were to autonomy and certain political and social freedoms within Israel, but not to self-determination or statehood).

The public airing of my concerns during the row might have been more entertaining than the Howard speech which followed, but it was hardly appropriate to the occasion. Greg Hunt from Downer's office eventually intervened. Before Downer spoke the following morning, the relevant part of the Downer speech was amended to remove the direct reference to the right of the Palestinians to choose an independent state. It referred instead to statehood as a 'possibility'. Although Australia's support for Palestinian self-determination was reaffirmed, self-determination and the ultimate shape of the Palestinian entity, including the possibility of an independent state, were said to be subject to the final status negotiations between the parties directly involved.

Arab reaction to the retreat from clear endorsement of the Palestinian right to a state was as negative as I predicted. Concerns were expressed that there was a shift in the Australian approach to one which gave primacy to the security of Israel in its Middle East policy.

Although Downer's speech on 2 July had emphasised the importance attached by Australia to the peace process, and in certain respects it sent a strong message that Australia looked to Israel to maintain the key elements of the Oslo process bequeathed to it by the Israeli Labour government, the balance in the speech had failed to register with key Arab interlocutors. The warmth of the Prime Minister's remarks at the dinner on 1 July, as reported in the Jewish media, had reinforced the conclusion that the Government was taking an approach to Israel that was demonstrably more sympathetic than that of its predecessor, and correspondingly less responsive to Arab concerns.

Adding to Arab concern over the Prime Minister's approach and the shift in Australia's stance on statehood in July was the fact that in public comments in April regarding Lebanon, in response to a massacre of Lebanese civilians at Qaana in an Israeli bombardment[7], Australia laid primary emphasis on Israel's security; limited itself to calling for restraint, and avoided criticising Israel's actions or calling for its withdrawal.[8] Howard said that Hezbollah attacks on northern Israel had aimed at wrecking the mutual confidence and trust necessary for a lasting settlement. In private, and in later remarks to the ZFA audience that were published, Downer made it clear that Australia supported UN Security Council Resolution 425 calling for Israel's withdrawal; but realistically saw its implementation in terms of a comprehensive settlement in which Israel's security was assured.

With considerable justification, Arab ambassadors found these comments unbalanced and intended to overstate the extent of

---

[7]More than 100 Lebanese civilians were killed on 18 April 1996 when Israeli forces shelled the headquarters of the Fijian battalion of the UN Interim Force in Lebanon (UNIFIL) where upwards of 800 civilians were sheltering during fighting between Israel and Hezbollah. The mortar fire to which the Israeli shelling responded was from positions several hundred metres from the UN compound. While Israel insisted the bombardment was the result of 'operational mistakes and technical failures', upon investigation, the Military Adviser to the UN Secretary General concluded that the pattern of impacts made it 'unlikely that the shelling of the United Nations compound was the result of technical and/or procedural errors.' Letter from the UN Secretary General to the President of the Security Council, S/96/337 dated 7 May 1996.

---

[8]On 27 April, the Prime Minister had said Australians were appalled by the tragic events in northern Israel and Lebanon; supported the call for a ceasefire "in the wake of the displacement of many thousands of families in both countries and immense human suffering including the terrible loss of life at Qaana" (emphasis added).

material damage and human suffering experienced by Israel, and to understate the impact of Israel's actions on Lebanon. They were seen, in the case of the remarks about Hezbollah, as factually little short of fanciful, and clearly oriented towards a pro-Israel domestic audience. Australian support for UN Security Council Resolution 425 was seen as conditioned by our attachment to it of language we had not previously used about the circumstances in which the Resolution might be applied.

Accordingly, the assurances that I sought to deliver to Arab ambassadors, upon instruction, that Australia's position had not changed, lacked credibility in their eyes. The Arab side was not so much interested in the form of language Australia used. Rather, they saw a change having taken place that was emblematic of a tilt towards Israel. And they were right: Helene Teichmann rang me to say she had been told by Michael Thawley that there was a change in policy under the Howard Government; that he would have no reluctance about saying so; and that so far as the Security Council candidacy was concerned, the Arabs would have to learn to live with it.

The shift in Australia's position was almost certainly a contributing factor when we did indeed lose the contest for a seat on the UN Security Council a few months later.

The debate over Australian policy during the transition to the Howard Government, and the public dispute at the dinner on the 1st of July in particular, were extraordinarily stressful. Although I enjoyed friendly and mutually-respectful relationships with both my Branch Head and the Division Head of the time, I had taken a stand that produced a deadlock within the Department that had to be resolved ultimately by the Foreign Minister.

At considerable professional risk, I had argued, successfully, for Australia to maintain a policy position that I knew was both sound in policy terms and appropriate in terms of the values with which I believed any government would wish Australia to be identified. I had failed, however, to appreciate sufficiently the political dynamics at Ministerial level within the Government, and to establish, accordingly, that the content of the Downer speech was fully consistent, in fact, with the Government's position.

The key lesson, for me at least, was that in the formulation of Middle East policy, including in the Australian context, expert inputs from diplomats, officials and analysts were unlikely to determine policy outcomes. There would always be debates, sometimes generational, between idealists and pragmatists, with some of the protagonists on both sides demonstrating questionable imaginative and moral capacities. Advocacy, and the intellectual and other skills it requires, would be at least as important for officials as analytical excellence. But, where Israel is concerned, even the best-honed presentations of officials and experts had little chance of shaping outcomes unless they happened to correspond, even fortuitously, with US presidential or Australian prime ministerial instincts.

As a public servant I accepted that the Prime Minister would determine policy, which on this issue was a defensible one, at both intellectual and political levels, even though I personally disagreed with it. I proceeded to outline and defend the Government's position to the best of my ability. But I was shattered, to a degree that went beyond mere disappointment, over the ultimate policy outcome.

Four years later, on attending a luncheon given by the Australia-Israel Chamber of Commerce at the same venue, the events of that night came flooding back, and I suffered an attack of post-traumatic stress disorder which needed to be addressed with the assistance of the Departmental Counsellor.

I also understood that my position within the Middle East and Africa Branch was now untenable.

Later in July 1996 I became the Director of Africa Section for a few months, mostly dealing with policy towards a crisis in Zaire. I found the experience interesting and rewarding. It was time, however, to move elsewhere.

Chapter 7

1997-98: UNRWA Headquarters Gaza and Jerusalem

I was sent a copy of an advertisement from the back pages of *The Economist* inviting applications for the position of Director, External Relations and Public Information, of the UN Relief and Works Agency for Palestine Refugees in the Near East—universally referred to by its acronym UNRWA, or simply the Agency. It was what was called a D1 level position—roughly equivalent in status and emoluments to a Branch Head in the Australian Public Service—based in UNRWA Headquarters in Gaza. With strong support from Alexander Downer and former Prime Minister Malcolm Fraser (Chairman of CARE Australia at the time) I was interviewed in Amman, selected for the position ahead of other international contenders, and given leave 'in the interest of the Commonwealth' to accept the job.

The D1 position had been created shortly beforehand, as a result of pressure from the donor countries, to solicit financial support for UNRWA more actively and effectively from the Arab states of the Persian Gulf. Created by the UN General Assembly in 1949, to provide education, health and other services to Palestinian refugees, while the political aspects of the refugee problem and Arab-Israeli conflict were supposed to be addressed elsewhere in the UN system, UNRWA was not a recipient of funding through the regular UN Budget. It relied entirely upon the financial support of governments, and especially the United States, which provided around 60 per cent of the Agency's budget, and other western governments and Japan. Operating in five 'fields' (Gaza, West Bank, Jordan, Syria and Lebanon) UNRWA was the key provider of humanitarian assistance to 5.5 million Palestinian refugees registered with the Agency, filling the needs of those refugees that governments in Syria, Lebanon and Jordan—and the Palestinian Authority in Ramallah—were unable or unwilling to meet.

The political sensitivities surrounding the Agency were immense. There were both political and security concerns, from the Israeli side, especially since UNRWA observers (Refugee Affairs Officers) were key witnesses to the behaviour of both Israelis and Palestinians during the first *intifada* or uprising against the Israeli occupation of the West Bank and Gaza that began in December 1987. There were allegations—usually spurious or unfair—that UNRWA facilities were used by Palestinian groups for weapons storage or transport. Pro-Israel commentators in the United States were fond of decrying the very existence of UNRWA as perpetuating a sense of refugee identity and entitlement that was, in their view, inappropriate.

The refugees, on the other hand, regarded UNRWA as not only essential for humanitarian reasons but also hugely important as a symbol of ongoing UN and international engagement in the Palestinian question, and of western responsibility, in their view, for allowing the creation of Israel and the refugee disaster in the first place. As I later discussed in my book *Palestinian Refugees: Mythology, Identity and the Search for Peace*, refugees saw every recurrent budget crisis of the Agency as yet further evidence of supposed US/Israeli conspiracies to abolish UNRWA, and thereby obliterate their identity and their right to return to homes and property in what is now Israel.

Operating in three Arab countries as well as the West Bank and Gaza, UNRWA was always careful not to present itself as a state within a state—although in some ways its education, health and other functions were exactly that. Acutely sensitive to any suggestion they might be willing to succumb to pressure to absorb the functions provided by UNRWA into their own education, health and (very limited) social welfare systems, none of which matched those of UNRWA, the governments of the region chose to maintain positive relations with the Agency. Moreover, the incomes of UNRWA employees (all but a handful of whom were Palestinian refugees) were a key contribution to economies within the region—although that made the budget crises for the Agency even more highly problematic.

In Gaza, especially, a complex concern for the Agency, arising in part from dealing with donors who in the aftermath of the first intifada rushed to fund major infrastructure projects which UNRWA undertook to deliver, was management of its relationship, on the one hand, with the Palestinian Authority (PA), under Arafat's leadership; and on the other hand, the unwillingness of donor countries to fund the recurrent costs of those projects. It was rarely difficult for the UNRWA Field Offices to secure donor funding for building schools or clinics—with plaques testifying to the largesse of the donor countries—but the salaries of teachers and other running costs were a different matter.

The major hospital built in Gaza with EU funding was a particular problem while I was in Gaza: neither the EU nor the PA had made budget provision for it to function on completion of construction and commissioning, which continued to be delayed while the wrangling went on. In the end, UNRWA told Arafat that unless the PA was willing to meet those costs, UNRWA would manage the hospital and—crucially—select its workforce: unable to countenance the loss of such a major opportunity for patronage politics, Arafat agreed to have the funds found within the PA's budget.

There were some aspects of my experience with UNRWA that I found rewarding, and many that were instructive—especially about working for the United Nations, about Palestinian refugee mythologies, and regarding attitudes of other Arabs toward Palestinians and refugees. Some of those lessons and insights I will discuss later. At a personal level, however, it was a very mixed picture.

The resilience, hospitality and composure of Palestinian refugee friends and colleagues with whom I lived, ate, worked and mixed throughout the time in Gaza deeply moved me. Living there was not easy, although I found Gazans exceptionally friendly, even by Arab standards, and helpful (including when I would manage to get lost, while driving, which was often). I had a heavy travel schedule around the region, and it therefore made more sense to have a bed in a rudimentary converted container and to use a communal bathroom at the UN Beach Club than to rent an apartment. The Beach Club was nowhere near as pleasant as it might sound, but I was only there to eat and sleep after 12-hour days in the office. Most importantly, it enabled me to breakfast each morning with Palestinian colleagues, and to absorb their advice and views of the meaning to them of being a Palestinian refugee—a learning experience which made an indelible impression.

The United Nations Beach Club, Gaza 1998

I absorbed some lessons about dealing with aid donors. As mentioned earlier, few donors were willing to provide funds to cover the recurrent costs of the schools, clinics and other facilities whose construction they were willing to fund. But there was almost universal recognition that UNRWA was providing services that were essential for the refugees, and was using donor project funds in a fully accountable and transparent manner. Accordingly, if a delegation from a donor country asked the Agency if they could visit some of UNRWA's field operations, the Agency made every effort to assist them.

A donor visit itself was a strong indication that further financial support was possible. It was therefore a matter of giving the visitors memories that made them feel good about themselves, and the role of their government, in addressing what they had seen. The approach I would take, which seemed to work rather well, was to ensure that visitors were taken to those parts of Gaza that were in greatest need (all areas were under stress, but some were worse than others). Delegations were taken to UNRWA schools that were double-shifted (almost all of them) and in some cases, triple-shifted. Intensely proud of their work and reluctant to admit to any personal discomfort, it was almost impossible to get UNRWA teachers to explain to delegations how difficult it is to teach primary school children under those conditions, let alone to appreciate the wear and tear of buildings being operated over 16 hours per day. It was sufficient, however, to encourage visiting delegations to draw their own conclusions on that score.

Dwellings that needed refurbishment (known in UNRWA parlance as shelters, since other terminology might suggest a degree of permanency which was not politically acceptable to the refugees themselves) had to be devoid of items such as satellite television dishes that might detract from the imagery required. All visitors had to step over at least one open drain. And, if we were lucky, they would be assailed by an elderly Palestinian lady in traditional dress dismissing their expressions of sympathy and telling them it was funding, not words, that was needed.

I made some wonderful, enduring friendships—Keith Walton, Sigrid Kaag, Richard Cook, Lex Takkenberg, Yvonne Haddad and several others—among the international staff of the Agency. I caught up again with my old friend from Damascus days, Ed Abington, now the US Consul General in Jerusalem, and I was on excellent terms with his British counterpart in Jerusalem, Richard Dalton.

On the other hand, without dwelling here on the subject, I struggled to cope with the incessant and vicious political infighting to which I was subjected by a clique of UN international staff around the UNRWA Commissioner-General, Peter Hansen. It was an experience for which I was quite unprepared, in a world far removed from the mutual respect and collegiality usually enjoyed in the Australian Public Service environment. Because I was not from the UN system but came to the position with ambassadorial experience and donor support, I found myself cast in the role of the unwelcome outsider, foisted on the Agency by donor countries. I was also, to some individuals around Hansen, a potential threat to their influence and status.

I was not comfortable with Hansen's antagonistic response to the donors to the Agency who insisted that the Agency should prioritise its activities to cope with its financial circumstances. (His usual refrain was to say he would await advice from the donors about how they saw the Agency's priorities—advice which never came, but which did not make my task of building the case for additional funding any easier either). Policy was for the Commissioner-General to make, of course. I was content to leave politically-sensitive dealings with the Palestinian Authority to Hansen and his astute Algerian deputy, Dr Abdel Moneim. But as a consequence of trying to explain to Hansen and others how donors perceived the Agency, and how we would need to respond to their concerns if we were to attract additional funding, I was depicted by those around Hansen (and was once referred to in a staff meeting by Hansen himself) as the 'donors' advocate'.

Adding to my discomfort was the fact that most of my division's staff had worked for Hansen in the past, and they continued to be supported by him when they disagreed with the direction in which I wished to take the external relations function of the Agency. Their comfort zone was limited to ensuring the transparency and accountability of project funding, activities which were obviously of considerable importance to UNRWA's dealings with major donors, but there were no serious problems from the donor side so far as the accountability of project funding was concerned. I insisted that it was no less necessary to strengthen our performance in regard to advocacy, including among Arab countries in the Persian Gulf, the function for which I had been recruited at the request of the donor countries, than it was to improve the Agency's performance in tying off project accounts.

For all those reasons, exacerbated by constant needling from Hansen's team, and because of personality differences between us, Hansen and I simply could not get along.

Although I had managed my role in Gaza and elsewhere effectively, immediately after I had successfully organised and managed an emergency funding conference in Amman in September 1997 which secured US$21 million in additional support from the donor governments to tide the Agency over one of its periodic financial crises[9], Hansen told me he had decided to terminate my appointment. He said he wanted to see more public information work undertaken by a person well known to him, and to go back to a separation within UNRWA Headquarters between the external relations and public information functions.

---

[9]For details of the 1997 UNRWA financial crisis and the political issues surrounding it see my *Palestinian Refugees: Mythology, Identity and the Search for Peace* (Lynne Rienner, 2003), pp. 183-208.

Donors who got wind that I was being moved out were told that I was finding life in Gaza without my family difficult—which was certainly true in one sense, but also far removed from the key facts of the matter.

With Jenny, Sam and Tabitha about to arrive in Jerusalem a week or so later, and with school fees pre-paid, and rental already paid in advance on their behalf for a house in Beit Hanina in East Jerusalem, I pushed back against Hansen's decision. I was concerned at the optics of my situation, despite the fact that I knew—and those donors and embassy officials who knew me also were aware—I had done my best: indeed I had lasted longer than some other international staff assigned to the Agency who had also fallen foul of Hansen and his team.

I had to contend with some malice as negotiations continued, but with the help of good friends who knew the workings of the UN much better than me the upshot was that I continued in Gaza for several months while a new D1 position was created in Jerusalem (Senior Advisor, Policy Research) for another six months. I used the time to prepare a detailed policy paper on the future of UNRWA, which probably never saw the light of day beyond Hansen. However it provided, on returning to Canberra, the research component for my PhD at the Australian National University on the place of UNRWA in Palestinian refugee political mythologies.

Gaza was difficult, professionally and personally, but it was not without its humorous moments. UNRWA Field Offices in Gaza and the West Bank operated, with considerable success, a program whereby single women heads of households (usually widows or divorced wives) were provided with a small amount of start-up funding to run portable stalls selling pens, drinks, tissues and so on. The income earned by their sales was modest, but the loans were guaranteed by lending circles of the women themselves, repayment schedules were met, and the income helped enable the families to live with at least a modicum of dignity. I liked to extoll the virtues of the program to donors.

In the lead-up to the emergency conference of donors in September 1997, mentioned earlier, there was considerable agitation, especially in Gaza, at the prospect of the financial crisis further constraining the Agency's capacity to deliver its education, health and other services. A demonstration was organised, most probably by the Palestinian Authority, since Arafat would never have permitted an unauthorised demonstration. My suspicions were heightened when, most unusually, the sandy street outside the UNRWA HQ was graded and a marquee set up for high-ranking visitors to the protest event.

Demonstrators were bussed in (reportedly on UNRWA buses) to encourage the UNRWA staff going to Amman for the meeting to do their utmost. Before long, rocks and bottles were flying across the perimeter wall towards my office. And, as I gazed out through my window, there were the ladies of the microenterprise program, selling soft drinks to the crowd.

On a more personal level, when returning, exhausted, to my office on being dismissed by Hansen, I suffered chest pains and was taken to al-Shifa Hospital in Gaza. The cardiologist who examined me had problems getting his electro-cardiograph equipment to work on me, so he tested it on himself. He sent me away and admitted himself instead.

There were also moments of insight into Palestinian society that reflected some of the most admirable qualities of the people in Gaza with whom the Agency worked. One instance of this arose from the problems that had to be addressed when a donor-funded sewerage dam failed repeatedly, and the fact had to be faced that the contractor who had been awarded the project clearly was not up to the task. On learning that his contract was about to be terminated, however, the other engineering contractors in Gaza (I recall there were only two of them) met with the Gaza Field Office Projects Committee (of which I was a member) and made it clear that if the contract were cancelled, then as a matter of principle they would not tender for the job. The contractor, they said, was inexperienced, but they would not allow him (and by extension, Gazans) to be shamed. They would lend him whatever assistance was required to ensure the work was completed properly—which in due course, it was.

From a professional perspective, my efforts to persuade Arab governments in the Persian Gulf to provide additional financial support to UNRWA gave me insights into the complex world of intra-Arab politics and tensions that few outsiders have opportunities to experience. The Gulf governments, especially Saudi Arabia, were significant donors already. Even Kuwait, where bitterness remained keenly felt towards those Palestinians, in Kuwait and elsewhere, who it was widely believed had cheered on Saddam Hussein when he invaded in 1990, always paid its contribution to UNRWA on time. (A senior Kuwaiti official told me that Kuwait did so because it wanted to show the Palestinians how Arabs ought to conduct themselves.)

There was a clear shift, however, among the Gulf states after 1990 away from employing Palestinians. Since the 1950s, Palestinians had been the main source of teachers, civil servants and other skilled professionals for the Gulf, but workers from South Asia and The Philippines were now considered less likely to be problematic to the local political and social order in the longer term. As a respected Emirati philanthropist explained it to me, it was widely felt that 'Palestinians are like worms moving through the ground: you never know where they will come up next.'

Gulf Arab governments were also fed up with Palestinian figures, both from the PLO and Palestinian Authority, and prominent Palestinian individuals, seeking financial assistance—and doing so, moreover, by seeking to present their case as a moral obligation on the part of those governments, but failing, invariably, to provide any acknowledgment, transparency or accountability for the use of those funds they received.

I argued the case for UNRWA as an organisation that was entirely tailored to meeting humanitarian needs, and which fully acknowledged the support it received. That was fine, but there was also, in some cases, a less than enthusiastic response to my emphasis on accountability and transparency of project spending—especially from individuals who I suspect may have had their own reasons for seeing support extended to Palestinian projects without such strictures. I observed instances where Gulf money was being funnelled into projects for Palestinians which rarely progressed beyond their announcement, through NGOs of which no-one had ever heard.

I look back at our time in Gaza and Jerusalem with mixed feelings. It was an extraordinary experience for the family, including for our younger children. In Gaza I could enjoy the warmth of ordinary people and appreciate their stoicism in the face of adversity, and I knew Jenny would make herself at home in Jerusalem. But I had concerns for our children, living in Beit Hanina in East Jerusalem and exposed, in travelling to and from school, to the challenges and humiliations facing Palestinians under occupation.

As a teenager, easily mistaken for a Palestinian, and in their daily passage with other, mostly Arab, students through Israeli army checkpoints, our youngest daughter in particular was exposed to abuse and harassment, including sexual harassment, that was commonplace for her friends. Nor were the children immune from the risks faced by Israelis: at one stage they had just left Mahane Yehuda market, close to their school, before a Palestinian suicide bombing took place.

Our children emerged from their time in Jerusalem with an enduring interest in and empathy for the region that reflected experiences few others could contemplate. As Jenny told the extended family in Canberra, in a letter shortly after her arrival:

> We have almost adjusted to the Ramallah checkpoint (probably only fifty metres away as the crow flies) but I still feel trepidation when the deep Quaaak-quaaark-quaaaaaaaaark klaxon is sounded. The Israeli soldiers use it to stop a car with people to be interrogated. Occasionally it goes a step further with an announcement in Arabic, then "Come out of the car with your hands up". The first time we heard it we all sat bolt upright. It was a strong American accent and there was a sense of having strayed into the set of a sleazy cops and robbers video-only production. Now we are almost used to it and it is obviously a recording—or the Israelis are all taught by the same English language tutor who sounds like John Wayne after a heavy night. That act was topped last night by a barrage of machine gun fire so now we are awaiting the next act. It is not far away but there is a very large and solid building or two between them and us so it feels okay. The security on this house feels amazing. Everything is double locked and padlocked, and I suspect that we would miss a real emergency while trying to get out to see what it was.

Jenny pursued her textile art, taken up while I was in Gaza, inspired especially by the human stories of Palestinians she met. We enjoyed the history, archaeology and visual spectacle of the Old City. With the assistance of our dear friends Tania and Hanna Nasser, and funding from UNDP arranged by Tim Rothermel, we arranged for Jenny's nephew Grant Chamberlain to teach at the Palestine Music Conservatory in Ramallah. In addition to teaching, Grant formed a jazz band with Hanan Ashrawi's husband Emile sometimes playing the drums.

Jenny with one of her quilts featuring Syrian fabrics, at the Church of the Holy Sepulchre, Jerusalem 1998.

My time with UNRWA was shorter than I had expected, but the experience, on balance, was worthwhile. I did my best to deliver what the donors to the Agency had asked UNRWA to do. I left with the greatest admiration for the talents and dedication of UNRWA Palestinian and international Field Office staff, the Heads of UNRWA education and health programs based in Amman, and the directors of UNRWA field operations in the West Bank, Gaza, Lebanon, Syria and Amman. I was impressed by their unmatched ability to deliver projects and programs in deeply problematic political and sometimes physically challenging environments. It was, and remains, a truly remarkable organisation. My only regret was my inability to surmount the political machinations in the Office of the UNRWA Commissioner General.

Chapter 8

Canberra 1999-2000: the Palestinian Authority, the second Intifada, and the Australian Wheat Board (AWB) Affair

Returning to Canberra, I headed the OECD Section for a few months, and was simultaneously the Administrator of the Trade Policy Division. The OECD-related work mostly concerned giving legislative effect to Australia's obligations, as a member of the OECD, to the recently-adopted convention against corruption. It was valuable experience for my later role, post-DFAT, as a company director. I then resumed my familiar role as Director of Middle East Section. Once again I was acting, much of the time, as the Assistant Secretary, Middle East and Africa Branch.

In October 1998, in a guest lecture to Middle East politics students at the Australian National University, I reviewed the Middle East situation since the Oslo Accords of September 1993, providing an assessment, in the context of those Accords, of the utility of what was popularly known as Track Two diplomacy.

I argued that both the Palestinians and the Israelis had gained initially from the Accords. The PLO, soon to become, for all practical purposes, the Palestinian Authority (PA), acquired a legitimate international persona and established power in its own right over most of the urban populations in the West Bank and Gaza. With Oslo, Israel's international standing rebounded from the darkest moments of the intifada. There was also a sense in Israel that peace and regional acceptance were within reach. Peace with Jordan was placed on a secure footing.

There was little evidence that the Israeli Labour Party would have been more willing to compromise on territorial issues than Likud, but, by accepting its obligations in regard to a partial withdrawal from Hebron after coming to office, the Likud government ended its ideological commitment to Eretz Israel and adopted in its place the Labour Party's formula of land for peace and security. From that moment on, the key issues for the credible Right in Israeli politics were to be the depth of PA control in the West Bank and Gaza, and the form of that control, and the means by which Israeli security concerns could be met. It appeared that whether the PA had a right to rule in some part of that area was no longer an issue.

Then the reactions had set in, as those who stood to lose the most from the revival of the flagging peace process went on the attack.

Terrorism proved it could be effective as a political tool. Shimon Peres was guilty of a colossal political miscalculation in failing to take early advantage of the political opportunity that the assassination by a Jewish settler in November 1995 of Prime Minister Yitzhak Rabin presented to crush the extremist settler movement. And, in addition to failing to set the seal on Israel's commitment to the peace process along the lines the authors of Oslo envisaged, Peres compounded his error by failing to address the fallout among Arab Israelis of the deaths of 106 Lebanese civilians subjected to shelling by Israeli forces in Qaana, south Lebanon in April 1996. Peres lost the election to Netanyahu shortly thereafter when Arab Israelis, as a protest over that atrocity, largely chose not to vote.

Terrorist attacks, including the massacre of Arabs in Hebron in 1994, and the cycle of attacks and counter-measures by Palestinians and Israeli security forces in following years ultimately boosted the urgent efforts of the rejuvenated Israeli Right and their external supporters to wind back the momentum of the process, including through expanding settlements. The political timidity of Arafat in dealing with Palestinian critics of his acceptance of the Oslo deal; his inability to avoid being caught by Israelis saying different things to different audiences, and the rising tide of violence all took their toll.

The Track Two process was shown to be a dialogue between the like-minded, without a political platform capable of withstanding the combination of the terrorist onslaught, deliberately provocative settlement policies and efforts by the Netanyahu government to lower Palestinian expectations of what Oslo could deliver them. It could not overcome the ongoing resistance of several key parties to genuine, but painful compromise.

A few brief windows of opportunity for Australia to make a positive gesture arose, however, in 2000. Ehud Barak had replaced Benjamin Netanyahu as Prime Minister of Israel; and agreement had been reached in September 1999 on the timing of implementation of measures that had been agreed in 1998 with Netanyahu to progress the implementation of certain elements of the Oslo Accords. Most important of all, Barak was keen to have evidence of external support for the peace process under his government—which led him to see advantage in tolerating western outreach to the Palestinian Authority.

John Howard was planning to visit Israel in April 2000. On learning that Barak was in favour of him doing so, and with the encouragement of Jewish community leaders in Australia,

Howard agreed to meet Arafat in Gaza. As part of his visit to Gaza I arranged in his itinerary for Howard to visit an UNRWA-backed small business enterprise (a metal fabrication factory) to show the Prime Minister that, if given the opportunity, Gazans were entrepreneurial rather than welfare-minded.

It was fortunate the Howard visit took place in April, because in May 2000 there were further serious clashes between Israel and the Palestinians (the Land Day confrontations) which would have presented insurmountable political arguments against making a positive gesture toward the Palestinian Authority at that juncture.

In a similar piece of fortunate timing, one of my few positive achievements at a policy level came about when, as acting head of Middle East and Africa Branch and working with Deputy Secretary John Dauth, we persuaded the Howard Government to agree to the opening of the Australian Representative Office in Ramallah to strengthen relations with the Palestinian Authority, and to oversee the Australian aid program in the West Bank and Gaza. The Representative Office opened in September 2000, after the failure of the Camp David summit meeting in July (see below), but shortly before the outbreak of the second intifada in September. (John Dauth told me my name could be put forward for the position as the first Australian Representative, if I so wished. Having only recently finished my time in Gaza and Jerusalem, and not overly attracted to the prospect of living in Ramallah, after discussion with Jenny, I declined.)

I was away from the Department for most of June 2000 following the death of my brother from mesothelioma, but I had returned by the time of the ill-fated meeting between Clinton, Ehud Barak and Arafat at Camp David in July. The summit had been doomed from the outset by a range of factors, which better planning and preparation on the part of the Clinton Administration, firmer direction on Clinton's part including advancing US positions on key points in dispute, and less US tolerance for the antics of both Barak and Arafat might have avoided or mitigated. But as the summit crashed and burned, amidst accusations directed entirely against Arafat for refusing to respond to proposals from the Israelis (as conveyed by Clinton) it was painfully clear that the prospects for restoring the political momentum necessary to make progress toward a two-state solution were dissipating rapidly. As my friend and colleague, the late David Hennessy said, while we watched on CNN the final moments of the press conference at the end of the summit, 'The Palestinians are fucked.'

The second intifada erupted at the end of September 2000, triggered by frustration with the Israeli occupation and the domestic political posturing of then Israeli opposition leader Ariel Sharon and his much-publicised visit to the Haram al-Sharif (Temple Mount). But it was fuelled not only by Palestinian frustration with Israel but also by the growing tensions on the Palestinian side between Arafat's political and security establishment (sometimes referred to as 'the Tunisians') and its marginalised critics within Fatah.

I was frustrated by Arafat's failure to impose his authority over those who were at the forefront of the uprising, but not surprised: since our first meeting in Beirut two decades earlier I had observed his flair for achieving the semblance of political consensus while avoiding critically important decisions. I was angered not only because the scale of deaths on both sides was deeply disheartening, but also because Arafat's utter failure to exercise leadership sacrificed the efforts, both personal and professional, of many of us to advocate for, and maintain the possibility of, achieving a two-state solution.

I watched some of my Israeli friends, and academic and other contacts who, like me, had risked their reputations and careers by persisting in advocating for a two-state approach, and who in some cases had been criticised for seeking agreed solutions to the refugee issue, walk away from the search for peace. Henceforth, if it were to be found at all, Israelis and Palestinians would want peace from each other, not with each other.

To many of those who, like me, saw the only prospect for a durable settlement of the Israeli-Palestinian conflict resting in the emergence of two sovereign states whose governments would be willing to face the challenges of building political support for painful mutual concessions, the second intifada marked the moment when the Oslo peace process had irretrievably run its course. With it evaporated the possibility for a two-state solution. For all its inadequacies and ambiguities, the Oslo process was the last best chance for either side.

The Australian Wheat Board (AWB) Affair

Although discussing my part in the AWB affair was a major preoccupation for me in 2006, while I was in Cairo and then appearing as a witness at the Cole Inquiry in Sydney, the events that were the main focus of the Inquiry and my testimony to it took place around March 2000. I am therefore outlining them here.

Following the invasion of Iraq in 2003 to overthrow the Saddam regime, evidence was published in 2005 in a UN Independent Inquiry Committee into the Food-for-Oil Program (known as the Volcker Report) that the regime had sought, under the so-called Oil-For-Food Program, to evade or minimise the financial effect of the economic sanctions imposed on Iraq by the UN Security Council. The Australian Wheat Board (AWB) as a major supplier of wheat was alleged in the Volcker Report to be involved in that process, to the tune of over $US200 million, through the payment of 'trucking fees' to a company controlled by the regime.

The allegations of impropriety and the evidence accumulated against the AWB were of such seriousness that a judicial inquiry—the 'Inquiry into Certain Australian companies in relation to the UN Oil-For-Food Program', generally known as the Cole Inquiry—was established by the Howard government to ascertain the facts, and to review the performance of the government in regard to the AWB affair.

Based on a misleading claim that I had 'cleared the AWB with one phone call', I was subjected to a vicious campaign, notably by Caroline Overington in *The Australian*, the Fairfax newspapers and also in a Four Corners documentary on ABC television in which—to my total incomprehension—my part was played by a professional actor who depicted me as having a pompous English accent. The general effect of the media coverage was to portray me as naïve and incompetent, and possibly complicit in the AWB's corrupt behaviour. I was also the subject of negative questions and claims in the Australian Parliament.[10] To my immense gratitude the ever-robust Alexander Downer firmly defended my character and record as a public servant to the media. However my own version of events and the rationale for my decisions and judgments received no coverage.

The media onslaught was deeply frustrating for me, and hurtful for Jenny who had to watch me go through it. I had no avenue to defend myself against those attacks. I was advised informally by DFAT against suing the Murdoch media for defamation because my financial resources would not be sufficient to pursue a successful case. I was assured that my performance would be given a thorough evaluation by Justice Cole, and that I should allow the outcome of the Inquiry to speak for itself. That proved to be wise advice.

The Department paid for legal advice to be provided to me and other departmental witnesses. The members of the Iraq Task Force, headed by Marc Innes-Brown and including John Quinn

---

[10] See for example the comments of Michael Danby MP https://parlinfo.aph.gov.au/parlInfo/search/display/display.w3p;query=Id:%22chamber/hansardr/2006-11-29/0172%22

(a 1979 trainee), and officers of the Legal Division were personally supportive, as between colleagues. But the Department was entirely professional and circumspect, as was appropriate, in presenting the facts of the case. I managed to make a detailed explanation of the rationale behind my actions to the Cole Inquiry, both in an affidavit[11] and then in oral testimony.[12] I then endured rigorous, sustained and critical examination and cross-examination over almost three hours. (My testimony got away to a somewhat inauspicious start when my mobile phone, which I had forgotten to turn off, rang—and its ringtone was the Collingwood theme song. Justice Cole was not amused.)

In his lengthy findings on the case, Cole determined the AWB had deliberately hidden or disguised the payment of fees to Iraq and knew that neither the UN nor the Australian Government was aware of it making those payments, which clearly contravened UN Security Council sanctions and Australian law. Cole noted, briefly and correctly, that I had not made independent enquiries to determine the veracity of the advice I received from AWB when it denied making such payments. However he also noted that in my discussions with Nigel Officer, AWB's General Manager, Global Sales and Marketing, in December 1999 I had been informed that AWB was 'fully aware of, and respected, the obligations of the Australian Government and would continue to act appropriately'—despite the fact that AWB had already agreed to the payment of kickbacks to the Iraqis.

Cole also noted that on 18 January 2000, when I had raised the detail of a Canadian allegation against the AWB with Andrew McConville, AWB's Government Relations officer, McConville

---

[11] Available at https://web.archive.org/web/20130513020429/http://www.oilforfoodinquiry.gov.au/exhibits/images/DFT.0013.0057.pdf

[12] My testimony to the Cole Inquiry can be read at https://web.archive.org/web/20130515094802/http://www.oilforfoodinquiry.gov.au/agd/WWW/rwpattach.nsf/VAP/(2A296B295C1E058B328FED2164E40B7D)_OFI060315.doc/%24file/OFI060315.doc

responded, without making any inquiry, 'This is bullshit', and further rejected the allegations, saying, 'AWB would continue to uphold its responsibilities towards the Australian Government in Iraq'. Cole pointed out that if McConville had made any inquiry of anyone in AWB before responding to me or following his conversation with me, or had looked at the contracts entered into after July 1999, or the conditions of tendering for such contracts, he would have observed that AWB had indeed agreed to pay, illegally, 'discharge', or inland transport, costs of US$12.00 or $14.00 per tonne.

Cole said DFAT's approach was 'explicable' for several reasons. These included the fact that it regarded AWB as 'a company of the utmost integrity' and saw its role (as I had testified) as 'supporting Australian economic interests and Australian companies'. He said it was 'difficult, if not impossible, to see what possible motive DFAT would have for turning a blind eye, or how DFAT could conceivably see that turning a blind eye would advance either AWB's or Australia's interests.' Without mentioning me by name, although it was clear from my testimony and cross-examination I had certainly done so, he recognised that on several occasions during the Oil-for-Food Programme the Australian Government had warned and advised AWB that the provision of funds to Iraq outside the framework of the Food-for-Oil arrangements would breach UN sanctions.

In short, Cole found that at no time did the AWB tell the Australian Government or the United Nations of its true arrangements with Iraq. The UN did not know AWB was paying to Iraq surcharges or after-sales-service fees or had inflated prices to encompass such payments. When the United Nations, through Australia, inquired of AWB whether it was making such payments to Iraq, AWB had emphatically denied that it was; and on receipt of a copy provided by the AWB of the standard terms and conditions it said were applying to its wheat trade with Iraq, the UN Office of the Iraq Program advised that this 'clarifies the matter and removes any ground for misperception'. And when inquiries were mounted into its activities the AWB took all available measures to restrict and minimise disclosure of what had occurred.

I remain comfortable overall with the actions I took in regard to the AWB, in response to the questions about allegations raised with, and as reported from, the Australian mission in New York. I acted in good faith on the basis of the advice available to me at the time from the AWB and our mission at the United Nations. Although a UN official later claimed to have referred to trucking fees in her discussion with the Australian official in the Australian mission in New York, Bronte Moules, the enquiry from the UN concerning alleged payment of kickbacks by the AWB, as conveyed by Moules by cable, made no refence to trucking fees. Instead, it referred to the AWB allegedly opening a bank account in Jordan into which kickbacks would be paid. I had no reason, on the basis of that advice, to raise any concern about so-called 'trucking fees'.

As I explained in testimony to the Cole Inquiry, I also saw no reason to question the advice which I received from AWB, both in late 1999 and in January 2000. I had been assured by AWB it was not facing any unusual problems in maintaining its business with Iraq. Moreover, paying kickbacks to Iraq made no sense when the supply of wheat was essential for the regime's security, and disputes with suppliers arising from corruption posed too great a risk of supply interruptions for the Iraqis to have persevered with their threats.

My experience of dealing with the AWB, and similar bodies such as the Queensland Grain Growers Association, also led me to believe the Australian side would be too wary and sophisticated in their marketing strategies to become entrapped in such schemes. Not least because the Iraqis would probably insist that other suppliers followed suit (as the Canadian-raised objections quickly demonstrated), engaging in corrupt behaviour would become known instantly around the wheat trade. As a business strategy it would be not only illegal, but profoundly stupid.

What I had not taken into account was a shift in corporate culture within the AWB in a new era of deregulation and the end of the previous single marketing body approach to wheat sales. I was not aware that shift had combined with generational change within the AWB which had seen the departure of experienced senior officials who, I believe, would have dealt with any such pressures effectively: if faced with Iraqi pressure they would have been careful, above all else, to preserve the confidence of Australian government ministers and officials in the AWB's integrity.

Instead, AWB's assurances that it was facing no unusual problems in the Iraqi market obscured the fact that its management was now determined to sell the crop at any cost. But even if I had been made aware of those changes and taken them into account, I would not have been able to penetrate the veil of secrecy within which the AWB had decided to operate, and which it tried to maintain even throughout the Cole Inquiry. As Alexander Downer put it, in response to Justice Cole's report, the AWB had practised a deliberate policy of deceit, hiding key information from the government and the United Nations.

The AWB chose to mislead me. If it had sought my advice over its concerns the AWB could, if it so wished, have had government and UN support in dealing with the Iraqis according to the approved terms of the UN oil-for-food arrangements. Though perhaps sometimes inconvenient for the AWB at an operational level, there was nothing incompatible between selling wheat to Iraq and respecting the rules laid down by the UN Security Council.

Instead, the AWB panicked. It allowed itself to be bullied. It then chose to deny it had acted illegally. In every respect, each decision it took was contrary to its own corporate interests, with extraordinarily damaging consequences for the AWB itself, and at considerable cost to the reputations of those associated with it.

Looking back some 20 years later, I believe I gained some valuable lessons from the experience, albeit more in regard to the nature of corporate and human affairs than in regard to the AWB. Two lessons stand out that I wish I had learnt before the AWB affair came about.

The first, is that one should never underestimate the power of fear, greed and stupidity in human affairs—which can be difficult for those who are not especially fearful, greedy or stupid themselves to appreciate.

The second lesson is that just because an answer to a problem seems logical, or even inescapable on the basis of whatever insight and experience one might possess, it is dangerous to assume others will necessarily arrive at the same conclusion, or even understand the problem in the same way.

Chapter 9

2001-2004 Centre for Defence and Strategic Studies, and returning to the Australian National University

In late 2000, I was seconded to the Department of Defence as the DFAT officer on the Directing Staff of the Centre for Defence and Strategic Studies (CDSS) at the Australian Defence College. It proved to be one of the happiest and most rewarding assignments of my career. Indeed, I enjoyed it so much that as the end of my two-year appointment approached, I asked for and was granted an extra year at the Centre.

My work at CDSS focussed mainly on two areas: providing insights into how certain international security and foreign policy issues tend to be viewed from a diplomat's perspective; and overseeing the selection of Australian and international scholars and other specialists to provide a world-class learning environment for Australian and international military officers, and the creation of suitable course material for officers about to advance to Brigadier ('One Star') level. Although I took responsibility for the Asia-Pacific modules of the courses, there was scope to include Middle East political and security concerns within the curriculum. Because I had published at an academic level on the larger topic of international security in *Beyond Peace: the Search for Security in the Middle East*, I also oversaw the modules dealing with International Relations theory.

The time at CDSS was an excellent opportunity to gain insight into the intellectual and practical challenges surrounding strategic thinking and the provision of advice to government. In their desire to seek solutions, diplomats tend toward unquenchable optimism, and may be tempted—especially if they are not area specialists—to neglect the value of sober reflection on the lessons of history. Strategic thinkers, in contrast, are required to make judgments about defence needs, and weapons technology platforms and associated capabilities to service those needs. They are required to make projections about circumstances and capability requirements several decades hence. Worst case scenarios tend to figure rather prominently: optimism is a scarce commodity when it comes to formulating strategic policy.

In addition to its application to analysis of Middle East issues, I found the interaction between the two disciplines of strategic policy and diplomacy, and the discussion of issues within the context of real-world bureaucratic and military processes, both fascinating and professionally illuminating. The intellectual calibre of the Australian Defence Force officers and their overseas counterparts, as well as the Defence civilians who undertook the courses, impressed me. It was a pleasure to be in their company and to gain insights as a civilian from their operational experience. I also enjoyed the travel within Australia and across the Asia-Pacific region through which the course members were exposed to a range of governments, businesses and think tanks.

On completion of my assignment to CDSS at the end of 2003 I took a year's leave of absence to rejoin the Centre for Arab and Islamic Studies at the ANU as a Visiting Reader (Associate Professor). My PhD on Palestinian refugee political mythologies and UNRWA, which had been awarded in 2001, was rewritten and published in 2003 as *Palestinian Refugees: Mythology, Identity and the Search for Peace*. I created and taught graduate courses on the dynamics of the Israeli-Palestinian conflict, and on Persian Gulf security. I also tutored the undergraduate courses on Politics in the Middle East, and Politics in Central Asia, and gave lectures for the Middle East politics course on Nasser's Egypt (including reference to the Islamist Sayyid Qutb and the advocacy of *jihad*), all accompanied by the music of Um Kalthoum. I also lectured on Ataturk and Turkey, and, of course, the Middle East peace process.

In mid-2004, I contacted the head of Corporate Management at DFAT, Penny Williams, to say that if the Department was willing to make use of my Middle East experience once again, I would be keen to return. Penny (who had also served in Damascus) was supportive. To my delight, I was advised almost immediately that Alexander Downer had decided to appoint me as ambassador to Egypt. The appointment carried with it accreditations to Syria, Libya, Sudan and Tunisia (I had already been accredited to Tunisia from Jordan in 1989-92).

Chapter 10

Iraq 2003 and its Implications for Australia

Because I was on secondment to the Centre for Defence and Strategic Studies at the Australian Defence College, I was outside the orbit of Middle East policy-making at the time of the Howard Government's decision (probably made in principle by Howard in 2002, but not announced until 2003) to commit Australian forces to the overthrow of the Saddam Hussein regime. However, I accepted an invitation from Hugh White at the Australian Strategic Policy Institute (ASPI) to contribute a working paper to a policy briefing, prepared by Elsina Wainwright, on the likely implications for Australia of the impending conflict (*Building the Peace: Australia and the Future of Iraq*, ASPI, May 2003).

In my paper, I expressed a range of concerns at the course upon which the United States and its partners were embarked. In addition, I highlighted key risks to Australian interests, notably discussing in detail possible threats to the future of wheat sales to Iraq—unaware as I was of the impending revelations about the role of the Australian Wheat Board in Iraq in the previous few years. I discussed how Australia should be positioning itself to pursue opportunities in Iraq and defend its interests there and, with that in mind, I recommended the early resumption of an official Australian presence at ambassadorial level in Baghdad. I also recommended that the limits to further Australian support for US objectives in the wider Gulf region should be quietly but firmly established as soon as possible.

Since it is not an official document, and because it has proven to be reasonably sound in its assessments and predictions (including regarding Syria's likely concerns about US aims after Saddam's removal) I am reproducing here those unpublished elements of the paper dealing with Iraq and the Middle East outlook.

The morning after?

Saddam Hussein, his immediate entourage and his closest relatives will die, disappear or flee at some point in the present campaign. That may not mean, however, that conflict in Iraq will have a clear-cut end point. There will be a range of ongoing issues from which localised conflicts could break out, including the settling of scores within Iraq. There will be pockets of resistance from those remnants of the regime who face extermination by the wider population, and possibly from those linked to them by tribal or other connections who anticipate sharing their fate.

There will be intense competition for new opportunities for power and privilege from those who were disadvantaged during the Saddam era. Those who flourished in exile but see even greater opportunities under an incoming US-backed administration will have to compete for their share of the spoils. As will be discussed, US-led efforts to change fundamentally the nature of Iraqi political culture that gave rise to Saddam Hussein will add to the unpredictability of the outcome.

The incoming administration may be led into a political labyrinth as it is forced to choose among those elements in Iraq who proffer their support. Those it chooses not to support will quickly label their rivals as extensions of Western influence and values. Be that as it may, the United States seems destined to have an extensive and enduring military presence in post-Saddam Iraq. Popular antipathy throughout the region towards the American presence in the region will have a new target.

The credibility of the incoming administration and the government it establishes will be shaped to some extent by its economic performance. Much will depend on how quickly Iraq's oil fields and associated facilities can be restored and expanded. The expected speed of recovery of Iraq's oil production is the subject of considerable debate.

Given the current downward trend of production and the likelihood of a prolonged recovery process, a build-up within six months after a successful US invasion and the subsequent lifting of UN sanctions, as predicted by some analysts, seems unlikely. A duration of some two years to bring production capacity back to 3.5mln b/d would appear more realistic, given the current devastated and decaying state of the oil infrastructure. If Iraq is to regain past oil production capacity it will need to assure and sustain multiple export routes and streams currently closed down or only in temporary use (such as those in Saudi Arabia and Syria).

The condition of Iraq and its population when Saddam is removed can only be guessed at. Humanitarian relief may or may not prove adequate. Refugee flows may or may not occur. The UN, the United States and its partners, and the NGO community may cope, or they may not, largely depending on how quickly events develop and the levels of violence that will be associated with the final days of the campaign.

The imagery of the war as viewed through *Al Jazeera* and *Al Manar* will compound an already palpable popular discontent with the American role in the region. Most regional leaderships however look set to manage successfully the internal tensions arising from their role in the lead-up to the conflict. There will be pockets of discontent with their performances, but barring a cataclysmic event in the final stages of the battle for Baghdad, each regional regime is capable of dealing with internal threats to its stability.

All regional countries will continue to hope and aim to move their relations with Washington forward. But some countries may also prefer, at the same time, to keep the United States off balance in its newly-established presence. Those already anticipating renewed American pressure would not wish the United States to become too comfortable with what many would regard as a new and potentially threatening beachhead of US influence in the Gulf and the wider region.

Habits of intervention in Iraq by neighbouring countries are likely to continue, essentially to protect their own interests, and also because few can afford not to be involved lest their clients look elsewhere for support. Iran will want to shape the nature of the future regime, but relations between Iranian Shia and Iraqi Shia are complex. Both elements are affected by factional rivalries, historic rivalries between centres of religious learning and political manoeuvring within Iran. An ongoing US presence in Karbala and Najaf—holier even than Mecca for many Shia—will serve as a rallying point for opponents of President Khatami.

Arab states in the northern Gulf, in control but not necessarily certain of the loyalties of their Shia minorities, will be nervous about the future shape of an Iraq where Sunnis comprise less than 20 per cent of the population. Kurdish rivalries and uncertainties surrounding the future involvement of the Turkish military in the light of Kurdish reactions to the fall of Saddam will continue to draw in external players.

Key risks

Peacekeeping and Re-inventing Iraq.

While Australian and US interests in the conflict with Iraq have had much in common, they have not been identical. Concern to achieve the removal of Iraq's weapons of mass destruction, albeit ultimately achieved through the use of armed force bringing about regime change, has principally driven the Australian approach.

Australia has interests in the restoration of stability and security within Iraq. It does not have an interest, except perhaps a defensive one, in the sorts of re-engineering of Iraqi society and Iraqi institutions that are envisaged in some parts of the US Administration.

There is a fundamental dilemma for the United States that remains unresolved. It is seeking to bring about a government in Iraq that will enhance the security of the region—and perhaps serve as a model to others—in a country that has neither a tradition of democratic rule nor a political culture to support such values.

To acknowledge that the Iraqi system, despite the abuses of power to which it gave rise under Saddam, is basically irreplaceable would be unacceptable to the United States. To bring about fundamental change in Iraq, however, an incoming administration will be confronting existing and traditional networks in Iraqi society that are the key to the functioning of the Iraqi system. Those forces have everything at stake in resisting their loss of power and being stripped of the privileges that accompany it. Any attempt to reallocate power will pose threats to the interests of individuals, families, clans and tribes—as well as posing larger questions of the balance between and within the Shia, Sunni and other communities—within Iraq. As demonstrated by the discussion below of the issue of wheat sales and distribution—relatively simple at one level, highly complex at another—if the United States does seek to bring about a thorough redistribution of power in Iraq, there is a high risk of domestic chaos.

The competing interests of regional countries in the unfolding of the post-conflict situation, and possible secessionist pressures, will also pose serious challenges to the stability of the post-war order within Iraq. Moreover, the prospect of an extended foreign military presence in Iraq is bound to generate regional anxieties, especially against the background of US concerns about Iran. There are also signs the United States may take a more robust approach to Saudi Arabia and Syria in the aftermath of the conflict, placing pressure on the leaderships in those countries whose performance it considers inadequate in terms of vital US security interests.

Australia has significant economic relations and generally cordial bilateral dealings with Saudi Arabia. It has strong economic relations with Iran, and despite clear differences and a robust dialogue on some issues—including on weapons of mass destruction—it has enjoyed positive and constructive dealings with Iran on a range of issues affecting Australian interests. Australia's close relations with the United States have not, in the past, been a problem for either the Iranians or any Arab country. In some cases (such as Kuwait) they have been to Australia's advantage. An ongoing Australian military presence in Iraq, however, which would be seen as signalling support for a more assertive US foreign policy and the lengths to which the US Administration might go to achieve its goals, could change that perception.

The factors discussed above, and the difficulty of defining clear Australian objectives or exit strategies under such conditions argues strongly against further Australian military involvement in Iraq. A substantial effort in support of economic development would be more consistent with Australia's overall interests in Iraq, and in the region. ... Rehabilitation of Iraq's agricultural sector (in which Australian firms were active in the 1980s) and enhancing the capabilities of Iraqi ports and associated grain handling facilities would seem obvious starting points. Beyond that, supplying environment technology, dryland and dairy farming consultancies, water management, and promoting livestock and grains production are all areas in which Australian firms have a reputation for competence and integrity, and a high level of commercial competitiveness.

Chapter 11

2005-2008: Cairo

Nothing could have been better than Cairo, the most remarkable of Arab capitals, as a final posting in the Arab world. Its fading late 19th century elegance matched its fading salon culture; but its sense of its own importance, indeed of its centrality to the Arab world, was unlike anything I encountered elsewhere.

My first visit to Egypt for work purposes was a familiarisation visit from Jeddah in 1976; and I had been back several times from Canberra, usually accompanying foreign ministers. We had taken leave there with children while on postings to both Damascus and Amman. During the Gulf War Jenny, Sam and Tabitha had spent a few weeks in Cairo, enjoying a break from Cyprus and staying with the ambassador, John Creighton at the embassy Residence on Zamalek. Its trees, lawn and flowers, lovingly tended by Gamal the gardener were waiting for us in 2005.

Cairo had its challenges, some of which I will discuss later, but it was professionally and personally exhilarating to work in the Arab world's most extraordinary blend of multifaceted culture, Pharaonic, Coptic, Arab and Islamic history, hospitality, humour, conspiracy theories, political and social conundrums and foreign policy sophistication.

Whenever opportunities arose, we would delight in taking sunset sailboat (*felucca*) rides on the Nile to escape the continuous noise and vibrant street life. Among the many micro-societies which comprise Egypt we enjoyed exploring and becoming familiar with the Tentmakers of Cairo, the grave attendants and silk spinners of the City of the Dead, camel traders and street markets far removed from tourist attractions. We were fascinated by *zar* music, and the ecstatic ritual performances of Sufi Egyptians, deeply embedded in Egyptian culture but explicitly rejected in orthodox Islamic circles.

Egypt was also an opportunity to return to desert camping, mostly in the spectacular White Desert with our good friend Magdy Badramany and his colleagues from the oasis town of Bahariya. Although I was unable to be out of contact for any length of time while I was ambassador, we returned to Egypt in 2010 and explored with Magdy and our son Sam and other friends as far Gilf Kebir and Jebel Oweinat on the border with Sudan and Libya, a 14 day round trip taking us beyond the Great Sand Sea, marvelling not only at the desert scenery but also the pre-historic artwork, and other, even older evidence of human activity long before civilization arose along the Nile.

With our son Sam, after crossing the Great Sand Sea, 2010. Sam is an international authority on Islamic art, including the work of the Tentmakers of Cairo.

For Jenny, Cairo was an opportunity initially to engage with, and in due course to support the Tentmakers of Cairo. By working closely with those men, whose artisanal skills and traditions were endangered, understanding the complex politics of their society and giving international exposure to their amazingly skilled applique work, Jenny almost single-handedly achieved the rejuvenation of a unique Egyptian art form. In doing so, she also restored a community to something approaching sustainability. After leaving Cairo, Jenny was awarded the Officer in the Order of Australia for her role. As the then Australian ambassador, Neil Hawkins, wrote to the Governor General in 2017 in support of Jenny's nomination for the award,

> Preserving and boosting a traditional art form, securing the livelihoods of hundreds of Egyptian artists and their families and promoting Australia's reputation, all done singlehandedly and as a volunteer, is surely an achievement to celebrate and to give due recognition as an extraordinary Australian.

The bilateral relationship between Egypt and Australia was cordial, but in the absence of strong economic ties, and without an aid program other than the modest amount of discretionary funds available to me as ambassador, not very substantial. Egypt's foreign policy priorities were concerned, appropriately enough, with managing its relations with the Arab world, the United States, major European countries and Israel. The intellectual calibre of those Egyptian officials around Mubarak with whom I mostly dealt on those issues—including Suleiman Awad in the President's Office; and Mubarak's legendary advisor, Osama al-Baz—was simply exceptional. So too were the insights of my good friend, Hisham Yusuf, at the Arab League. On the other hand, there were others around Mubarak—apparatchiks of the old guard of the regime, such as Safwat al-Sharif and Kamal al-Shazli—whose imperiousness left me cold.

To my quiet amusement, the Secretary of DFAT, Ashton Calvert had asked for me to be told, on being advised of my appointment as ambassador, that I was not to 'get involved with the Palestinians'. I largely followed his instruction, and refrained from reporting to any great extent on Egyptian involvement in the Middle East peace process—although it turned out I was to have some interesting encounters with PLO figures visiting Cairo, especially the Fatah personality Mohammed Dahlan, and Arafat's bag man, Mohammed Rashid, with whom I got along well. I had a private lunch in Cairo with Dahlan and Rashid during the seizure of power in Gaza (Dahlan's power base) by Hamas in July 2007. As I reported back to Canberra afterwards, it was like having lunch with *The Sopranos*.

Domestically, it was a time of strong but unbalanced economic growth as a younger generation of businesspeople close to the President Hosni Mubarak's son, Gamal, sought to increase their access to opportunities to profit from movement toward deregulation of the Egyptian economy in response to advice from the International Monetary Fund. The tensions generated within the Egyptian system by that movement—necessary as it was— and by changes of attitude, growing capability to mobilise for political ends outside the straitjacket of the traditional military-backed power structure, resentment at corruption and rejection of the ambitions of Gamal Mubarak to succeed his father were to unfold shortly after we left.

As I found elsewhere in the region, Australia's relationship with Egypt was surprisingly unburdened by historical baggage. The Egyptians displayed no ill-feeling toward Australia's unfortunate record so far as the Anzac presence in Cairo during the First World War was concerned. No-one I met raised the part played by Australian forces in the suppression of the Egyptian nationalist movement in 1919 (I had viewed those matters with some personal trepidation, as my grand-uncle was part of the Anzac force that trained in Cairo before he was killed in Gallipoli; and my grandfather was part of the British occupying force in Egypt after the war). Nor did Egyptians seem to recollect that Egypt severed diplomatic relations with Australia in November 1956 over our support at the United Nations for the British position in the Suez conflict, and that those relations were only restored in 1959.

The relationship with Australia was shaped in Egyptian minds mainly by the success of the wheat trade which, until the 1990s, saw Australia provide the bulk of Egypt's wheat imports, and the notion (perhaps shaped by the extensive connections of the Egyptian Coptic community with Australia) that Australia was well-disposed toward Egypt and Egyptians. There was also some recognition that Australia represented a potential source of expertise in such areas as mining and agriculture, although, as discussed below, the Egyptian side was reluctant in practice to pursue the systemic changes that would be required to apply such expertise to best effect.

With Presidential Counsellor Osama al-Baz and Australian Defence Minister Robert Hill 2006.

I relished the opportunity to investigate and reflect on Egypt's foreign policy activities and its insights on regional affairs, including Iraq, the dynamics of its internal politics, and the Middle East peace process. Egyptian humour was on full display when, at a donor conference in 2006 on Iraq convened in Sharm el-Sheikh by the United States, the music played during the conference coffee break was the theme song from *Titanic*. But as mentioned earlier, the intellectual calibre and sophistication of the upper echelons of the Egyptian foreign policy machinery, which included the Presidency and the Arab League, the Foreign Ministry, and a select group of individuals still active in those domains as analysts and advisors, was extraordinarily impressive.

Aside from managing the embassy, however, and dealing with consular problems I discuss elsewhere, most of my routine activity focussed on expanding the scope for Australian business to take advantage of the opening up of the Egyptian economy. I spent a lot of time encouraging the Egyptian ministers for Planning, Industry and Finance to determine their pricing policy for natural gas according to whether it was to be allocated for export, domestic industry or domestic consumption, since their decisions on that issue would determine whether a major Australian company would proceed to make a significant investment in aluminium refining (a decision was not forthcoming in the time frame required, unfortunately). I also discussed possibilities for joint ventures in education and public hospital management.

Given Egypt's extensive gold resources, which had remained undeveloped because of an antiquated mining code that ruled out investment in the sector by mining companies of international standing, I urged attention be given by the Egyptian government to updating that code. I also became heavily engaged in seeking to put the trade in live cattle with Australia on a humane and sustainable basis.

In both these areas, however, I found that whereas Egyptian ministers would be positive, and even enthusiastic in some cases, in our discussion of reform, their capacity to move forward in practice was determined mainly by the level of resistance to change they encountered, especially within the Egyptian civil service. Wherever one turned in Egypt, there was likely to be a system beneath the dysfunctionality, if not chaos, that was part of daily life, and the determination and capacity of those Egyptians adept at operating within the systems with which they were comfortable and familiar, to outlast and thwart the ambitions of reform-minded ministers, was quite remarkable.

As someone from a farming background (I was probably one of very few Australian diplomats who in his youth could kill, skin and butcher a sheep) and with a deep concern for animal welfare, I was strongly opposed to any trade that did not reflect Australian values in regard to the treatment of exported livestock. I had no problem with live animal trade, provided the conditions under which animals were transported and slaughtered met the standards most Australians would expect. Because it was in the commercial interest of sellers and buyers alike for sheep and cattle to arrive in healthy condition, they usually did. Indeed, in the case of sheep, a common problem was that they were inclined to gain weight beyond the contracted weight limit during shipment to the Middle East. The main problems, however, were usually associated with slaughter arrangements, especially for live cattle.

Whereas most Australian cattle shipped to Egypt were processed through a purpose-built facility on the Red Sea coast, evidence emerged in the Australian media of gross maltreatment of Australian cattle at the main slaughterhouse in Cairo. As I investigated further, I found that the reasons for that situation, which was truly deplorable, were mostly systemic.

The slaughterhouse was owned by the Cairo municipality, but its operation was left to the butchers and wholesalers whose focus was entirely on the speed with which animals could be killed and processed. As with the ploughing contractors in Jordan, those casual employees doing the killing therefore resorted to practices that were unacceptable (including, in all likelihood, to many Egyptians, if they were aware of them) and needlessly cruel; but there was no inclination by any of the parties to prevent such practices from being pursued. Nor, in all probability, would anything by way of government regulation which affected the commercial interests of the users have been sustained for more than a brief period. I therefore recommended the trade in Australian cattle be halted until there were improved facilities for identifying and tracking the movement of the cattle, and ensuring that none were destined for processing at the Cairo municipality facility.[13]

On the mining code front, as mentioned, I paid particular attention to encouraging the Egyptian government to move expeditiously toward adopting an international best practice mining code that would see major Australian companies attracted to the sector. It was an uphill, and ultimately fruitless, battle.

Gamal Mubarak and his coterie were the darlings of the western economic media and the IMF for driving reforms made in comparatively new areas, such as banking, information technology and telecommunications. Investment flowed from Gulf states into such areas as gated real estate developments (where in some cases one square metre of land sold for the equivalent of the annual income of most Egyptians), private hospitals, shopping malls and hotels. They believed that contemporary economic orthodoxy, as promulgated by the IMF, if not the tide of history, was on their side.

But Egyptian ministers, and their senior staff who, like their ministers, were usually drawn from outside the bureaucracy,

---

[13]The outcry in Australia over the live cattle issue was accompanied by a demonstrator from PETA turning up at the embassy in Cairo to deliver a protest—dressed in a sheep costume. Fortunately, the long-suffering Consul, Andrew Macksey, was alerted to the planned demonstration, and whisked the demonstrator away before the Egyptian security people, not known for their sense of humour or empathy for demonstrations of any kind, detained him.

rarely received the political support they required from the presidency to achieve and implement policy reform within existing institutions. Moreover, they often had to face the problem of being associated with the presumed ambitions, and perceived corruption of those who, like Gamal, were the face of reform.

Even in the operation of the tourism industry, the system was bound to prevail. The tourism industry focussed almost entirely on two targets—pre-packaged tours of major sites of pharaonic Egypt, and resort holidays on the Red Sea and southern Sinai. Both operated very well, in terms of tourist satisfaction, and were highly profitable for the military-owned or backed hotel, transport and other operators involved. But there was almost no promotion or development of other worthwhile tourism opportunities that fell outside the accepted model, such as visiting artisanal workshops and monuments in Islamic Cairo in underprivileged areas. Tour operators were directed specifically not to take tourists to the City of the Dead where in addition to visiting spectacular examples of Mamluk architecture and artisanal workshops and activities they would witness some of the poverty that is the daily reality of many Egyptians.

Tour guides, also, were highly reluctant to take groups to the Street of the Tentmakers, not because of supposed health risks, but because the guides, who were reliant for their own income on kickbacks from sales of marked-up merchandise from so-called carpet weaving schools and perfumeries, were unable to obtain commissions there. And on such a seemingly minor matter as improving the inadequate labelling of exhibits in the Cairo Museum, attempts by the museum director to do so were thwarted by an outcry from tour guides, supported by museum employees, complaining that to do so would deprive them of their living.

In short, the prospects for reform reaching to the fundamentals of the Egyptian system were poor. Few Egyptians believed systemic reform would work better than time-honoured practices to which they were accustomed. Some were inclined to question the motives behind calls for greater integration into the global economy. Mubarak senior shared the aversion of his military, security and intelligence apparatus to the posing of open-ended questions about the intent and consequences of reform for the relationship between citizens and the state.

Moreover, as a practical matter, the process of bringing about restructuring within the civil service itself was bound to be constrained by the resources made available to the minister concerned: as the head of the Egyptian nuclear affairs agency told me, it would require economic growth in excess of 6 per cent of GDP annually to generate enough funds for him to promote, and then to retire on enhanced pensions, the 90 per cent of his officials who he believed were non-productive.

Political Islam and the Muslim Brotherhood

My longstanding interest in political Islam led me to take a close interest in the Egyptian Muslim Brotherhood and its more conservative rivals—the venerable Sunni centre of Islamic learning, al-Azhar, traditionally respected for its excellence in Islamic jurisprudence and education; and the Salafist phenomenon often referred to as Islamism, which was politically quiescent and closer to similar schools of thought in Saudi Arabia at first, but which had become more organically Egyptian by the middle of the decade and had turned to political activism.

Political Islam, represented by the Muslim Brotherhood, arose in the 1920s in the context of a political struggle against secular, foreign-influenced forces which were widely seen among Egyptians beyond the ruling circle and its cosmopolitan, mostly foreign, supporters as inauthentic. But whereas the Brotherhood operated mostly within the rules of the political system, alternating between experiences of repression and co-optation according to the personalities and politics of the time, Islamism under the guidance of its best-known ideologue, Sayyid Qutb, represented an anti-establishment force seeking to build a society outside the existing frameworks. The extremist movement was bitterly opposed to the Muslim Brotherhood, which it regarded as compromised by its accommodation of the regime. It was deliberately unresponsive to notions of constitutionalism, civil liberties, freedoms and electoral accountability.

In contrast to the extremists, both the Brotherhood and the Salafists were politically savvy at a tactical level. Both were adept at spreading their influence where state power was weak or non-existent, as was the case in most of Egyptian village society—in practice, the Salafists did rather better than the Brotherhood at the village level because the Brotherhood members, who tended to be better educated, were prone to assuming airs and graces less on display from the more traditionally-attuned Salafists who formed the al-Nour party. Politically, the Salafists often outflanked the Brotherhood by being prepared to attack the Copts with their rhetoric, which the Brotherhood was unwilling to do, although it was probably no less sectarian in its private views of Copts and Jews.

Although technically still banned, with over two million members and a nation-wide network the Brotherhood was clearly a political and social force in Egypt which, as ambassador, I needed to understand—not least to gain some idea of its view of foreign investment in Egypt—and where possible, seek to build an appreciation on their part of Australia and its role in Egypt. Since it dominated most of the Egyptian professional associations, I began to call on those leaderships, and in the immediate aftermath of the success of the Brotherhood in the 2005 parliamentary elections, where running as independents but under the slogan 'Islam is the Solution' it won 20 per cent of the allocated opposition seats. I also entertained some of the

Brotherhood's senior figures to lunch (noting, sometimes, the absence of fingernails).

I soon found there were divisions within the movement regarding economic policy, notably on the issue of welfare. Some traditionalists, focussing on the fundamental duty of *zakat*, or tax to support the poor, argued Islam encouraged state-sponsored welfare programs. Others, notably the successful businessman Mohammed Khairat al-Shater, observed that the Prophet was a trader, and advocated for a growing economy as best meeting Islamic criteria of both social responsibility and adhering to the example of the Prophet's own role. In any event, so far as Australia's interests in the issue were concerned, it was also clear that the Brotherhood took a positive view of foreign investment, provided it was environmentally responsible (another factor consistent with Islam), equitable as a business, and socially responsible. There was a generally positive, albeit hazy, view of Australia in Brotherhood circles.

It was no surprise to me that the Brotherhood was unprepared for the events of 2011. Although its leaders claimed to be ready to accept the responsibilities of power, it lacked a concrete program for political action. Though famous for its party discipline, there were gaps between its members over whether it should focus on creating an authentic Muslim society from the grassroots (*da'wa*) and eschew politics, or to aim for political power to use the institutions of the state to achieve their goal, with the compromises and dilution of the Brotherhood brand that would require.

There were bitter divisions between the old guard of the Brotherhood which was focussed on accommodation (or perhaps just survival) with the Mubarak regime—and who could argue that repression by the regime justified their maintaining strict discipline within the party, and therefore an absence of leadership challenges—and a younger generation of Brotherhood activists upon whom the burden of regime's repression mostly fell.

The Brotherhood eventually joined the 2011 uprising and took advantage of the incoherence of the secular forces, and a brief period in which the Egyptian military cut it some political slack, to win control of the government through parliamentary and presidential elections. Once President Morsi was in power, however, oppositional politics proved much easier than government. The Brotherhood failed to build political constituencies capable of challenging the fundamental power structure of the state system—the military, security, judicial, business and other systems that sometimes contested each other's turf, but that also shared an overriding interest in preserving their privileges within it.

Moreover, instead of reaching out effectively to Copts and others who did not share its vision of developing an Islamic society, and building a support base through achieving equitable economic management, if not economic growth, the Brotherhood's early unsophisticated steps toward building an Islamic identity for Egypt engendered a level of popular resistance that contributed significantly to its downfall in 2013. One close friend objected to finding his daughter prevented from swimming training by regulations separating the sexes introduced by the Morsi government. Another friend, being considered for the post of foreign minister, was told the only question Morsi asked, when his name was suggested, was 'does his wife wear *hijab*?' (He accepted a post in Saudi Arabia instead.)

Though more devout, in my experience, than most Arabs, Egyptians, in general, do not appreciate being told how they should behave, let alone being dictated to by governments on matters of religion.

Sectarianism and the Politics of Development Assistance

Although the discretionary aid program funding for Egypt was very modest, it provided opportunities to make a positive difference at the village level in Upper Egypt (that is, to the south of Cairo) and in the slum areas of Cairo. In both areas, however, there was a need to take careful account of social and other dynamics.

In Upper Egypt, our focus was on the provision of funds to support NGOs connecting village houses to piped water supplies, which enabled them to install indoor toilets. Without such facilities, villagers either used the cattle pens under their living areas for toilets, or had to walk some distance to a communal facility, with attendant risks for women. The projects had immediate benefits not only in terms of hygiene but also for the dignity of the recipients. The problem with this, however, was not the nature of the project but its social context.

In Upper Egypt frictions between Egyptian Muslims and Copts—who share more or less equally bad living standards—are endemic, and so care needed to be taken not to be seen to be according priority to one group over another. But added to that concern was the fact that the most articulate proposals we received, carefully matched to the embassy's aid criteria, almost invariably came not from Coptic or Muslim NGOs, but rather from US-backed evangelical Christian groups. The evangelicals were astute enough not to be seeking to convert Muslims, which would have been both illegal and unacceptable behaviour in the deeply conservative village milieu: instead, their evangelical appeal was mainly to the Copts whose authoritarian, conservative Church hierarchy stood in the way of such human needs as divorce for those seeking it. At a minimum, we sought assurances that the facilities we were funding were made available to all, irrespective of whether the recipients were Muslims, Copts or evangelicals.

In Cairo, one of the programs we funded provided for the pottery kilns in the area known as Fustat to be converted to the use of gas, instead of the combustible rubbish collected by street children at considerable risk to themselves. It was a pilot project, because its implementation on a large scale would have been beyond our funding capabilities, but it brought to light the social and other complexity of the issues that would have to be addressed if it were to be successful (which in due course, with EU funding, and the support of the Cairo Municipality, it was).

Among the issues it highlighted were that although the risks to the children of gathering hazardous waste, including used medical supplies, were real, and the environmental benefits of shifting to gas were obvious, the children were nevertheless providing an income to their families that would now be lost. Moreover, if the plan was now to give those children an opportunity to go to school, it would be necessary to have teachers who were specially trained to cope with children who were much older than the usual school entry age, and who had little comprehension of school discipline. In other words, to be sustainable, the changes in one area—the fuel for kilns—had to be part of a larger program which took account of local conditions and was integrated with established education and other programs overseen by the Municipality.

Accreditations

In addition to dealing with the responsibilities of the embassy in regard to Egypt, I especially enjoyed engaging with Sudanese ministers and officials in Khartoum. Although there was little substance to the relationship between Australia and Sudan, there was concern in Australia in regard to the humanitarian situation in Darfur, and Australian churches had been important supporters of the progress toward independence for South Sudan. Australia had a modest but useful contribution of peacekeepers to the UN mission in Sudan (UNMIS). It was important to demonstrate the government valued their efforts, and the wider efforts of the UN force, not only in regard to the program for demobilising and disarming rebel forces, but also for the efforts to protect South Sudanese from the depredatory behaviour of the Lord's Republican Army straddling the southern border region.

I also urged an Australian contribution to efforts to address the tragic situation in Darfur. On the latter, I took a particular interest in the performance of the World Food Program, to which Australia is a major contributor, in the refugee camps, and observed with a great deal of pride the role that Australians were playing both in WFP and through World Vision Australia as one of the implementing agencies for the delivery of WFP food aid. Having seen the chaotic conditions on the border between Iraq and Jordan during the exodus of foreign workers from Iraq in the latter half of 1990 before the liberation of Kuwait; and aware of the less chaotic but still unruly situations encountered in the distribution of food aid by UNRWA, it was a pleasure to see the professionalism and discipline imposed by World Vision (with local police support) on food distribution procedures.

Of all the ceremonial presentation of credentials occasions I undertook, none was more memorable than that in Khartoum. It began normally enough, with a police escort of a protocol vehicle to the presidential place (the site of the British residency where General Gordon was killed on the 26th of January 1885 by the forces of the Mahdi). A guard of honour was in place and a military band provided an approximate rendering of the Australian national anthem. Unfortunately, however, the red carpet on which I had to walk to inspect the guard was laid over an uncut grass lawn. My arthritic hip was always a problem, but as I progressed along the carpet, my lurching from side to side grew exponentially. By the end of the walk. I was lucky not to find myself catapulting into the guardsmen.

My revenge upon President Omar al-Bashir for the atrocities being committed by his tribal proxies in Darfur was to give my speech on presentation of my credentials in Arabic.

With Sudanese President Omar al-Bashir. (MFA Sudan)

I relished the opportunity to return to Syria and resume contact with networks there. I enjoyed the delights of Tunisia once again (President Ben Ali had a better head of hair in 2005 than when I presented credentials to him in Tunis in 1990: mine had long since begun to disappear, but he had married a hairdresser). Although the PLO leadership had departed from Tunis, the foreign policy interests of the Tunisians straddled both the Arab Middle East and North Africa, and they provided valuable insights on both counts. They were also more willing than many Arab countries to benchmark their notions of social progress against the standards, if not of Europe, then certainly of the Mediterranean countries to their north with whom they retained close economic, cultural and civil society connections. The Bardo National Museum in Tunis still had one of the finest collection of Roman mosaics in the world, and the Roman ruins at Dhugga and the spectacular Roman amphitheatre at el-Jem were magnificent.

The utter chaos of Libya under Ghaddafi tested my capacity to meet the challenges of working in a dysfunctional government system, but as will be recounted later, getting things done there also provided moments of light relief. Leptis Magna in Libya was the location of some of the most spectacular Roman ruins in the Middle East, and Libya's Amarzigh (Berber) villages were a reminder of the flows of people and vibrant cultures across the Sahara, from Morocco to Egypt, as well as from South to North.

Compared to the Egyptians and Syrians, there was an element of volatility among the Libyans I met, combined with a remarkable reluctance to deal directly with each other, or to take responsibility for making decisions. But Libyans were also engaged in the business of survival as the subjects of a capricious, violent regime sitting on top of a daunting complex of historical, geographical, political and tribal divisions. For Libyan officials, Ghaddafi's rule combined a draconian security system with a fundamental calculation: that in the absence of a direction from Ghaddafi himself, the only safe course was to avoid taking a decision. The consequences of taking any decision without authority were certain to be more severe than making a wrong decision, or even a correct one. In an interesting contrast to Egypt, the traffic in Libya would actually stop immediately when traffic lights changed.

Life in Cairo

Of all the places we lived, Cairo was surely the most entertaining where daily life was concerned. It also had some extraordinary moments as we undertook the routine business of hosting social events for Egyptians to meet Australian visitors and businesspeople, and to reciprocate hospitality from fellow ambassadors.

Many older Cairo buildings still operate elevators from the 1920s, with their considerable aesthetic qualities somewhat marred by their unreliability. The elevator in the building of our dentist would frequently get stuck between floors, requiring the son of the *bawab* to climb in through the ceiling and restart it by disconnecting the fluorescent light fitting. Changing light globes in the Residence—a wonderful building from the 1920s with high ceilings and deep stairwells—was as awe-inspiring as it was death-defying.

One of the delights of my time in Cairo was being introduced, by my astute Irish colleague and good friend Richard O'Brien, to a small group of Arab ambassadors and European ambassadors with considerable experience of the Arab world, who would meet regularly for a very informal dinner. We would discuss freely the issues of the day, as well-informed friends, each speaking in whichever language he preferred. Australian government bans on smoking in the workplace notwithstanding, cigars after dinner were obligatory.

Jenny is a superb cook, and under her guidance Ahmed, the talented chef at the Residence produced the finest meals one could expect. But during a somewhat lengthy pause during drinks ahead of a casual dinner with our friends and colleagues, including the Canadian ambassador Phil MacKinnon and his wife Mary, Ahmed (who normally remained in the kitchen) came over and drew Jenny aside. 'The waiter' he said quietly, 'is unable to complete his duties tonight'. 'Is he sick?' Jenny asked.

'Ma'am, he is very tired.' Hint taken, and assuming there had been a quarrel in the kitchen, Jenny dispatched me to sort things out.

The waiter, a charming Nubian, was prone on the floor. He had had an epileptic seizure, and as he collapsed, had triggered the fire extinguisher. Everything in the kitchen, including the waiter, was covered in white powder. Gamal the gardener was reciting a verse from the Koran over him. I sat the waiter up and called the doctor. Jenny sorted out the remainder of the dinner and served it with Ahmed's help. At least we kept our guests entertained.

We relished the warmth of Egyptians toward those who respected and liked them. I adored my Egyptian embassy staff, and the staff at the Residence. It was always a pleasure to catch up again with them, and with the State Security guards who were still on duty at the Residence, long after we left the post. And through the extended families of our local staff, Tentmakers and other Egyptian friends we were introduced to a much wider range of ordinary and extraordinary Egyptians, from camel traders to retired military officers, who would invite us to join with them in the celebration of family weddings (at ear-splitting decibel levels) as well as convivial, relaxed, delicious dinners at their homes.

My colloquial Levantine Arabic was adequate for conversational purposes and, where necessary, for understanding the gist of media and other material, but my more formal use of the language suffered when confronted with the idiosyncrasies of the Egyptian dialect. Although my Egyptian staff and friends were gracious in tolerating my efforts, on one occasion, to the amusement of our daughter Tabitha, when I asked a young man in absolutely correct standard Arabic for directions to the road leading to Hurghada, he replied with a broad smile, 'I am sorry. I do not speak English.' I suspect it may have been the only sentence he could say in English, and he was determined to seize the opportunity to practise it.

I was disappointed when Canberra, in its wisdom, decreed that all ambassadors in the region would henceforth be required at all times to use only government-provided armoured BMW vehicles. I was in the habit of hopping into Cairo's ancient black and white taxis wherever possible, both to have some Arabic practice and to soak up the local atmosphere. I was quite sure that if the Egyptian security officials were aware of any specific risk to me I would be quickly informed and protected accordingly. I also varied my travel timing and routes to work on a daily basis, as an additional sensible precaution. But my drivers (who had to go to Germany for training, at the expense of the embassy travel vote) were pleased at what was clearly a status upgrade for the embassy in the diplomatic corps driver pecking order.

With Jenny, al-Azhar Park, Cairo, 2008

Farewell to Cairo: Australia Week 2008

As the expected end of my posting to Cairo drew near (although because of the conflict in Lebanon it was then extended by a further few months) I marked Australia Day in 2008 with rather more celebration than normal. It fell to three wonderful, talented and hard-working people—Third Secretary, Sarah Kirlew, my Executive Assistant, Dagmar Emery, and Jane Smythe, an Australian archaeologist living in Cairo—and the embassy public affairs officer, the delightful Heba Sharaf, to make it all happen. It was a great success.

We decided it would be appropriate to introduce Egyptians to indigenous and non-indigenous Australian culture through holding an Australian film festival at the Cairo Opera House, featuring classic Australian movies, mostly from the 1970s. The major reception we had organised to be held at the Opera House, with Australian wine and meat for the occasion, was thrown briefly into jeopardy on the morning of the event when the director of the Opera House was confronted by his religiously-conservative staff insisting that no alcohol should be served. The Director and I quickly agreed, however, that of course no alcohol would be served—and indeed no gin or whisky went around that evening—but wine was ok.

Whereas Egyptian responses to *Gallipoli* and *Strictly Ballroom* ranged from polite to curious to positive and appreciative, the empathy between the Egyptian audience and the key indigenous figures in *Rabbit-Proof Fence* was immediate and powerful. In a reminder of what matters most deeply to Egyptians, after a century of unequal and unfair treatment at the hands of foreigners, and despite probably having no background knowledge of the historical events depicted, the audience applauded the determination of the indigenous girls to prevail against their white European oppressors.

Since 2008 was also the 25th anniversary of archaeological cooperation between Egypt and Australia, it was also appropriate to set up a display of key events in the relationship at the Egyptian Museum. Zahi Hawass, the Minister of Antiquities; Wafaa

Sadik, the impressive and charming director of the Egyptian Museum; the distinguished Egyptian Australian archaeologist Naguib Kanawati who worked at Saqqara where some of the earliest pyramids are located; and friends from Macquarie University excavating near Luxor were all more than willing to assist Jane Smythe in putting the exhibition together. It was an impressive display.

In addition, we secured the participation of the wonderful indigenous singers, Nardi Simpson and Katleena Briggs, known in Australia as the Stiff Gins but performing in Cairo under their alternative, more politically-correct name Sweetwater. At the opening in the evening of the display at the Museum, among dimly-lit colossal statues of Ramses II and others dating back nearly 4000 years, Nardi and Katleena performed a Welcome to Country (complete with smoke!) danced and sang. Alongside walking through the gorge into Petra to see the Nabatean façade known as the Treasury for the first time, and seeing the Great Sand Sea by moonlight, their performance in that extraordinary setting was among the most evocative and memorable moments of my career.

Chapter 12

The 2006 Cairo Bus Crash and other Consular cases

Working through bilateral and other issues with Egypt and the opportunities and frustrations arising from them was endlessly fascinating, if not always rewarding. Ultimately, however, my time in Cairo came to be dominated by the management of complex consular situations.

2006 Cairo bus crash

On the night of the 10th of January 2006, I had a phone call from Consular Operations in Canberra advising that a busload of holidaying Australian police and their families had crashed on the highway between Cairo and Alexandria. Six were killed and 24 seriously injured. The injured had been taken to the al-Haram public hospital.

Although I maintained an informal relationship with my embassy staff, all Australia-based and Egyptian staff knew I operated on the principle that when circumstances required, all were part of the embassy team, under my direction, without regard to their nationality or the department in Canberra to which they were attached. I was fortunate to have an exceptionally able, rock steady Consul, Andrew Macksey, in charge of the embassy administration and consular affairs, and a dedicated and experienced consular team, both Australian and Egyptian. The sense of community across the embassy was wonderful.

I asked Ross Wilkie, the First Secretary (Immigration) to go immediately to the crash site 49 kilometres from Cairo to make sure there were no Australians unaccounted for, and to return the following morning to check in daylight there were no body parts or baggage remaining at the scene. I asked another officer to proceed immediately to the hospital, while Andrew Macksey went to meet the uninjured Australians who were being taken back to their nearby hotel. Andrew's immediate tasks were to identify those killed by going to the mortuary and examining the corpses against the passport documents issued in their name; preparing lists of the injured, and beginning the process of collecting the permissions required for DFAT to advise the next of kin. He also began to establish the whereabouts of personal belongings, the securing of which we knew would soon become a concern for the families of the injured.

With the initial response tasks delegated, I went to the public hospital. I found that although the emergency department had stabilised the situation of most of the injured, there was almost no pain control on offer to those who had, in most cases, suffered fractures or worse. There was an urgent need to have the injured transferred to Dar el-Fouad, a private hospital a few kilometres away where treatment more akin to western standards was available.

The charming and superbly professional head of the emergency department at Dar el-Fouad, Dr Hany Moro, had just run a training session for his staff based around a bus crash situation, and the facilities available at the hospital were excellent. The immediate problem, however, was to arrange for the transfer of the patients from the public system to the private hospital.

The management of al-Haram were unsure whether they as civil servants had the authority to allow the move to be made, and they expressed concern about possible issues of liability they might face if the transfers went awry. I also needed to be careful not to cause offence to the staff at al-Haram who had in fact provided support to the best of their ability and according to the requirements and expectations of the Egyptian public system. It was important to have their cooperation, including the provision of the documentation on individual cases, for the transfer to Dar el-Fouad to succeed.

With Australian patients still without pain relief, and some wandering the hospital corridors in shock, and with little prospect of the public hospital being able to meet their needs or agreeing to anything else, I worked with our Egyptian consular officer, the wonderful Amani Shenouda, to create over several hours a document in Arabic which absolved al-Haram hospital from responsibility for the transfer of its patients. By dawn, all but one critically-ill Australian had been transferred by ambulance to Dar el-Fouad, together with their medical records.

I then went to meet with the uninjured members of the group to brief them on developments and introduce the consular team. I said it was up to the party members to decide whether they wished to continue their tour, but assured those who wished to remain in Cairo with their partners and friends they would be welcome to lend their assistance to the embassy if they wished (several did so, and made a valuable practical contribution to our efforts). I promised to ensure that their representatives would be briefed as far as patient confidentiality allowed about the condition of their friends and family members, and the steps being taken to arrange medical evacuations. I fielded calls from the media; and had a strongly supportive phone call from Alexander Downer.

Andrew Macksey set up a crisis centre at Dar el-Fouad, at which I gave briefings twice daily to the embassy team and visitor representatives. Stuart Campbell made sure any relatives arriving in Cairo to support injured family members were met at the airport and escorted through immigration and customs, and those who left also had embassy escorts. The Egyptian staff of the embassy, from drivers to senior clerks, were simply magnificent.

The Australian community in Cairo rallied around. Our friend, the Reverend Canon Jim Doust, the interim Dean of All Saints Episcopal Cathedral in Cairo, came by to offer pastoral support and spiritual comfort to those who might ask for it. I am not a religious person, but I deeply appreciated Jim's support, and that he, his wife Elaine and many others were praying for all of those involved in the accident and its aftermath, myself included.

Jenny and others donated blood, before she had to leave to fulfil a long-standing commitment to the opening of a display of Australian textile art in Tripoli in Libya. Others donated clothing, phone chargers, comfort food and other items to assist the injured. The Consul in Amman, Roz McKenzie, arrived to help. DFAT sent in additional staff from Brussels and elsewhere and the Australian contingent to the Multinational Force and Observers based in the Sinai lent us two warrant officers to relieve exhausted embassy staff, to help with the management of victims' property and to assist as medical evacuation arrangements to London were made through the travel insurance companies. The Victorian Police Commissioner, Jim Hart, and other senior police from Victoria arrived to liaise with their Egyptian counterparts concerning the circumstances of the accident, and to support their colleagues and their families.

In the end, we successfully managed the largest non-military evacuation of Australian civilians from a post in the history of the Department. DFAT awarded the post team a 2007 Australia Day citation in respect of their outstanding response, saying that staff had worked 'with particular dedication and professionalism under very difficult and stressful conditions.'

Two memories from those days remain especially vivid. I grappled with the question of when to move the last, critically-injured patient from al-Haram, a decision which her partner, who was also injured and hospitalised at Dar el-Fouad, had left to me. As concern about her condition grew, her supervising doctor at al-Haram hospital rang me to advise that she would have to be moved but might not survive the transfer. Knowing that I was acting on the best medical advice available to me at the time, I authorised the transfer, while knowing that she might die before reaching the new hospital. (Jim Doust came with me to al-Haram, and gave the final sacraments to the patient before she left). The transfer was completed successfully.

My other abiding memory, which still causes me difficulty at times, was going to the Haram public mortuary, with Roz McKenzie, to search the adult corpses for specific items including a police badge, and the substantial amounts of money which individual victims were believed to be carrying. Andrew Macksey, as Consul, had already done more than anyone could ask of him in visiting the morgue twice and identifying the victims, some of whom were severely disfigured. Roz aside, I would not, and could not, ask others to do so when I felt up to the task.

Out of respect to the families of those concerned, I will not dwell on the conditions we encountered in searching through the blood-soaked remains of the six Australian victims in the facility, in the dimly-lit vault alongside the mouldering remains of other corpses. The cooling system of the mortuary had failed some time before. In appalling conditions of stench, amidst the blood and bodily fluids with which the floor of the mortuary storage area was awash, we followed an intrusive process of going through each of the bodies, trying to disentangle flesh from clothing to look for their belongings. Although the money had disappeared from the belts worn by the victims, I did manage to find a police badge, which was displayed at a memorial service at the hospital arranged at the initiative of Jim Doust and the travelling party. Roz burnt her clothes afterwards.

Other Consular Cases

I found myself dealing with a range of other consular problems, including the abduction of children by their Egyptian father and the desperate efforts of their mothers—almost always unsuccessful—to find and return them to Australia. The most time-consuming consular case, however, was the disappearance of an Australian citizen whose wife believed he had been taken by the Egyptian security services and who she believed was being held secretly in various prisons.

On the basis of several meetings with him, I felt the person informing us and the wife regarding the supposed whereabouts of her husband was sincere in his expressed desire to help. Nevertheless, our repeated attempts to contact the husband, and questions posed to the relevant Egyptian authorities through the Foreign Ministry concerning his whereabouts and welfare came to nothing. We were told, at one stage, that the husband was actually being held in a prison but was able to be released if a ransom was paid to the family of a prominent Egyptian.

Faced with ongoing stories about the alleged transfer of the husband between various locations we asked our informant to come up with evidence the husband was in fact alive—by answering a question to which only the husband and his wife would know the answer. When the informant came back some time later with a correct answer, I took up the issue directly with the Egyptian Foreign Minister, but once again drew a blank.

Since we expected that the Muslim Brotherhood's networks of prisoners in the prison system would keep them abreast of the whereabouts of their members and sympathisers, and taking care to let the Egyptians know beforehand through intelligence liaison channels what I was doing and why, I made enquiries of individuals known to be close to the Brotherhood. They too said the husband was not known to them. The only clue to his possible fate was a passing comment, by a family member in the course of a judicial enquiry instigated by his wife, that he thought the husband had been killed in Afghanistan—but there was no evidence to support that conjecture either.

A case with a happier conclusion was that of Douglas Wood, an Australian kidnapped and held for ransom in Iraq in May 2005. My involvement in the case was through liaison on behalf of the Emergency Response Team in Canberra with Sheikh Tajeddine Hilali, a prominent and sometimes controversial figure in Australian Islamic circles, who had offered himself as a go-between with the kidnappers. We enjoyed a positive personal relationship, but Hilali was a controversial figure in some respects, and staying in contact with him as the situation evolved proved challenging. At times I resorted to the decidedly Egyptian method of interrogating the caretaker (*bawab*) of his building to determine his whereabouts.

On 15 June Wood was found and rescued by Iraqi troops without a ransom being paid. The Secretary, Michael L'Estrange, wrote to say my dedication and professionalism reflected great credit on the Department, and that this had been recognised by the Prime Minister and Mr Downer and Mr Wood's family. The embassy consular team received a performance citation from the Department.

Dr Hany Moro and his colleagues at the Dar el-Fouad continued to provide exceptional service to the embassy and Australian visitors throughout our time in Cairo. On Anzac Day 2006 three bombs were detonated in the Sinai Peninsula resort city of Dahab, killing 23 people and injuring around 80 others, including two Australians. As I was hosting the pre-dawn service at the Commonwealth War Cemetery in downtown Cairo that morning, I had to alternate, in the darkness, between fulfilling that responsibility, wreath-laying and giving a speech to those who had gathered for the event, and arranging for the helicopter transfer of the injured Australians to Dar el Fouad.

Once again, Hany Moro supervised the reception of the injured Australians as well as many other victims of the attack. While I was in the Emergency Department I heard a woman screaming in grief, and when Hany came by, in surgical scrubs, I asked him what was happening. He took me aside and said he had just come from the operating theatre, where he had amputated the leg of a two year old Swedish boy: the screams were those of the mother when he broke the news to her. Hany then burst into tears, and I wept with him.

Chapter 13

Under the Hangman's Tree: the George Forbes case[14]

In May 2007 George Forbes, a decent Australian citizen based in Kenya, was arrested, together with two Kenyan and one Sudanese colleagues, following the death in a room in their compound in Rumbek, southern Sudan of a Ukrainian flight engineer, Mykola Serebrenikov. The latter had broken into Forbes' compound late at night, dead drunk, and saying someone was threatening to kill him. He committed suicide early the next morning by hanging himself from a towel rail.

The local police could not decide what to do; the doctor who examined the body wrote that the death was 'suspicious'; the police did not want to get involved but the deputy governor may have told the governor and the local press that some expats had been arrested for murder; and it all went downhill from there. Forbes chose to stay in Rumbek rather than clear out while waiting for the trial, as he was certain that leaving would have meant his colleagues would be executed.

---

[14]This account is based on a background document I prepared for Julie-Anne Davies of The Bulletin in July 2007, at the request of the Department. See Julie-Anne Davies, 'Out of Africa' The Bulletin, 19 June 2007. A more colourful account, 'Our Man in Sudan', by Cameron Stuart appeared in The Weekend Australian Magazine September 15-16 2007.

From my perspective as the Australian ambassador accredited to Sudan, the core of the Forbes consular problem comprised several elements. Our goal was to secure due legal process for George and to protect his health and well-being. That involved several challenges. First, we had to understand the complexities and sensitivities of the dynamics that were in play between the judicial and political elements of the government in southern Sudan, at both the local and regional level. We had to work out how best to pursue our key objectives in that context. We had to help George access the best legal support available while that process was being completed. And we had to do whatever we reasonably and legitimately could to help him survive.

Within that framework, we had to coordinate and obtain maximum value from the inputs that were offered from the Australian side. There was a constant risk of being seen as overplaying our hand as a government. However there were also ambiguous and sometimes directly contradictory messages coming to us from the South Sudanese side about how far we could and should go. We had to make some delicately balanced judgements—often amidst a range of conflicting assertions and rumours—about the reliability and capability of certain key people. We had to respect the rights of George and his family and friends to their privacy and their freedom to choose how they wished to proceed. We needed to coordinate a range of players between Canberra, Rumbek, Juba, Cairo and Nairobi. We had to manage the mishaps and communication problems inevitable in a place emerging from 20 years of armed conflict. And it had to be a team effort throughout.

It would be fair to say you have not seen the end of the Earth until you have been to Rumbek. It was a pretty tough place in which to survive, let alone as a prisoner. The government hospital had nothing, not even a mortuary. Absolutely everything was imported, at very high prices, from Kenya and Uganda.

There was no sign of the national government. Even Sudanese currency was unwelcome.

It was not the physical appearance of the place—mud and thatch round houses, red dirt roads, the usual goats and donkeys—or the local Dinka inhabitants who were friendly and physically quite striking (very tall, heavily scarified men, and brightly dressed women). It was not the heat and humidity, malaria, typhoid, smoking piles of garbage or the torrential rain. It was, rather, the extraordinary challenge—for the locals—of starting from scratch to build a country out of the ruins (literally) of the civil war; and (for both the locals and for ourselves) the complications of trying to work within the framework of law upon which good and sensible governance had to be built.

In those cases where commitment to that objective was genuine, it was painfully apparent that the South Sudanese authorities did not have, and without assistance perhaps never would have, the means of putting those principles into effect. To give just one example, the president of the Court of Appeal—a serious man with close connections to Australia, hard-working and sincere—had exactly six books in his court library (I counted them). He had no reliable means of gaining computerised access to decisions, precedents etc. The police commissioner had very little fuel for his vehicles—so the next of kin of the accused had to transport the four accused, their police guards, and the defence and prosecution lawyers to the court. Only satellite phones worked—and not always. There were no fax machines, and only very limited internet access. It was in some ways an inspirational experience to meet the locals, but it was also something which left me feeling for the enormity of their situation.

George Forbes and his colleagues (Kenyans James Mayao and Bernard Alumasa and Sudanese Joseph Nyakot) had been briefly imprisoned when first arrested, but released following several phone calls from me to the Interior Minister of the Government of Southern Sudan, Paul Mayom, and from our Consul in Nairobi, Leann Johnston, to the State Governor, Daniel Awet. The British Consul in Juba, Ian Ross, worked effectively and with great dedication to help secure their release. The downside of this outcome, however, was a heightened degree of sensitivity on the part of the Rumbek judiciary to any further pressure on them at the political level.

We stayed in a tent camp beside the airport, which I found comfortable enough, although it meant there were a few unwelcome insects and other bits of fauna sharing my space during the rain. (I told the Vice Consul, Nermeen Nabulsi, in response to her question, that her job was to patrol at night outside my tent in case there were lions—and for a horrified moment she believed me.) A greater problem was that even with taking some care, I came down with a nasty case of gastro which developed into a bout of colitis by the time I returned to Cairo because I tried to ignore it.

Having been assured by the court that the High Court trial would begin on the 7th of May, and having had that reaffirmed to me by the acting governor and the police commissioner the day before, when Forbes's relative, Orson Taylor, went to get the police prosecutor he was nowhere to be found. The senior prosecutor had gone to Juba and then to Cairo. The other had headed off to an assignment in a town 30 miles away the previous day.

Less than amused, the judge wrote an order directing the latter to return (I had someone take it to the police commissioner to get it countersigned by him). The judge told Orson to deliver it, as the police had no way of doing so. Orson found the prosecutor, and brought him back to Rumbek that night. The next morning, the judge heard him for less than two minutes and dismissed him from the court (Orson had to drive him and his family back to his new assignment). The judge took over as prosecutor himself.

For all the strangeness which we had observed at the High Court trial on 7/8 May, we were taken aback when on 21 May the court found the group guilty of murder of the Ukrainian flight engineer. The judge who had taken over the prosecution was well satisfied with his own case—notwithstanding a complete absence of motive or forensic evidence linking the accused to the victim. Even worse, as we were reasonably confident the verdict would be overturned on appeal, was that all four who were convicted had been returned to Rumbek prison pending advice from the Ukrainian family of the deceased regarding the sentence to be passed.

After a phone call to me from Simeon Gilding, head of Consular Operations on the 22nd of May while I was outside Cairo visiting an aid-related project, I went to see the Sudanese ambassador in Cairo to give him a diplomatic note asking for Sudanese assistance and to brief him on the situation. I then flew to Khartoum at 0230hrs the same night arriving at 0530hrs on the 23rd of May. In Khartoum I went to see the British ambassador, Ian Cliff, key players in the Sudanese MFA, and the Ukrainian Honorary Consul, seeking to have any advice from the relatives in Ukraine of the deceased passed on quickly, and getting some local advice on how best to tackle the problem. The Ukrainian Honorary Consul was especially helpful, offering to set up meetings with lawyers in Khartoum who Third Secretary Hugh Robilliard went to see when he arrived a few days later from Cairo.

I had toured the Rumbek prison on my earlier visit to attend the opening of the trial in May. It was truly appalling: bombed repeatedly throughout the civil war, it held 520 men in an area about half the size of a hockey field, with one tree for shade, no medical facilities, no kitchen and no working latrines. Most men lived, ate and slept in buildings without a roof—the buildings with roofs were controlled by those whose tribes were the strongest—

in rain and in the burning sun. The stink from open drains and sewerage and men relieving themselves was incredible.

Murderers were kept in shackles, and if two were guilty, they were shackled together. Only a small proportion of those in the prison had been convicted: mostly they were being kept there as witnesses, or awaiting charges, or in some cases because they were relatives of those who had been convicted but who could not be found. There was an outbreak of chicken pox, and when I went to the prison on 31 May it was evident that a lot of men were affected.

I saw George and the others twice while they were in prison during this second visit to Rumbek. They were feeling the effects of being there. In addition to sweets, biscuits and dried fruit Jenny had sent down with me from Cairo, I gave George some insect repellent and most of my anti-malaria tablets. I then went to see the President of the Court of Appeal, Justice Kukurlopita. He was not around on the first afternoon, part of which I spent sitting under a mango tree waiting for him to turn up (you spend a lot of time sitting under trees in Southern Sudan, partly because it is cooler, and partly because you never know when or if anyone will turn up). Eventually I wrote him a note highlighting my concerns and the need to see him urgently, and left.

Going back again the next morning I finally met Kukurlopita. I told him the Australian government fully respected the legal process in Southern Sudan and admired his efforts to strengthen the system within his jurisdiction. It would be inconsistent with that approach to seek exceptional treatment for George Forbes, and we would not do so. But Forbes's health, and the conditions he was enduring posed a serious threat to his life. We had the gravest concerns about his well-being. Moreover, any chances of Australia contributing to the goals the judge had of developing the judicial system would be severely affected if Forbes should die in prison. I stressed that that was now a serious possibility.

Kukurlopita appreciated these arguments. He said he would direct that the case be taken from the High Court and considered in the Court of Appeal, based on the fact that the defence lawyer had presented a memorandum to the Court of Appeal seeking a revision of the wording of the High Court decision. As he had taken charge of the case, it also meant he had responsibility for the welfare of the prisoners.

He said he would visit the prison himself the following day and make arrangements for George to have a medical examination by a doctor from the government hospital. If that doctor's report recommended that George be taken to hospital for treatment, he could be taken to any hospital that could provide such treatment as was needed. As the government hospital almost certainly could not treat him, he would agree to George going to a small hospital run by a Christian NGO.

Happy enough with that outcome, I drafted a letter from George to the judge asking to be transferred to hospital, which George's friend Jenny Fletcher typed up for George to sign. I also wrote out my concerns and gave them to the judge so he had the official Australian position on record for a second time. I then told George and the others the news, filled in Simeon and his team using the satellite phone from outside the prison (while being yelled at by a particularly feisty character telling me to go and sit under another tree) and left for Juba to lobby at the government level.

With the generous help of a Sudanese Australian, Manyang Parek, I charged around on the afternoon of the 25th of May, seeing in rapid succession the Minister for Legal Affairs, the Minister for Cabinet Affairs, the Vice President, the Interior Minister and the Minister for Regional Cooperation. To each of them I underlined the gravity of our concerns for George. I said that while we respected their legal system, and were aware that it would correct its mistakes in due course, it would be a disaster in both human and bilateral terms if George were to die in prison.

The Sudanese ministers were all at pains to assure me how deeply they valued the relationship with Australia. Almost all of them had lived in, or had visited Australia, which has the second largest South Sudanese diaspora after the United States. They hoped we would see from this situation the dimensions of the development challenges they were facing, including the problems of changing guerrilla fighters into police, judges and lawyers. They were full of assurances that it would all be sorted out. In the nicest possible way, I delivered the message it had to be.

The following morning (Saturday the 26th of May) I went to meet Ruben Madol, the Senior Registrar of the Judiciary of Southern Sudan at his home (under the trees again). Madol made it clear that he wanted his judiciary to take care of this problem without recourse to any external interference (including when disguised as support). This was a problem, because Kukurlopita had told me he would appreciate assistance with access to source material, including briefing which the legal team from Melbourne (comprising Alex Danne, Lex Lasry QC and Julian McMahon) had prepared to supplement the submission made by Forbes's lawyer Kiir Chol. Ultimately, I had to balance the two opposing approaches somehow.

Then I had a phone call from Jenny Fletcher saying that the judge, Kukurlopita, had not turned up at the prison or made arrangements for the medical examination. He was said to have gone to Juba that morning. Moreover, Jenny had not been allowed to visit the men in prison that day, and had been threatened (by the acting officer in charge, backed by the chap who had been yelling at me - who turned out to be the prison executioner) with being jailed herself if she did not go away.

Manyang and I went back to sit again under Ruben Madol's trees - he had chosen a different one for this time of the day. When I explained the information I had been given he appreciated the seriousness of the situation immediately. He doubted that the judge would have come to Juba, but he asked that enquiries be made at the home of the judge's brother in Juba to check. Later that night I heard that he was definitely not in Juba.

Back we went to see Madol the next morning (Sunday the 27th of May) with the latest story—that the judge had gone to Wau, and that his satellite phone had been stolen (this story was also untrue: the judge was actually in Rumbek all along, but holed up writing legislation that the State government was urgently demanding). Madol said he had briefed the Chief Justice, and the case would be resolved very soon. The Chief Justice was sending judges to Rumbek to sit with Justice Kukurlopita to hear the case. We then settled into an interesting discussion about Islamic extremism and why Australia was less affected by it domestically than most western countries, and we were getting along pretty well by the time we finished.

I then managed to find the Chief Justice, Ambrose Thiik. After a cordial discussion about the right of judges to make errors and the importance of a system being able to fix them, and strong representations again from me about the health threats facing Forbes, he confirmed he would be sending judges to Rumbek to expedite hearing the case. In response to my concerns about George's health, he said he believed the four should be allowed to return to their compound on bail, and that George should be admitted to a hospital.

Later that day I rang Pagan Amum, Secretary General of the Sudan Peoples Liberation Movement (SPLM), probably the second or third most powerful person in Southern Sudan, who was a good friend of a very helpful Australian businessman, Bryan Grasby and briefed him on the situation. Pagan, who had recently visited Australia, undertook to help wherever he could.

That night, Ruben Madol gave me and barrister Kiir a letter signed by the Chief Justice to Kukurlopita ordering that the men be released on "strong bail" and that George should receive proper medical attention until the conclusion of the hearings. As the Chief Justice left it to us to advise the Court, and the Ministry of Legal Affairs had no means of sending the letter by fax or phones or radios, I scanned it in at a nearby compound and sent it as an email from my account to Kukurlopita and Jenny the next morning. Also, as the judge who was in Juba had no way of getting to Rumbek, I went to the World Food Program HQ near the airport and arranged for him to travel on a WFP/UNHAS flight the next morning (since local officials are prohibited from booking themselves on UN flights).

Instruction from the Chief Justice of South Sudan, Justice Ambrose Thiik, to Justice Kukurlopita for the release of George Forbes and others on 'strong bail'. Forbes is incorrectly identified. May 2007.

The instruction from the Chief Justice enabled Jenny Fletcher to get the men out of prison to the hospital, under police guard, around 1200hrs on the 28th of May. However at around 5pm the police had had no further instructions from the police chief, who could not be found. They therefore insisted that the men had to go back to the prison. Jenny rang me. I told her to delay things as long as she could, by any means she could, without getting shot. I then rang the Minister for Legal Affairs, who was in Khartoum at a meeting. He said he would look into it. Fortunately, Pagan Amum of the SPLM answered his phone when I called him as well. At my suggestion he immediately phoned Jenny's phone, and spoke to the police when they were 100 metres from the prison, stopping them in their tracks. George and the other men were then returned to their compound.

The bail issue however had not been resolved. Because the Chief Justice had specified "strong bail" Judge Kukurlopita had advised the police chief (whose responsibility it was to set the bail terms) that it would be appropriate to impose a bond equivalent to the amount payable under customary law if relatives accepted cash instead of insisting upon a death penalty. No-one seemed to know how much he had in mind—amounts seemed to vary between US$30,000 and US$180,000—but in any event it was going to be difficult to resolve the issue if that advice were applied. And, once again, the police chief was nowhere to be found. I spoke to the Chief Justice, who said a bail bond was not necessary, but he had no means of advising the police to that effect, physically or procedurally. He had to work through Kukurlopita, whose phone was either stolen or turned off.

Incidentally, throughout all this day the DFAT communications system in Canberra was not functioning either. But I knew I had Greg Hunt in Downer's office supporting me, and that Simeon Gilding and his Consular team would be willing to back my judgement if I had to take some risks.

The Chief Justice spoke to the judge travelling on the WFP flight I had arranged for him, instructing him to tell Kukurlopita to tell the police chief there was to be no bail bond. It is not clear whether that message ever reached the police chief—there is no evidence they met that day—but Jenny delayed the meeting with him to allow as much time as possible for the message to get through. (There was another bit of drama when the judge could not find his name on the WFP manifest—the Chief Justice rang me at 0730, and I had hopped into a utility from Mango Camp in Juba heading to the airport trying to sort it out, with Hugh Robilliard working feverishly at the Khartoum end, when the Chief Justice rang back to say it had been resolved).

Fortunately Hugh Robilliard had arrived in Rumbek that morning, so I dictated to him a letter couched in very vague terms referring to Forbes's undertaking to remain in the company of the (Acting) Vice Consul and attend court with him. I had no authority to suggest anything of the sort, of course, and I doubt Canberra would have allowed me to offer, in effect, Hugh as surety—if I had asked the Department. The unflappable Hugh took it all calmly enough.

Jenny Fletcher stood as surety for the two Kenyans (James and Bernard), and Joseph's father stood as surety for him. The police commissioner was persuaded by Hugh to accept my letter. He was understandably a bit underwhelmed by its generality, but I had had a couple of conversations with him in early May about assistance to his police force, and I suspect he was not inclined to put me too far offside at that juncture. The upshot was that no bail bond was paid, and the four men were released on bail formally on 29 May.

I arrived in Rumbek from Juba on 30 May to see the men, and to do a round of calls on the police and the prison and of course on Kukurlopita. The court accepted the submission from the Melbourne lawyers, including the material prepared by Professor Stephen Cordner reviewing the Kenyan forensic pathology analysis. Over a quiet beer with the clerk of the Court, Hugh Robilliard had put the Cordner material on the computer of Kukurlopita so the judge could cut and paste from it—which he duly did. I then returned to Khartoum and Cairo, while Hugh remained in Rumbek to ensure there was an ongoing consular presence until the verdict was heard, and Forbes had left.

With George Forbes, May 2007. Photo courtesy of Are Media Pty Limited / aremediasyndication.com.au / 'The Bulletin'. 19 June 2007.

I had lost 5kg with a dose of Rumbek races, gone a bit greyer, and learnt a lot. I had nothing but admiration for almost all the people involved (maybe not the executioner, although I thanked him profusely as well "for doing all he could"). George Forbes and Jenny Fletcher were amazing in their resilience and courage in extraordinary circumstances. I appreciated that the senior South Sudan judiciary with whom I dealt—Registrar Ruben Madol and the Chief Justice, Ambrose Thiik, and Justice Kukurlopita and the Police Chief, Brigadier Sabit—were serious people with a strong vision for the future, even if their systems sometimes let them down.

Besides a range of political and other pressures, they all had to cope with the lack of the physical means of making their nascent system work consistently well. They suffered particularly from the lack of reliable communications. The Rumbek prison was dreadful, but changing that required changing a large number of other things as well—such as the administration of the justice and policing systems, and the improvement of the health care system generally. Setting up a decent clinic at the prison when the public hospital was inadequate, for example, would simply not be a sustainable approach. As always, development, if it were to happen at all, would be a slow and complex business. It was a pity that the consequences of that situation sometimes affected Australians such as George Forbes, and pointlessly put lives at risk in doing so. But for almost everyone in Southern Sudan, the daily reality was not much different.

Exhausted, at Rumbek airport, May 2007.

Chapter 14

Libya: Touring Tobruk by Moonlight

Of all the Arab countries in which I lived and worked, or to which I was accredited, none could match Libya's blend of chaos and impenetrability under the Ghaddafi regime. In March 2005, with a visit by the Australian Minister for Defence, Robert Hill, impending to celebrate Anzac Day by holding a dawn service at the Tobruk Commonwealth War Graves Cemetery in eastern Libya, I set out from Tripoli to check the venue and make the necessary plans. It was an experience.

On arrival in Tripoli a couple of days earlier to present my credentials as non-resident ambassador, I had mentioned to Protocol officials that I would be flying to Benghazi, about an hour away, planning then to head on to Tobruk by road. 'Oh,' they said. 'You have to leave from the domestic airport, Mantega, not the international airport.' I went ahead and purchased a return ticket on Libyan Airlines. Heba Shenouda, the consular manager in Cairo, had already done a marvellous job in sorting out my overnight accommodation in Benghazi for the return journey, and road transport. She did the latter through the Egyptian consul-general in Benghazi, after the hotel car drivers wanted to charge exorbitantly, and insisted on staying overnight in Tobruk as well because it was, after all, a five-hour journey and a 10 or 11 hour round trip. The consul general, who for reasons that will become obvious, shall remain nameless, also fixed up the local security escort arrangement (ambassadors could go nowhere in Libya without such arrangements, although the security people were supposed to be invisible).

I headed off to the airport to catch the 0800 flight. I had mixed up the times—it was a flight for 0900, so I settled back to read a book in the completely deserted Mantega airport. As is the case throughout Libya, there were no signs in English to guide the traveller, but my Arabic was up to the task of reading what was around me, there was a Libyan airlines office nearby (unstaffed) but there was a Libyan airlines plane on the tarmac, a crowd was drifting in and all seemed normal. At 0830, the queue formed at the check in and up I went, only to be told that I was queuing for Buraq airlines (the other local carrier) flight to Benghazi at 1000, not Libyan airlines, which used the international airport for flights to Benghazi. The Libyan air flight was leaving at 0900, and the airport was at least 30 minutes away. Blast.

I swung around to the Buraq ticket office, bought a ticket to Benghazi and rejoined the queue, which had barely moved anyway. Frantic mobile messages (the Libyan mobile network is not exactly the world's best) around Tripoli went unconnected or unanswered until I managed to raise Heba in Cairo (at home, on a Friday, at Easter). Heba went into action, ringing around until she had the number of the VIP Lounge at Benghazi airport, who in turn alerted the Egyptian Consul General to what had happened, and asked them to expect me at 1115.

The Buraq flight was ok, using an old Algerian 737, which rattled a bit but stayed in the air. The passengers applauded on landing. I bounded down the steps of the plane to be met by my Egyptian colleague, who proceeded to regale me with an urgent proposal for an Australian company to secure undreamt of wealth through being party to an illegal, immoral and probably downright dangerous business arrangement which he knew was being put together with the involvement of some Egyptians in Alexandria.

After hearing this out for about 30 minutes, including over a cup of tea at his residence, I gently suggested that perhaps it might be difficult to find a company in Australia that preferred to operate in such a manner. 'Ah,' he replied, 'if it is honesty you are looking for, you have come to the wrong country.' He went back to outlining his proposal. In response to a further question, as to why the Egyptians and Libyans did not simply do the business between themselves, he suggested it was because the Egyptians did not fall into the Libyans' traps, but Europeans were usually gullible enough not to argue.

We parted friends, with his driver setting off to reconfirm my Libyan airlines return flight booking and to drop the tickets off at the hotel for my arrival that night (no Libyan airlines offices are open on Fridays, except at the airport, and because I had been taken out from the VIP area there was no chance to do it myself). I was left pondering what, if anything, I could do with my Egyptian friend's business proposal without appearing to be party to the scheme. I decided it would have to die of less than benign neglect.

Off I went with Ali, a driver with the protocol department of the Benghazi governorate, who was borrowing his official car, an Audi, for the negotiated price of Libyan Pounds 160, plus tip, plus petrol. We collected my minder, Ahmed, who turned out to be a relative of Ali's, a little later. Neither spoke any English at all, but that was no problem, as my Syrian/Palestinian Arabic seemed to work better in Libya than it did among Egyptians, and it was time I put in some Arabic practice anyway. There is very little English spoken in Libya—my dealings with Protocol were invariably in Arabic, and there was no English signage on roads etc.

Ali was a good driver, if one used the concept loosely, and had no qualms about doing 150 kph down main streets. I was running late as we did not leave Benghazi until 1230 and I was concerned to make it to Tobruk in plenty of time to see the cemetery, and some other sites of importance to the Australian record there (such as Hill 201, and Fig Tree). In response to my question, Ali happily admitted he had no idea where the Australian war cemetery in Tobruk was, but Ahmed said he had seen it.

The drive across was fascinating, with scenery rather like the hill country of Cyprus, intermingled with flat, stony desert. That is where the car chose to run out of petrol. Ahmed flagged down another security vehicle and headed off, returning 20 minutes later with petrol in plastic bottles. He poured it into the petrol tank, and the car immediately decided to run on five instead of six cylinders. That was fine for speeds over 120 kph, but every time we came up to a check point (which was very often) or had to stop at traffic lights (which Libyans do, unlike most Egyptians), the car sounded very sick indeed. Ali's answer was to get someone to top up the oil. It did nothing for the engine, now clogged with plastic laden petrol, but it was something he needed for reassurance.

On to Tobruk we went, with the sun sinking lower. As we approached the town, I noticed a war cemetery off to the right, but Ahmed said it was not the right one, and we had to go further. Ahmed and Ali proceeded to ask anyone passing by the roadside where the Australian cemetery was to be found. Everyone thought for a while, was deeply surprised to learn there was any such thing in Tobruk (there was a general awareness that the British had been there, but not that there were also Australians present) and then produced contradictory answers. Then we followed an authoritative piece of advice—and found ourselves looking at the German war cemetery sign. Ahmed asked if it would do anyway—Germany and Australia were friends, weren't they?

We traversed rubbish dumps, wheat fields, and suburban roads dug up for sewerage work. We reversed up the highway because we could not get around road dividers. Deciding that the first cemetery we had seen was perhaps the right one, we doubled back again, asking advice along the way. As it was getting quite gloomy, we had trouble spotting the cross in the distance, across a wheat field. It turned out to be a British cemetery, known as Knightsbridge, not the Tobruk cemetery.

At that point, things were looking good humoured but grim. It had been a long day already. In the local tradition, Ahmed took us off to consult his mates in the *mukhabarat* (the domestic intelligence service). The usual round of headshaking followed, but then someone thought he might know the spot. He piled into the car, and off we went again—this time to discover the French cemetery. At least this suggested we were in a cemetery-rich environment.

We pulled up outside a building site, and the local mukhabarat fellow (Abdul Qadir) interrogated the supervisor. Ten minutes later, with the full moon above us, we had another fellow traveller. The five of us went another 200 meters down the road, and turned in at a place I thought might be a possibility because it had a couple of limestone pillars (but no sign) on the roadside. Indeed it was the place.

The cemetery caretaker had long gone away, so we squeezed through a gap between the cemetery wall and the fence, walked around a bit and found a gate I could scramble over. The others, somewhat younger and less arthritic, came as well. I checked out the site, which was particularly beautiful by moonlight, noted the space available for laying wreaths, where a catafalque party could be positioned, the distance from the front entrance etc. There was nothing more I could do, apart from making mental notes about making sure that someone would be pre-positioned in Tobruk to lead the drivers of the Ministerial cavalcade to the right cemetery at the right time on the right day.

It was time to head home, but first Abdul Qadir had to get a copy of my passport and to prepare a report, presumably on why this ambassador chap had been scoping out the port area and surrounds of Tobruk, especially the high ground overlooking the harbour, quizzing locals about the layout of the urban area, and doing so in execrable Arabic. He and Ahmed remained in animated discussion and waved bits of paper at each other for quite a while. Then we left Abdul Qadir behind, but Ali was flagging. Ahmed wound up driving while Ali recovered, and we kept stopping for tea, Pepsi (*Bebs*) and coffee.

Finally we made it back to Benghazi at 0130, and I had to be up at 0500 for my return flight. But Ahmed, bless him, shook my hand and planted kisses on both my cheeks. When you are kissed by a Libyan security official, you know it is time to go home.

By way of a postscript, I should add that the Robert Hill visit and the ceremony at Tobruk proved well worth the effort invested in bringing them about. The minister and his accompanying party coped remarkably well with somewhat chaotic, sometimes life-threatening experiences of long distance high-speed motorcades, substitution of a decrepit and decidedly malodorous Libyan Air Force plane for the RAAF plane which had gone unserviceable en route to Benghazi; hotel accommodation that was barely fit for the most budget-conscious backpackers, and a farewell buzzing by a Libyan jet fighter only metres above our unsuspecting heads.

A week before the visit I had gone around with my good friend Brigadier Peter Daniel, the commander of the Australian Defence Force contingent serving with the Multinational Force and Observers (MFO) in the Sinai, seeking the location of significant sites where Australians had fought during the Libyan campaign, and using military maps to identify landmarks such as railway water tanks in some cases where the towns themselves had been relocated. Peter also managed to persuade his regimental sergeant major (RSM)—the font of all authority on military ceremonial matters—that whereas the rules of the Australian Defence Force required catafalque parties to have weapons, and the Libyans would not allow rifles to be brought into the country, and the swords on board the RAAF aircraft were not available either, the Australians could stand on guard with heads bowed instead.

Speaking at the Commonwealth War Graves Cemetery, Tobruk, 25 April 2005.

The dawn ceremony at Tobruk was an unforgettable experience. As I said in my address to the ceremony, looking out in the freezing cold over the almost flat, stony desert which had seen such remarkable heroism by Australians, Tobruk was a terrible place to fight and die. It was entirely appropriate, and long overdue, for them to be honoured, like tens of thousands of other Australians who had perished in times of war, with a dawn service attended by an Australian Cabinet minister. On a personal note, I later laid a sprig of rosemary on the grave of the father of Ron Barassi, as Ron was a friend of my aunt Mealor.

Without telling us, the Governor of Tobruk had sent a bugler to the ceremony, and so I asked the Australian and Libyan buglers to perform a duet, which was riveting. Recognising not only the Australians who had made their sacrifice, but also the fact that Indian and other Muslims had died in the campaign, and Libyan officials had made the dawn ceremony possible, I read a translation from the Koran which urges patience and prayer amidst fear and hunger and loss of life:

"Give good news to the patient who, when misfortune befalls them, say: Surely we are Allah's and to Him we shall surely return. Those are they on whom are blessings and mercy from their Lord, and those are the followers of the right course." (From Surah al-Baqarah (the Cow) Verses 153-157).

Chapter 15

Life after DFAT; ANU and Centamin

As my appointment in Cairo was nearing its end, and the timing of forthcoming vacancies in other Middle East posts ruled out any possibility of securing the ambassador position in Tehran, I decided to retire from the Australian Public Service. I had enjoyed 37 years as a diplomat, and with seven postings completed, it was time to pursue my interest in the Middle East in other capacities. My enthusiasm for the region was undiminished, but I felt Cairo was a suitable point at which to conclude that part of my career. After writing a series of valedictory cables from Cairo about what I saw as the outlook for reform and change in Egypt and elsewhere in the Arab Middle East I retired on 30 June 2008.

I was generously farewelled by the Department, which kindly acknowledged my service, and included me among the recipients of an Australia Day achievement award.

I returned to the Australian National University as Adjunct Professor in the Centre for Arab and Islamic Studies, where I completed *Egypt and the Politics of Change in the Arab Middle East* (Edward Elgar, 2010) in which I attempted to outline my sense of the social and political dynamics of the Arab Middle

East, in all its variety and complexity. I taught a graduate course on those issues, in addition to supervising PhD students, contributing to seminars and short-term courses for various government agencies and other academic activities, and giving guest lectures on the Palestinian refugee issue, all happily unburdened by the bureaucratic and budgetary concerns of regular academics. Until 2011, I combined my academic role with contract employment as a consultant on the Middle East for the Office of National Assessments.

Centamin

Shortly before leaving Cairo, I was invited by Sami el-Raghy, the Chairman of Centamin, and his son Joseph el-Raghy, the Chief Executive, to join the Board of the Australian gold mining company as a Non-Executive Director. I had the utmost admiration for Sami for his unswerving honesty and rectitude in dealing with the Egyptian authorities in his efforts to bring into production the first modern gold mine in Egypt, at Sukari, in the Eastern Desert near Marsa Alam. Centamin had also sponsored travel to Australia by Egyptian officials in an effort to encourage much-needed reform to Egypt's antiquated and unsuccessful mining code; and Sami had provided funding from Centamin enabling Jenny to arrange the first exhibition of Egyptian Tentmaker work in Australia.

Now one of the largest producing gold mines in the world (around 500,000 ounces of gold annually) the mine at Sukari came into being because Sami, who had graduated as a geologist in Alexandria before migrating to Australia, had always dreamed of returning to apply his knowledge to the moribund mining sector in Egypt. Sukari had been the site of alluvial and shallow mining since at least the Roman era, but both the British and the Russians mining engineers who examined the site had concluded that it was not a viable proposition for commercial development.

Sami and his friend Mike Kriewalt, however, envisaged its exploitation simultaneously excavating an open cut mine, as used in Australia, together with an underground mine targeting the higher-grade ore bodies.

It took over a decade of negotiation with the Egyptian authorities, but Centamin eventually secured a deal by which it exercised sole managerial authority (subject of course to Egyptian law). Under the agreement, which was given legislative authority by the Egyptian Parliament, Centamin's capital expenditure would be reimbursed, royalties would be paid on its gold production and all profits shared equally between the company and the Egyptian government. Production began in 2009.

By the end of my service on the Board in 2016, Centamin was employing over 1000 Egyptians, including a range of university graduates, and providing well-paying, safe employment to workers from Upper Egypt. After initial construction, it employed only a handful of expatriates, including some Australians, with several key operational areas staffed entirely by Egyptians. And in addition to its commercial success, Centamin helped the Egyptian authorities to arrive at a world-class regulatory framework of environmental management that was in marked contrast to the informal mining activities being undertaken around Sukari and elsewhere.

Serving on the Board of Centamin with Sami and Joseph and a remarkable group of talented fellow directors was a rewarding experience. I undertook the Australian Institute of Company Directors course for new directors, and enjoyed the challenge of finding my feet in committees dealing with budget management, salaries and recruitment and company law. Since I was particularly interested in the environmental management at Sukari I was responsible for chairing the Environment and Sustainability Committee of the Board, as well as the Health and

Safety Committee. I also served on the Corporate Governance, and Nominations and Remuneration Committees. I provided assessments to the Board of the likely direction of political developments of potential significance to the company, and offered advice on how best to position Centamin to address such risks as the Mubarak era drew to an end.

The director position with Centamin enabled me to return to Egypt every few months and, in addition to supporting the company's management, to stay abreast of the changing political environment. Few Egyptians outside the mining industry were aware of Centamin. The Egyptian media was inclined to be sensationalist and mostly antagonistic toward the project, usually with nationalist refrains along the lines of 'why are we allowing foreigners to mine our gold rather than doing it ourselves?', and the company eventually all but ceased trying to gain balanced local media coverage of its role. Litigation, and threats of litigation were frequent: one Egyptian politician, a serial litigant whose motives were decidedly open to question, led a campaign against the company, although he received little support among his parliamentary colleagues with whom Sami enjoyed constructive relations.

My experience with Centamin provided insights into the challenges of operating as a foreign company in a complex and corrupted political environment. I urged bringing the project and its achievements—not only in terms of revenue for Egypt from royalties and profit-sharing, but also its generation of jobs—to the attention of President Mubarak and senior ministers. Centamin had an exceptional story to tell on those counts. But while Sami agreed it would stand the company in good stead with the government to have President Mubarak visit, and thus to hear Sami's views and suggestions about the future of the project (indeed Sami had a helipad built at Sukari for that purpose) and to highlight the need for urgent reform in the mining sector, he was firmly against extending an invitation to Gamal Mubarak. A visit by Gamal and his coterie of predatory businessmen, Sami believed, would prove to be 'very expensive indeed'.

Politics aside, commencing and optimising production from the mine at Sukari required major changes across a range of Egyptian systems. As just one example, the quantity of explosives required for the mining operations (ideally using around 40 tons of explosive per day) was unlike anything the Egyptian security authorities had ever contemplated before: the only other mine in Egypt, an iron ore operation in the Western Desert, used around one ton of explosives for a single detonation each month. Getting the cooperation of Egyptian inspectors in the storage, release and accounting of such quantities of high explosive in a country facing security issues in the Sinai, Cairo and elsewhere was never going to be easy.

From my experience in Syria and Jordan, I had long believed that litigation was usually going to be fruitless in the Arab world for foreign companies. Even if, after a lengthy period, a court might decide in favour of the litigant, securing the implementation of such a judgement would be problematic. Moreover, if against the odds both the judgement and its implementation were given effect, the company would probably never do business in that country again.

Centamin's experience showed, however, that under certain circumstances litigation against Egyptian government agencies in Egypt, and potentially against the Egyptian Government in Switzerland, for breach of contract could provide one of the few avenues by which Centamin was able to protect itself from unfair actions by those parties when, as was usually the case, support at the political level for the company was not forthcoming. Having a respected, capable, well-connected Egyptian Australian from Alexandria, and competent local legal advice, certainly helped in that regard.

I enjoyed the challenges, personal and professional, of being on the Board of the company. Witnessing and participating in the human dynamics of the Centamin Board, and learning the basic features of the gold mining business were novel and fascinating experiences. The operational and strategic challenges faced by the company, and its Board, in maintaining the company's reputation for integrity and its transparency in its dealings with Egyptian officials, were extraordinary.

In seeking to deliver the outcomes Centamin had undertaken to achieve to its shareholders and its Egyptian government partner, the Egyptian Mineral Resources Authority, the Centamin Board always met its statutory reporting obligations. However, with power games almost constantly played within the Egyptian system, and pressures occasionally directed against Centamin itself, it was often difficult to ascertain fact from fiction when, for example, instances arose where gold shipments would be delayed, inspectors would be reluctant to work according to the needs of the mining schedule, or disputes would arise with the sole, government-owned fuel supplier over diesel prices. There were some anxious moments, particularly when operational circumstances threatened to make a material difference to the company's profitability and shareholder value—a situation which, if it had come to fruition, would have required disclosure of the facts to the regulatory authorities in London, where Centamin was a FTSE 250 listed public company. However the Board kept its nerve, despite these challenges, and in due course, the crises would pass.

Sami el-Raghy, Chairman of Centamin, at Petra, Jordan, 2010.

PART II

REFLECTIONS

Looking back at my Middle East experience and observation of policy processes from 1974 onward, I can discern a growing appreciation on my part of the human, cultural, political and historical factors that shape key issues, and of the limits to the possible for western policy practitioners.

I found throughout my career that the sense of Arab agency and resistance to external pressure (real or perceived) was considerably more important in practice than the views and prescriptive ideas of external parties about what the region needed or should be expected to do. Coming to the region initially from a perspective shaped by comfortable assumptions about the nature of power in the Cold War era, I found the resilience of Arab leaderships in Syria, Jordan and Egypt, and among the Palestinian leadership, and the capacity at all levels of Arab politics and society to deflect and balance against attempts to corral their policy choices and practices—whether from fellow Arab governments, Israel or external parties—was a major revelation.

Where US Middle East policy was concerned, I was struck by the absence of interest in maintaining consistency between US rhetoric about freedom on one hand, and US practice on the other, especially regarding Israel. Obama's cautious personal approach to Syria was arguably a partial exception, but mostly because the soaring rhetoric surrounding his idealism was tempered by his sober public recognition of the limits to US power. Moreover, when policy decisions were made, notably in regard to Iraq and Syria, coordination between the various US agencies and instruments of US national power in the planning and delivery of those decisions was often imperfect.

Accordingly, where policy issues arose for Australia, I came to the view that it would be foolish for Australia, or any other western country, to assume a commitment of sufficient resources, planning and policy attention on the part of the United States to secure the fruits of any short-term successes, let alone to rebuild societies and foster support for a new order imposed by outsiders. As the catastrophe which unfolded in Iraq in 2003 clearly demonstrated, such a commitment by the United States to the sustained exercise of leadership commensurate to its power rarely happened.

As a practitioner, I acquired, over time, an understanding of the importance of cultural norms in Arab societies that were sometimes quite subtle, but extraordinarily important to one's professional effectiveness. Damascus, especially, was a learning experience in appreciating the importance of political culture to Arab identity. Partly through friendships with Syrian and Palestinian intellectuals, writers and artists, and partly through empathy with the sense of historical injustice to which most Arabs subscribe, I came to appreciate how effectiveness as a practitioner demanded an appreciation, not only of power relationships, but also of how interlocutors understood themselves as actors in their historical context.

It took me several years to appreciate that what I call the *hakawati* tradition (after the Damascene tradition of public storytelling) was vastly more important to popular perceptions of issues and events than the empirical facts beloved of western intellectual tradition. There were, and will always be, many versions of truth in the Middle East. And, as I learnt in various ways during service in the Arab world, because an answer to a problem may appear logical on the basis of one's own experience, others may not understand a particular problem or issue in the same way. Although objective facts were important, of course, the narrative message or the interpretation of those facts was always the more important aspect of any communication. In seeking the effective delivery of such messages, perceptions of the integrity, honesty and other personal attributes of the interlocutor mattered greatly.

It took time for me to understand how deeply the sense of

honour was ingrained, not only in the context of beduin society as I discussed in regard to Jordan, but also in terms of national sentiment. I came to realise the extent to which graciousness toward others defines, for many ordinary people, what it means to be Arab. In practice, of course, a range of personal and political factors would shape behaviour and outcomes. Subversion, rivalries, declamatory rhetoric, and even threats toward fellow Arabs would sometimes surface. But it was always essential, as an outsider, to bear in mind how Arabs believed leaders and officials should conduct themselves in a formal sense toward each other.

It was especially important to demonstrate the respect with which Arabs are entitled to be treated by external parties. For Arabs at all social and economic levels, perceived and alleged affronts to national dignity (especially from outsiders) remain potent mobilising factors, irrespective of whether criticisms or comments may have an objective or rational justification.

And finally, in terms of diplomatic practice, I came to learn to appear relaxed, however urgent the situation. In normal circumstances, most Arabs have a droll approach to the foibles of life, and can relate to and appreciate the circumstances in which others may find themselves. Being honest, calm and patient was almost always the best, or least bad, option. Open expression of anger or frustration was invariably counterproductive, whereas a quiet but never self-deprecating sense of humour, and a careful eye to what agendas might be in operation behind the scenes, not only relieved tension, but could also helpfully demonstrate and build empathy with shared problems.

Chapter 16

Issues

Both before and after retirement from DFAT in 2008, I wrestled with three core questions, which continue to underpin my reflections on the region and my experiences in it. The first is: How do you build peace between two peoples—Israelis and Palestinians—with compelling national rights, human rights and historical narratives, but who have a clear imbalance of power? My view, which I defended throughout my career, was that this could only be done through a process in which two sovereign, confident states could make and justify the accommodations that would be necessary for Israelis and Palestinians to achieve peace with each other, not from each other.

As someone who believes a rules-based international order with the United Nations at its core is both desirable in its own right, and certainly the system that best protects and serves Australia's interests, I have always supported Israel's rights as a sovereign state. Its establishment was foreshadowed by the United Nations in 1947, and its entry into that body was agreed to according to the rules and recommendation of the organisation Australia helped to create. The proposal to establish two states, one 'Jewish' and one 'Arab', as well as a *corpus separatum* for Jerusalem, arose as the least bad answer to an insoluble political problem. One can be disappointed by, and argue about, the events that preceded and followed that outcome, but the continuing legitimacy of Israel as a member of the international community cannot and should not be questioned.

Regrettably, the possibility of achieving two sovereign states, one Israeli and one Palestinian, has now ended. In the light of the failure to create the balancing factor of an 'Arab' Palestinian counterpart (and a *corpus separatum* for Jerusalem) as originally envisaged, what can, and should, therefore be questioned is the nature of the 'Jewish' state; and what our approach to Israeli policies says about ourselves, and what values we wish to be seen as supporting. In other words, we must address the consequences for Israel, and for the values with which we wish to be associated, of seeking to maintain an approach which was began with international support, but which has come to be defined by systematic discrimination along ethno-religious lines by Israel against what is, in effect, Israel's Palestinian majority.

I have seen enough of the Israeli-Palestinian conflict and its major protagonists to appreciate that there is nothing straightforward about the issues it embodies. It is a political, historical and moral conflict cast in shades of grey, not black and white. But it is increasingly difficult, in the context of the political and social values of the 21st century, including a renewed focus on racial justice in the US context, and in a global order whose face is also changing, to deny the universal application of the principle of equality before the law. And in the Israeli-Palestinian context, that is certainly true.

I have lived among the 80 per cent of Palestinians who can still see, occasionally drive through, and sometimes even smell the places from which their families and communities were forced to flee in 1947-48 and, in some cases, in 1967. So that the (undefined) 'Jewish character' of Israel may be preserved, they are not permitted by Israel to return, let alone to exercise the right to do so enshrined in the same body of international law and values of universal application that saw Israel formally admitted to the international community.

In contrast, a Jewish person whose family is of Eastern European origin, with no direct connection to Israel or Palestine, is entitled if they choose to settle in the West Bank, to aid from the Israeli government that includes free air travel, financial assistance, subsistence allowances for a year, rent subsidies, low-interest mortgages, Hebrew instruction, tuition benefits, tax discounts and reduced fees at state-recognised day care centres.[15] Confirming the status of 1.2 million Palestinian citizens of Israel as second-class citizens (to say nothing of the 4.5 million Palestinians who live under Israeli rule in the occupied territories with no civil or political rights at all) was the passage in 2018 of the nation-state law[16] a quasi-constitutional measure stipulating the right to self-determination in Israel belongs solely to Jews.[17]

According to a 2016 Pew Research Center poll (taken in a period of relative calm), 48 percent of Israeli Jews agree with the statement, "Arabs should be expelled or transferred from Israel." Support was especially high among Orthodox (71 percent) and ultra-Orthodox (59 percent) populations.[18] Rampages by Jewish mobs in Israeli cities with substantial Arab populations during May 2021 suggest the prospects for maintaining equilibrium within Israel between Jews and Arabs (or 48 Palestinians, as many now refer to themselves) are worsening.

---

[15] Nathan Thrall, 'A Day in the Life of Abed Salama', The New York Review, 19 March 2021. https://www.nybooks.com/daily/2021/03/19/a-day-in-the-life-of-abed-salama/?utm_medium=email&utm_campaign=NYR%20Online%20Nathan%20Thrall&utm_content=NYR%20Online%20Nathan%20Thrall+CID_0b0d244742d202df79a74695300276a3&utm_source=Newsletter&utm_term=freely%20available (accessed 21 March 2021).

[16] For a translation, see https://knesset.gov.il/laws/special/eng/BasicLawNationState.pdf

[17] Khaled Elgindy, 'Washington Has Enabled Israeli Extremism', Foreign Policy, 6 May 2021, https://foreignpolicy.com/2021/05/06/israel-palestine-united-states-extremism-netanyahu-lehava-jerusalem-violence-sheikh-jarrah/?fbclid=IwAR2B9dmM8ikGIBt7e74W-wz9XEgRvU2jG78oyi5EEdbV-2rGVb0qhhYxO7YI

[18] Michael Lipka, 'Among Israeli Arabs and Jews, limited optimism about a two-state solution', Pew Research Center, 9 March 2016, https://www.pewresearch.org/fact-tank/2016/03/09/among-israeli-arabs-and-jews-limited-optimism-about-a-two-state-solution/

While politically convenient, reaffirmation of support for the principle of a two-state solution with no prospect of achieving such an outcome has become divorced from political reality on the ground. It is a wilful prevarication regarding the fundamental question of whether, in the present era, a Jewish state of Israel ruling a Palestinian majority is an unacceptable anachronism. In my view, it is.

A second question is: How does one recognise and appreciate the importance of national and personal or familial mythologies as a shaper of Palestinian identity, connecting the present to the past, without succumbing politically if not intellectually to their poetic power? As I argued in *Palestinian Refugees: Mythology, Identity and the Search for Peace*, the answer, if there is one, lies in focussing negotiation on interests, not beliefs, because beliefs are organic, structural and fundamentally non-negotiable.

My third concern is whether the Arab world is able to expand the space for empowerment and critical debate quickly enough to meet the growing demographic, economic, environmental and social challenges it faces, while preserving its Arab and Islamic identity and protecting the advances that have been made in some areas over the last two decades? In more specific terms, can Arab countries move from a social focus on male-dominated authority, protection of family and close conformity with conservative social expectations, to rewarding creative talent and initiative with all the social and political consequences that may imply? How do Arabs affirm or develop values of constitutionalism, including the separation of powers; respect for difference, and widening space for critical thinking and political accountability—and yet manage the potential societal and political risks and unpredictability of such empowerment?

For the Arab world since 2011, the failure to achieve negotiated political transitions that constrained the coercive power of the state is both a cause and a consequence of the weakening of the institutional basis of government. It has exacerbated the polarisation (in some cases) and multiple fracturing (in most cases) of Arab societies.

For a brief period in the Arab uprisings we were tempted to believe such transitions could be achieved. But far too often we saw what we hoped to see, and failed to look beyond our preconceptions. We responded with human sympathy when shown the horrors being endured, but we understood very little about the actors in the conflict—on either side—and their motivations.

But even if one allows for a failure, by western advocates for change, to understand the complex reality of the popular Arab mobilization, the fact remains that in all too many cases, a generation of activists and optimists who arose briefly across the region to demand justice, dignity and empowerment have been imprisoned, or lost to exile. None of the current leaderships of the major Arab states, and Iran, have answers to the problems of legitimacy and governance, let alone the growing impact of climate change and other matters beyond their control. And it is upon the capacity of Arab regimes to harness and build upon the energy and creativity among that small, beleaguered, cohort of activists and cosmopolitan intellectuals that the future of the Arab world depends.

If Arab governments are not performing effectively among these existing and emerging challenges, and for the next decade few of them will, my fear is that they will grow more authoritarian, transactional, and violent in their instincts and behaviour. Even though regimes will probably survive, through recourse to violence and aided, most likely, by the absence of any credible, coherent alternative, that phenomenon of rule by oppression and co-optation, rather than genuine political authority, will further damage their capacity to realise the full potential of their citizens and resources. Nor will they address the trauma and depression they have inflicted upon those courageous individuals who challenged, at enormous personal cost, the structural dysfunctionality of the existing Arab order.

The cumulative effect of these prospects, if they come to fruition, will be felt at strategic levels. They will expand possibilities for external interference as neighbouring states, and others within their immediate strategic environment, seek to protect themselves from the consequences of a weakening of state power in those nearby countries.

We have witnessed that occurring already in the role played by the Saudi Arabia in Bahrain, and in UAE support of non-state actors in Yemen and Libya. Both the UAE and Saudi Arabia actively supported the overthrow of the Muslim Brotherhood government in Egypt. Syrian and Sudanese mercenaries have been used by Turkey and the UAE, respectively, in Libya. Turkey is determined, through the use of proxy Islamist forces and its own military resources, to control most of Idlib province, and as much as it can of the Kurdish-majority areas of northern Syria. In the worst of all scenarios, we may also witness, in Syria and possibly in Iraq, a re-invigorated threat of jihadist Sunni elements, exploiting economic collapse, ethnic and tribal tension, and failures of governments and regional authorities to meet the basic economic and other demands of those under their control.

Those possibilities cannot be separated from the outlook for Israel and the Palestinians, and the part played—or perceived to be played—by the United States in fostering a climate of immunity for Israeli actions that affronts the dignity of Arabs in general, and those whose identity is framed around Islam in particular. Whatever progress might be made, when the price is right, toward normalising relations at the government level between Israel and regional countries, without a solution to the Palestinian question that offers a sense of historical justice to the Palestinians, Israel and the United States will remain the regional execration objects of popular choice. That will be the case, especially, among those who cannot give vent at home to their frustration with their own lack of dignity, economic security and empowerment.

Paradoxically, I should note that I have gradually come to prefer less, rather than more, external intervention in the region in regard to the resolution of these questions. We are witnessing, as Fouad Ajami wrote more than two decades ago, 'a great unsettling of things, a deep Arab malady'[19] in which external involvement may serve to complicate rather than facilitate the search for indigenous solutions. And unfortunately, as I will argue in more detail in the chapters below, external military interventions in recent decades have contributed to making it harder for western countries to make a positive difference in the region.

For the United States and other western countries, the invasion of Iraq in 2003 and the mistakes made in its aftermath are among the most grievous miscalculations in the sad history of western engagement with the region. As the late David Gardner observed, it was seen in the region as 'the epitome of US unilateralism, powered by a deadly combination of arrogance and ignorance' which left the region shocked, disgusted and enraged by the unintended, but entirely predictable, bloody fiasco which followed.[20]

While always present in some form, sectarianism and identity issues enlivened by the Iraq conflict and its aftermath, in which Islamic State and other groups in Iraq and Syria exploited and exaggerated sectarian fault lines for their own purposes, have combined with, and exacerbated, the simultaneous rise of authoritarianism and the weakening of the political authority of Arab governments. In combination, those phenomena have become so central to the political dynamics of the Middle East that they may now be irreversible obstacles to progress toward conflict resolution, both within and between states.

---

[19]Fouad Ajami, *The Dream Palace of the Arabs: A Generation's Odyssey (Vintage Books, 1998)*, pp. 3, 123-24.

---

[20]David Gardner, *Last Chance: The Middle East in the Balance* (I.B. Tauris, London 2012) p. 13.

I still believe that prudent, carefully calibrated external engagement, based on a deep appreciation of the social, political, and cultural dynamics of the region, and combined with the ethical use of power, is preferable to standing back and hoping for the best. Turning away from the region will neither help it resolve its problems, nor will it prevent further serious challenges to our security and other interests emerging from the Middle East.

In the case of Israel, it is clear that ending the occupation of Palestine and providing equality and a degree of autonomy for all within an Israeli state will require an existential struggle within Israeli society. Success is improbable without both external pressure and incentives for Israeli politics to change course from their largely cost-free current direction. But it is time to turn from empty rhetoric about supporting a two state solution to addressing the repercussions of Israel's occupation, and insisting that the rights of both Palestinians and Israelis should be treated equally.

There is no value in the pursuit by western countries of political and strategic objectives that are poorly articulated, if at all, and bereft of any credible means, military, political or otherwise, of achieving them. I am deeply sceptical about the overall utility of external military intervention in the region, especially when such intervention is driven primarily by the pursuit of US domestic political agendas and concerns, with little or no connection to, or understanding of, the dynamics of the Middle East mentioned above.

Reality dictates our objectives in the Middle East should always be modest. Arab states have to find their own pathways to be both accountable and refreshed if the creative potential of their citizens is to be realised. But even as the risks of instability loom larger, our approaches should be shaped to reflect and, where possible, support the priorities and aspirations of those who we would wish to respect our values. It is they who ultimately must, themselves, address the tasks and challenges that lie ahead.

Chapter 17

The Israeli-Palestinian Conflict

As an Adjunct Professor, sometimes released and eventually retired from diplomacy, I would pose to my students two questions. With Israelis and Palestinians seeking the realisation of their conflicting versions of their respective national rights, where does justice lie? And, if one were confident in making such a judgement, and if one agreed with the view of Martin Luther King (however improbable it might seem in the Middle East) that the arc of the moral universe tends towards justice, how should justice in the case of Israelis and Palestinians be given concrete form?

My starting point for discussion of the Israeli-Palestinian conflict was that without a political solution to the conflict through the creation of two states, one Jewish and one Arab, in Palestine, willing and strong enough to be able to reach and win support for accommodations and compromises with each other, a measure of justice cannot be realised for the Palestinians. In other words, if justice is to be found at all, it will have to be through politics, not through appeals and demands for the observance of international law, or unilateral declarations of the Jewish character of the State of Israel. Nor will it be found through whatever reprehensible, illegal and self-defeating acts Israel, backed by an indulgent US Administration, might adopt in seeking to quash Palestinian aspirations and force acceptance of an Israeli-dictated 'reality'.

My intention was to encourage students to realise that at its core, the Arab-Israeli conflict is a puzzle that lends itself to multiple interpretations, but not solutions. I encouraged my graduate students to appreciate the diversity within the original Zionist movement, and to discuss the reasons why the bi-nationalist approach, advocated by certain leading figures in the Zionist movement such as Judah Magnes, failed to sustain political support. I encouraged them to read I.F. Stone, Arthur Koestler and Menachem Begin, not only to understand the determination and single-mindedness of those and other early Zionists, but also to appreciate that an Israeli who, against the odds, survived the Holocaust, managed to enter Palestine, and had the will and support required to prevail militarily, would have little inclination to appreciate the suffering and outrage of those Palestinians, and their descendants, who were forced to flee. Their respective notions of justice proceed from entirely different standpoints.

I insisted it was equally important, of course, for students to read Palestinian and other Arab perspectives—Rashid Khalidi, Edward Said, Yezid Sayigh and Albert Hourani among others—as well as the views and concerns of Jewish intellectuals such as Simha Flapan and Peter Beinart. And I urged them to appreciate the personal and professional dilemmas facing Israeli and Palestinian intellectuals and academics, many of them friends of mine, able to discern historical fact from political fiction.

I shared with students my outrage at the betrayal by Arafat and his coterie, and the Israeli Right and its supporters, of the idealism and personal courage of those Israeli and Palestinian academics and friends of mine who had risked their reputations by arguing for the two state approach. I lamented the corruption and venality and recourse to terrorist violence which overtook the Palestinian movement, and the opportunities for peace-building that Israelis ignored. Freed at last from the constraints of being a public servant, I lambasted the extraordinary ineptitude of US diplomacy as the Oslo process collapsed. I deplored US reluctance to counter Israeli malfeasance with the vigour required, not only for the sake of preserving a peace process, but also for the sake of the United States' own interests in defending the credibility of western pretensions to being balanced in our approaches to the Arab world.

I also argued that without strong and courageous political leadership the views of Palestine of Israelis and Palestinians, respectively, were fated to remain poles apart because history, real and imagined, and lived personal experience would remain at the heart of the Israeli-Palestinian contest. As I explained at length in *Palestinian Refugees: Mythology, Identity and the Search for Peace*, mythologies are structural issues. They build identities. They cannot be negotiated away. The task was to achieve accommodation on the basis of mutual respect—now clearly no longer possible via the fabled two-state approach—and it required meaningful responses from Israel to injustices.

The lesson that I hoped would be taken was that it was essential, for academics and diplomats alike engaged in seeking conflict resolution, to be aware of and to respond to the ongoing creation, on all sides, of memories and political mythologies surrounding historical events and personalities. Central to the political equation between Israelis and Palestinians, fundamental issues of identity and dignity and power and material worth would continue to permeate perceptions of each other in that sadly tormented parcel of land between Jordan and the Mediterranean.

To help my students on their way toward intellectual engagement with those questions, and perhaps discovering something about their personal values in thinking about them, I would tell the real-life story of two people—one Palestinian, and one Israeli—and a piano.

A Palestinian friend, Aida, returned in 1992 to Jaffa from Jordan, where her family had lived since 1948. She located the family home, and without prior warning, knocked on the door. She was greeted politely by the somewhat surprised Jewish woman living in the house, who graciously showed her around rooms that were distantly familiar. In the drawing room the family piano still stood. But when she opened the seat of the piano stool, and found the music she had played as a 10 year old, complete with her mother's handwritten notes, Aida wept.

Aida's Israeli hostess, trying to comfort her in her distress, said she could only begin to imagine how painful such memories had to be. But she wanted Aida to know two things. First, she had had nothing to do with the departure of Aida's family from Palestine. She had arrived in 1950. And second, she had spent much of her life since that time paying the Jewish National Fund for the house. It was her home.

One may debate whether the law can provide justice in such cases: whether Israeli legislation preventing Palestinian 'absentees' forced to flee in 1947-48 from returning to their homes contravenes various instruments of international humanitarian law; or whether Jews forced to flee Iraq, Yemen or Egypt should be no less entitled to the reversal of an illegal act. Extracted under strong US pressure, Israeli willingness, however provisional, to discuss a limited and strictly controlled return of perhaps 100,000 refugees to the newly-established Jewish state, in return for international recognition, disappeared within a few years. And whereas Jews are entitled under Israeli law to present claims to return to properties they were forced to leave in 1947-48, no such right exists for Palestinians.

UN General Assembly Resolution 194 (IV) paragraph 11,

recommended compensation for those Palestinian refugees who might choose not to return. It is an illusion. No government would ever be willing to provide the quantum of funding that might be deemed sufficient to satisfy the demand, even if the evidentiary and policy basis for such compensation could be agreed. Still-debated policy questions would include, in the case of the Palestinian refugees, whether compensation should be paid to those few wealthy individuals—such as Aida's family—who could perhaps demonstrate loss of property: or instead to the vast majority of Palestinians, without property, who lost their livelihoods.

In addition to the refugee issue (and not irrelevant to it) stands the question of sovereignty in Jerusalem. For anyone engaged in teaching or researching the Israeli-Palestinian conflict, Jerusalem is where the metaphorical rubber of peace-building, not only between Israel and the Palestinians but also between Israel and much of the Arab and Islamic world hits the realities of the political road. Whether we like it or not, Jerusalem will shape the contours of relations between Israel and the Palestinians for generations to come.

Jerusalem requires examination from many perspectives, including its historical record of occupation and contested claims of sovereignty; its place in national mythologies and identity-building; its significance to the three Abrahamic religions; and its importance as a key issue in negotiations toward a resolution of the conflict that has endured for almost a century. I recall being told by Zaid al-Rifai, the former Prime Minister of Jordan, that in 1977, he had a phone call from US Secretary of State Henry Kissinger during preparations for a summit meeting in Geneva between the United States and the Soviet Union on the Middle East. Kissinger asked al-Rifai if Jordan would agree to Jerusalem being at the lower end of the meeting agenda. 'Mr Secretary' said al-Rifai, 'I don't care whether it is at the bottom or the top. There will be no peace in the Middle East until the issue is settled.'

Whereas the refugee issue is centred on issues of identity and justice, Jerusalem encapsulates, in addition to those concerns, the relationships between power, ideology, messianic impulses, religion and religiosity in a struggle to control a space whose character, history and even whose physical dimensions are fundamentally contested. In its religious and cultural diversity, its cuisines, cultures and sub-cultures, its passions and tensions, Jerusalem remains, in the words of the 10th century Arab geographer, al-Maqdissi, 'a bowl of scorpions'.

In recent years, the focus of the contest for Jerusalem—in practice, the Old City Basin and the Arab suburbs, notably Silwan and lately Sheikh Jarrah in East Jerusalem—has been on Israeli efforts to drive out Palestinians and entrench Israeli control over territory it occupied since 1967. Because under Israeli law only Jews are allowed to reclaim property they owned before 1948, right-wing Jewish organisations have sought to locate the heirs of Jewish property in Sheikh Jarrah in order to evict the Palestinian residents. Jewish settler groups have succeeded, accordingly, in using the Israeli judicial system to achieve the legal (according to Israeli law) but entirely unjust eviction of Arab families from their homes in those areas. Meanwhile, Palestinians in East Jerusalem cannot reclaim their property in Talbieh and elsewhere that they had to leave in 1948, despite Israel's insistence that Jerusalem is reunified.

But this is only part of a picture of ongoing discrimination intended to prevent the growth of the Palestinian population, and to Judaise the city with a minimal Palestinian presence.[21] In pursuit of those objectives, since 1967 Israel has appropriated one third of the privately-owned land in East Jerusalem to build

---

[21] See Nur Arafeh, 'Which Jerusalem: Israel's Little-Known Master Plans', *Al-Shabaka*, 31 May 2016 https://al-shabaka.org/briefs/jerusalem-israels-little-known-master-plans/

homes for 225,000 Jewish settlers; but it is almost impossible for Palestinians to obtain building permits in Jerusalem, and buildings constructed without such permits are liable to be demolished (at the owner's expense). Palestinians living in Jerusalem do not have Israeli citizenship, and their residency permits may be withdrawn if they cannot prove that their 'centre of life' is Jerusalem.

In its urban planning, residency laws and minimal budget allocations, and its facilitation of Jewish takeovers of homes and settlement construction, the clear intent of the Israeli government, and its discriminatory practices, are in blatant contradiction to its obligations as an occupying military power. There is no moral equivalence between the occupier and the occupied in Jerusalem. But since the politics of identity in Israel revolve around upholding difference, the Israelis defend their behaviour as necessary to uphold the Jewish character of the state. In the reported words of a deputy mayor of Jerusalem, Fleur Hassan-Nahoum,

This is a Jewish country. There's only one. And of course there are laws that some people may consider as favouring Jews—it's a Jewish state. It is here to protect the Jewish people.'

In the course of the resistance by Palestinians to a seizure of Palestinian homes in Sheikh Jarrah, in May 2021, a Jewish settler (with an American accent) put it even more bluntly, in response to a Palestinian woman pointing out he was stealing her house:

Yes, but if I go, you don't go back. What's the problem? Why are you yelling at me? I didn't do this. If I don't steal it, someone else is going to steal it.

The contest for Jerusalem is more subtle and complex than the blending of state power and exclusivist visions of the city countering Palestinian claims to sovereignty, important though that behaviour is in regard to Palestinian lived experience. In addition to the deliberate, strategic use of land and settlement activity and barrier building to secure Jewish predominance Israel has done its best on the ground to blur, physically, the so-called Green Line which demarcated Arab from Jewish Jerusalem from 1948 to 1967. And in recent decades a shift of Israeli government economic focus toward the private sector has witnessed a government-sponsored capital investment, tourism and archaeology effort in and around Jerusalem whose aim is to capture the (non-Palestinian) public imagination, with the altogether improbable objective of supplanting one long-established, Arab, urban identity with another.[22]

Looking ahead, the optimist in me observes that the immediate prospects for survivability in the Middle East seems less problematic than once was the case. Reality dictates that the rule of existing regimes seems likely to continue. But the pessimist in me observes that if political longevity has increased, the scope to take political risks in pursuit of a package deal has not widened.

In practice, unfortunately, the willingness, on both sides, to take political risks has diminished. The path of Arab politics since 2011 has been one of ever more-entrenched authoritarianism, amidst periodic upsurges in popular mobilisation over inadequate economic performance, corruption, and joblessness. In the case of Israel and the Palestinians, the Palestinian Authority is more likely to slide into irrelevance than either to cede control to its rival Hamas, or dissolve itself. It would appear that Right-wing governments in Israel can outlast almost anything, including, if necessary, by shifting coalition partners and policies even further to the Right.

The greater concern now is that the very notion of a two-state approach to resolution of the conflict has been fatally undermined, especially by Jewish settlement activity in the West Bank and East Jerusalem, as well as by the direction taken by

---

[22]These concerns are addressed in more detail in Anne B. Shlay and Gillard Rosen, Jerusalem: The Spatial Politics of a Divided Metropolis, Polity, May 2015.

Israeli and US politics in recent years. Although an upsurge in settlement building took place under Israeli Labor governments in the 1990s, the 12-year period of Benjamin Netanyahu as Israel's prime minister saw the settler population increase from 490,000 to 700,000. After more than five decades, Israel has mastered the art of an occupation to which the Palestinians have no hope of mounting serious resistance, whether peaceful or violent.

The Israelis have made effective use of checkpoints all over the West Bank, sealing off Gaza, subcontracting security in cities to Palestinian security forces, recruiting Palestinians to report on their neighbours, pre-emptive raids into Area A (under Palestinian security control) and Area B (where control is shared with the Palestinian Authority), and arresting and imprisoning organisers of peaceful resistance. They have no reluctance to use overwhelming violence against Palestinians and there is zero accountability for IDF or police violence against Palestinian civilians. No Palestinian is beyond the reach of Israeli military courts. The cavalier approach of the Trump Administration to principles the responsible international community hold sacrosanct hastened the erosion of US credibility as a peacemaker. And despite the election of Joseph Biden as US president, political momentum for a two state approach is unlikely to be recovered in the foreseeable future.

For our part, we have persisted in seeing the Israeli-Palestinian conflict within an intellectual and diplomatic framework shaped less by the facts on the ground than by our desire and strong political preference to see a two-state solution come to fruition. Like John Cleese's famously deceased parrot, it is politically easier and personally tempting to deny the death of the process, or to hold out hope that a meaningful process will be found, rising Lazarus-like in its place.

The facts suggest we should change our approach.

Ninety-one per cent of Israel-Palestine, excluding the annexed Golan Heights, is ruled by Israel. The areas of limited Palestinian autonomy, in Gaza and the West Bank, make up the remaining nine percent.[23] As mentioned, there are over 700,000 Jewish settlers in the West Bank and East Jerusalem—nearly a quarter of the population of those areas. More than 7.3 million Palestinian Arabs live either as citizens of Israel or non-citizens in the West Bank, Gaza and Jerusalem alongside 6.8 million Israeli Jews. Importantly, the demographic imbalance in favour of Arabs is set to widen: Palestinian Arab fertility rates (4.3 children per woman in the West Bank, and 4.5 children per woman in Gaza) are far greater than the Israeli Jewish fertility rate average of 3.1 children per woman. Equal rights for Palestinians would be a moral imperative, even if the Palestinians were a clear minority, but demography will make demands for those rights impossible to ignore.[24]

Understanding the forces ultimately and immediately at work, and even pointing to the demographic and other factors that will affect Israel's international standing in the absence of two sovereign states, does not, of course, provide an answer to the problem of how justice may be found on any of the central issues of the conflict.

For the first 50 years of its existence, the exact nature of Israel's identity was, for most Jewish Israelis, an intellectual issue to which no answers were needed: the Holocaust provided the justification for a Jewish state. It was also accepted without question (and with a little help from Hollywood) among westerners deservedly suffering historical guilt in the aftermath of that abomination. I suspect the vast majority of Israelis remain reluctant to address

---

[23]Nathan Thrall, 'A Day in the Life of Abed Salama', The New York Review, 19 March 2021.

---

[24]Marwan Muasher, 'After the Two-State Solution: New Israel-Palestine Peace Efforts Must Focus on Equality', Foreign Affairs, 27 April, 2021 https://www.foreignaffairs.com/articles/israel/2021-04-27/after-two-state-solution .

the existential issue of whether they wish to be a Jewish state (and what that means in practice), or an Israeli nation providing equality for all its citizens.

Instead, and especially in recent years under a succession of Right-wing Israeli governments, there has been a determined effort to obfuscate or obliterate, both physically and politically, the historical record and associated issues surrounding the birth of Israel. As Abe Silberstein, paraphrasing the Israeli academic Avi Shlaim put it, 'the problem isn't that the new historians (such as Shlaim) believe in original sin, but that the old historians believed in immaculate conception.'

The first intifada broke out in December 1987 because a new generation of Palestinians, no longer prepared to accept Israeli occupation, felt both humiliated and abandoned by the Arab world. The Oslo process degenerated as Israelis lost interest, and Palestinians lost hope, not for want of American activity but for want of strong US leadership (including over the issue of settlements) during Oslo's implementation phase. The second intifada broke out in 2000 because, by that stage, the vision of Oslo had finally been trampled into the mud by a combination of Palestinian terror, the continuation of settlement expansion in the West Bank and Jerusalem, Israeli political insouciance, Palestinian leadership fecklessness and the abject failure of American diplomacy. But the undermining, and then the collapse of the Oslo process meant that as a result, since 2018, Israel now rules, as a demographic minority, over the Palestinian majority living between Jordan and the Mediterranean.

The tragedy of the present situation is that Israeli fears of Palestinian irredentism, and the vastly superior coercive power of Israel, sustain Israeli determination not to make concessions to Palestinians under threat of violence; but the Israeli approach all but guarantees the Palestinians, determined to demonstrate their authenticity in response to Israeli military dominance and communal supremacism, will not concede to the humiliations of occupation.

In reality, those who see a tide of history running in favour of anti-colonial struggle may not be entirely wrong. But they are making heroic assumptions about Palestinian capacity to sustain a violent struggle. And, despite the lessons of the Syrian conflict, advocates for the Palestinians, including the handful of courageous Israelis in that category, probably under-estimate the likelihood that the primary beneficiaries emerging from such struggles may be forces that are deeply antagonistic toward values of human rights, gender equality and secularism that they envisage for Palestine.

They also under-estimate the unifying effects of such threats of a return to conflict on Israeli politics and Jewish society, particularly as tensions grow between Jews and Palestinians within Israel itself. Jewish settlements in the West Bank and East Jerusalem are contrary to international law, an affront to the international community and a humiliating daily reminder to Palestinians that they are under occupation. Over the past decade, the number of Jewish settlers in the West Bank has reached around 500,000—an increase of 43 per cent compared to an 11 per cent increase in the Israeli population. But in the absence of a comprehensive, durable prior agreement between the two sides, any serious attempt by an Israeli government to remove those settlements—or even to act forcefully against those who perpetrate acts of violence against the Palestinians among whom the settlers are living—would probably divide Israelis even further along their political and societal fault lines. It simply will not happen.

Many Israelis may despise the settlers and their supporters, but few are willing to support government action that might call into question the premise of Israel as a Jewish state. Nor would moves in that direction be likely to attract strong support from within the Palestinian community in Israel, which remains inclined, however reluctantly, to accommodate itself, for the most part, to the present reality.

However, the international environment is less conducive now to ascribing the blame solely to the Palestinians for the situation in which they find themselves. The generations whose perception of Israel were shaped by historical guilt regarding the Holocaust are passing. With the Democratic Party in the United States responding to and fostering calls for racial justice, we are witnessing the gradual emergence of criticism of specific Israeli practices among members of the US Congress (despite overwhelming Congressional and state level support for Israel in a general sense).

There is greater focus on issues of human rights among western countries than ever before, and the passing of the generation in the United States and other western countries that grew up with the positive mythologies surrounding Israel will make it harder to sustain an argument for treating the case of the Palestinians as exceptional. It is difficult to see how Israel and its supporters can reverse that shift.

In April 2021, Human Rights Watch (HRW) released a compelling, 213 page report arguing that Israel's policies toward the Palestinian population in the West Bank, Gaza Strip, and Israel have met the definitions of apartheid and persecution—and thus, of crimes against humanity.[25] The HRW report, and the effective use of real-time imagery from conflict situations lent legitimacy to public discussion of whether Israel is an apartheid state. Then, in February 2022, Amnesty International not only affirmed and reinforced the evidence and conclusions presented by HRW, but argued that discrimination, dispossession, repression of dissent, and the violence to which Palestinians were subjected were "all

---

[25]Human Rights Watch, 'A Threshold Crossed: Israeli Authorities and the Crimes of Apartheid and Persecution', April 2021, https://www.hrw.org/sites/default/files/media_2021/04/israel_palestine0421_web_0.pdf

are part of a system which is designed to privilege Jewish Israelis at the expense of Palestinians. ... This amounts to apartheid as prohibited in international law."[26]

Notwithstanding such criticism, if asked to decide between a Jewish state and an Israeli nation now, it is likely most Israelis would strongly reaffirm their preference for a Jewish identity—not defined in terms of religious observance (on which Israelis will remain forever divided) but given practical expression in favour of Jews in such areas as discriminatory housing, social infrastructure and political rights.

But if, subject to political trends within Israel, the coming generation of Palestinian Israelis should choose to firmly reject such discriminatory treatment—and if the responses generated within the Israeli system to such a challenge insisted upon affirming Jewish identity, by force if necessary, rather than ensuring equal rights for all—the consequences would be deeply distasteful for many of those who have hitherto supported Israel from abroad.

When facing serious questions about the legitimacy of ethno-religious Jewish rule over a Palestinian majority—possibly amidst ongoing, mutually-degrading blows and counter-blows—the foundation myths of Israel, and its security concerns, are unlikely to provide meaningful answers to a polarised Israeli society, or to its supporters elsewhere.

Conclusion

Israelis and Palestinians may be condemned to seek but not to find a satisfactory outcome to the issues between them. There is a substantial political, diplomatic and self-serving infrastructure surrounding the two-state approach that few credible political actors are willing to challenge, despite the fact that the two-state approach, in the form it has been pursued since the 1990s, is dead.

---

[26] Amnesty International, Israel's Apartheid Against Palestinians: A Look into Decades of Oppression and Domination, https://www.amnesty.org/en/latest/campaigns/2022/02/israels-system-of-apartheid/

In Jerusalem, Jenny ran out of bottled gas. Taking her almost new, bright blue cylinder to the nearby Palestinian bottled gas factory, just beyond the Beit Hanina checkpoint, she found the plant was closed but there was a vendor selling beaten up old gas cylinders from the back of his truck. As he was about to take her cylinder in exchange, Jenny pointed out that her cylinder was new, and beautiful, and perhaps she deserved something better than the battered old specimen he was offering. 'Yes,' he agreed thoughtfully, Jenny's canister was indeed more beautiful, 'but mine is so full'.

As I mentioned earlier, Palestinians are yet to address a fundamental conundrum: if the two-state approach underlying the Oslo process is unacceptable to most Palestinians or simply unworkable as a basis for pursuit of a Palestinian state, for a range of deeply-held reasons; and if it is also clear that Israel is not going to disappear, the only pathway to securing a measure of justice for Palestinians must entail active Palestinian outreach to Israelis in the hope of building a foundation of advocacy for Palestinian rights and dignity *among Israelis*. However gratifying, and appropriate, many Palestinians and their supporters find the rhetoric of steadfastness, and despite all the risks attached to the supposed 'normalisation' of relations, the absence of such outreach, especially beyond the Israeli Left, has worked to the disadvantage of the Palestinian cause.

There would be a high degree of resistance, especially among the Palestinian diaspora, to the notion of people-to-people programmes, arguing that they threaten to undermine international law and Palestinian rights, and fail to address the root causes of the conflict.[27] Those are legitimate concerns, which defend values and interests important to Australia, as well as the Palestinians.

---

[27] See for example Yara Hawari, 'The Revival of People-to-People Projects: Relinquishing Israeli Accountability' *al-Shabaka*, 6 April 2021, https://al-shabaka.org/briefs/the-revival-of-people-to-people-projects-relinquishing-israeli-accountability/

But they do not provide a path forward for the Palestinians that connects ends to means.

There is nothing incompatible between calling Israel to account for its abuses of human rights (and vice versa, where Hamas is concerned) and violations of international law; and striving for a process of building a sense of shared futures between a majority of Israelis and Palestinians, based upon principles of respect for dignity, security and equality before the law.

The future for those Palestinians upon whom the burden of occupation falls hardest—those who endure house demolitions, humiliation at checkpoints, settler violence, travel restrictions and a host of legalized forms of discrimination—will depend, to a large degree, upon Palestinians galvanising support for a process exposing more Israelis to the possibility, despite grievances, of mutually respectful, rather than permanently conflictual relations with their Palestinian neighbours. There are indications, moreover, that a clear majority of Palestinians in East Jerusalem (84%), the West Bank (60%) and Gaza (62%) agree that Palestinians should encourage direct personal contacts and dialogue with Israelis in order to support the efforts of those Israelis advocating a just solution to the conflict.[28]

There are also ways Israel could facilitate the emergence of a new, more positive future for Palestinians and Israelis alike, without raising existential questions on the Israeli side. The absence of sovereignty is a legitimate grievance for Palestinians, but in practice it is the absence of dignity and economic security that matter much more. Palestinian exclusion from highways used by Jewish settlers; the humiliation of Palestinian property being vandalised and lives threatened by Jewish youths in the West Bank; and the daily indignity associated with border controls could all be addressed by Israel, in cooperation with the

---

[28] Dylan Kassin, David Pollock, 'Arab Public Opinion on Arab-Israeli Normalization and Abraham Accords' Washington Institute for Near East Policy, 15 July 2022, https://www.washingtoninstitute.org/policy-analysis/arab-public-opinion-arab-israeli-normalization-and-abraham-accords

Palestinian Authority, if it should so choose.

There is no reason why Palestinians should be prevented from using roads that could be shared with settlers, with security arrangements agreed between both sides. Whereas the Israeli military presence in the West Bank is maintained there ostensibly to protect Israeli settlers from Palestinians, there should be no tolerance by Israeli civilian police of disturbances of the peace and other breaches of the law by those settlers. And instead of the ritual humiliation of Palestinians crossing into the West Bank via the Allenby Bridge, or into Israel via the Eretz checkpoint from Gaza, officials of the Palestinian Authority could undertake the security and other checks required by Israel, with discreet Israeli supervision, to avoid unnecessary delays on the Israeli side.

Ultimately, as David Shipler wrote several decades ago,

> Whatever happens in war or diplomacy, whatever territory is won or lost, whatever accommodations or compromises are finally made, the future guarantees that Arabs and Jews will remain close neighbours in this weary land, entangled in each other's fears. They will not escape from one another. They will not find peace in treaties or in victories. They will find it, if they find it at all, by looking into each other's eyes.[29]

Meanwhile, however, even as parties external to the conflict and without any appreciable influence over how Israelis may come to see themselves, how we respond to attempts by Israel, and its supporters in the United States, to resort to the palliative of repression, and bury the core issues of the conflict, rather than resolve them, will say a great deal about ourselves and our values. We should not add to scepticism in the Arab and Islamic world concerning our commitment to the principles we espouse by treating such moves with indifference, even though we probably will do so.

---

[29]David Shipler Arab and Jew: Wounded Spirits in a Promised Land (London: Bloomsbury, 1987) p. 16.

Policy choices aimed at ending the Israeli-Palestinian conflict have to take the poetic power of myths on all sides into account, even as we must take care to measure the dosages. Achieving outcomes that are reasonably balanced between principles and pragmatism will require the political reconditioning of both Israeli and Palestinian popular audiences. That is something for which neither side has an appetite.

But if there is to be a solution, with at least some degree of justice for all sides, it will be through recognition of the essentiality of politics, not raw power, in bringing Israelis and Palestinians to an acceptance of each other.

Chapter 18

Syria: When a regime outlasts a country

Australia and other Western governments have to decide the relationship they wish to have with Syria, and its neighbours and friends, including Iran—and how they wish their values to be reflected in their approaches to that relationship. Questions about what western governments wish Syria to become—including where it fits in terms of their strategic interests, its humanitarian and population movement ramifications, and the values to which those governments pay lip service—have never been directed with the vigour they deserve toward western policy makers. And, as Syria slips below the waves of international attention, such questions are increasingly likely to go unanswered.

The immensity of the Syrian tragedy—around 640,000 deaths by UN estimates, including the deaths of some 306,000 civilians, 90 per cent of which were caused by the Syrian government and its allies—should not lead to assumptions Syria will engage the attention of governments beyond present levels. The temptation to avert one's gaze from the mess to which the absence of critical thinking, and questioning, in western capitals has contributed is powerful. But those questions remain important in defining the sort of Middle East western countries would wish to see in coming decades.

There is a risk, moreover, that declining western attention to the gridlocked Syrian conflict, including as a consequence of failure even to articulate their objectives, let alone to devise ways of achieving them in that context, will lead to tacit acceptance of existing policy settings that are fundamentally at odds with the human values western countries espouse.

To those of us who knew Syria, it is above all else a human tragedy—half the population of pre-conflict Syria is displaced or living in neighbouring countries, often in appalling conditions, or have fled further abroad. Thirteen million people have been displaced. Surveys of Syrian refugees suggest up to 75 per cent of those living in camps show symptoms of post-traumatic stress disorder. A million children have been born outside Syria's borders, and are therefore probably stateless. A generation of what was among the most sophisticated, educated, entrepreneurial societies in the Arab world has effectively been lost. The societal wounds of the conflict go much deeper than its physical consequences, and may never be healed.

Our understanding of the Syrian conflict was influenced, inevitably, by those urban activists in Damascus and Aleppo who articulated to western audiences, often in English, an agenda for change that resonated with the values and notions of democracy with which those external audiences identified themselves.[30] But the majority of those Syrians who rose in the brutal, complex turmoil of 2011 did so for reasons of personal or local grievance that were genuine, but essentially situation-specific. Whereas family and tribal and religious factors were extremely important in the mobilisation of popular resistance,

---

[30]Similarly, in the case of Egypt, a documentary by the Australian film-maker, Kim Beamish, *The Tentmakers of Cairo*, captured superbly the mood of initial excitement, and then ambivalence, disconnection and scepticism as events unfolded, in one of the many micro-societies that comprise Egypt. But most western media and analysts focussed almost entirely on the daily drama of Tahrir Square.

there remains little evidence of a sense of empathy or ideological connection in Dera'a, let alone Idlib or other semi-rural, tribally-oriented localities, to those urban actors who sought to capture western imaginations.

Aron Lund captured this problem superbly when he wrote that early U.S. and European descriptions of the Syrian uprising:

> skewed very heavily toward a focus on (its) civil-society, universal-values aspect ... at the expense of locally rooted, identity-based, economic, and social forces ... while erasing the Syrians who do not fit into that narrative—the poor, marginalized, and angry young men of the Sunni countryside, who would go on to form the backbone of Syria's uprising. You may not like them, but this history is theirs, too.'[31]

The core fact of Syria since 2011, or perhaps since the Russian military intervention in 2015, is that Bashar al-Assad's regime has outlasted the country. Its bedrock is its brutality. It is one among several Middle East regimes which believe that repression, if not used in moderation, provides a necessary answer to challenges to the existing political and social order. Bashar al-Assad, like his father before him, proved determined to avoid the asking of open-ended questions about the appropriate relationship in Syria between state and society. Meanwhile, from its more inclusive early character, the multi-faceted ideological disposition of opposition groups within Syria has been reduced, since mid-2011, to an Islamist-inspired rejection of the existing social and political order. The externally-based Syrian opposition no longer matters.

---

[31] Aron Lund, 'The Politics of Memory: Ten Years of War in Syria', The Century Foundation, 15 March 2021, https://tcf.org/content/commentary/politics-memory-ten-years-war-syria/

Outlook

Suffering the effects of US economic sanctions and the collapse of the Lebanese economy, and unable to find the funds required for the provision of basic fuel and food requirements for the bulk of its population, let alone reconstruction, the regime can point to the suffering of its citizens as an argument for western countries to ease those sanctions and re-engage with it. It can continue falsely to deny its part in causing the displacement and horrendous suffering that are matters of public record. And it can argue, and is doing so with some effect, to the Gulf Arab countries that if those countries are concerned not to see Syria become ever more reliant upon Iran to secure the minimum of human decency and dignity for its people, sanctions must be eased.

Meanwhile, for the foreseeable future, Assad will pursue the restoration of central government control; and manoeuvre between Putin and Turkey's Erdogan over the future of Idlib province and North East Syria. He will aim to deal with Arab tribal leaders in the Euphrates valley bitterly opposed to Damascus at present, but also potentially at odds with the Syrian Kurds under the banner of the People's Protection Units, generally referred to as the YPG. Kurdish–Arab tribal frictions in Deir ez-Zour, and Kurdish resistance to ethnic cleansing and Turkish proxy occupation will probably grow.[32]

In the absence of a reconciliation between Ankara and Damascus, the respective interests of Russia and Turkey, in Syria, are largely misaligned. The relationship between Iran and Syria is complex. But each of these external parties sees strategic benefit in mutual accommodation on key concerns beyond the Syria issue. For the foreseeable future, therefore, irrespective of their longer-term goals, the overriding objective of Iran, Russia and Turkey will probably be to manage their respective

---

[32] Fabrice Balanche, 'The Assad Regime has Failed to Restore Full Sovereignty Over Syria', PolicyWatch 3433, Washington Institute for Near East Policy, 10 February 2021. https://www.washingtoninstitute.org/policy-analysis/assad-regime-has-failed-restore-full-sovereignty-over-syria

differences and conflicting interests in the Syrian context, rather than to engage in fruitless attempts to resolve them through military means.

Although Assad will not abandon the goal of restoring central government control of the Islamist-dominated Idlib province the military limitations of the regime are obvious. The Syrian regime's capacity to deal with an IS regrouping near Palmyra, as well as around Deir ez-Zour has been impacted by unrest in the South, potentially creating a security gap in that region if fighting in Idlib should intensify. Meanwhile, determined to prevent the YPG, which has close ties to the PKK Kurdish terrorist organization which has been fighting the Turkish government since 1984, from gaining territorial contiguity along the Turkish border, Erdogan has effectively achieved the long-term implantation of Turkish military outposts, especially in Idlib province. He has sponsored Islamist forces, with appalling human rights records but antagonistic to both Damascus and the Kurds, in Idlib and elsewhere in northern Syria.

Within the areas under the regime's overall control, in addition to the economic and societal effects of corruption, sanctions and the destruction caused by the conflict, there is a power vacuum at the local level. Its main symptom is the growing entrenchment of local militias—and in areas of traditional regime dominance, larger bodies such as the Fourth Armoured Division of the Syrian Army under the command of Assad's younger brother Maher—dominating and extracting gains, instead of the highly centralised patronage arrangements of the previous order. As government institutions have weakened the production and smuggling of captagon, an illicit narcotic, has grown exponentially, with members and close associates of the Assad family exploiting weakness in governance across the region in

---

[33]Caroline Rose and Alexander Soderholm, *The Captagon Threat: A Profile of Illicit Trade, Consumption and Regional Realities*, Newlines Institute for Strategy and Policy, 5 April 2022. The estimated potential retail value of the illicit trade in the Middle East and Mediterranean in 2021 was $5.3 billion. https://newlinesinstitute.org/terrorism/the-captagon-threat-a-profile-of-illicit-trade-consumption-and-regional-realities/

collaboration with criminal networks, militant groups, mafia syndicates and government officials.[33]

Whether it was ever capable of realising the potential of ordinary Syrians is a matter for academic debate, but the old system—a combination of coercion and co-optation—offered predictability, albeit at a price, and at least the possibility of reforms in some areas. Now, writing about Aleppo, but in a comment applicable to areas under regime control in general, International Crisis Group wrote in May 2022 that Syria is:

> ... gravitating toward a patchwork of territorial control propped up by warlords-turned-entrepreneurs. ... (M)ilitias are entrenched to the point that no single edict from Damascus – much less one from outside powers – can root them out. Aspects of militia rule have been incorporated into state institutions and wartime tycoons have become deeply integrated into parts of the Aleppan economy.[34]

The Assad regime has a range of challenges arising from beyond its borders as well. The economic meltdown of Lebanon and the loss of Syria's hard currency held in Lebanese banks; uncertainty surrounding future Iranian oil revenues; and questions about Hezbollah's capacity to field combat-ready forces beyond Lebanon present issues that Syria has no power to control. And as Israel seeks to deny Iran a deeper foothold in Syria it will continue to strike at facilities, and welcome the elimination of individuals from whom the Assad regime has drawn benefit—such as the Iranian Revolutionary Guards commander Qassem Suleimani, who supervised not only Hezbollah but also Afghan (Fatemiyun) and Pakistani (Zeinabiyun) Shia militias supporting the Syrian regime.

Meanwhile, the effects of coronavirus, drought and rising food

---

[34]International Crisis Group, *Syria: Ruling Over Aleppo's Ruins* Report No. 234, 9 May 2022. https://www.crisisgroup.org/middle-east-north-africa/east-mediterranean-mena/syria/234-syria-ruling-over-aleppos-ruins

insecurity on public health in Syria, in addition to the traumatic stress inflicted upon its civilian population, can only be guessed at.

External parties

Although their interests conflict in Syria and Libya, Putin will continue to attach greater importance to the strategic relationship of Russia with Turkey—a fellow revanchist actor and a thorn in the side of NATO and Europe—than addressing the threat of jihadist activity, let alone more tactical considerations relating to meeting the desires of the Syrian regime regarding Idlib. Although he has had no hesitation striking Turkish forces embedded with their jihadist proxies, Putin has no desire to engage in direct military confrontation with Turkey.

Putin would probably prefer to settle for the preservation of the Assad regime as a viable but vulnerable Russian asset. Addressing the role of Turkey, the Kurds and the Iranian involvement in Syria are lesser order concerns. The Russians are comfortable for their strategic interests to be protected through repression, despite its known costs and risks. However, it remains to be seen whether the Russians are prepared to invest in attaining the levels of manoeuvrability, intelligence gathering and other capabilities required to deal conclusively with IS remnants. Although it has conducted some air strikes lately against IS elements in desert areas east of the major cities, Russia to date has shown limited interest in taking a more comprehensive approach to doing so.

While the survival of the Assad regime is of great strategic importance to Iran, its stance on Turkey is less straightforward. Hezbollah is a major factor in Iran's defence posture toward Israel. It has also been a key element in the Assad regime's combat efforts. There is historical rivalry between Iran and Turkey, and some residual Turkish nationalist sentiment calling for redress of the loss of oil-rich Mosul in northern Iraq in the post-World War I carve-up of the Ottoman Empire. Periodic Turkish military incursions into Kurdish areas of Iraq are resisted by Iranian-backed Kurdish forces.

But Iran's approach is also shaped by the need to use Turkey to reduce the economic impact of US sanctions. Moreover, neither Turkey nor Iran nor Iraq want to increase the risk of Kurdish irredentism in Syria impacting on their own Kurdish populations. And, as with the Russians, it remains to be seen whether the Iranians have the interest in and capabilities required to deal conclusively with IS remnants so long as they pose no direct threat to the Assad regime, or the sustainability of a government in Iraq that broadly suits Iranian interests.

For its part, the United States will not have the capacity to deal conclusively with an Islamic State resurgence in NE Syria and south of the Euphrates without the Kurds as their primary partner. But US and Turkish interests in, and approaches to, the PKK-linked Kurds are, and will probably remain, irreconcilable.

From an ethical perspective, US policy towards Syria and Syrians should not be treated as an extension of the contest with Iran. But the United States will not have a clear and credible policy toward Syria until it determines its preferred approaches to Iran, Turkey, Saudi Arabia and the Kurds. And although the United States has very limited capacity to shape the political outlook for Syria, in practice the humanitarian outlook for most Syrians living within Syria or abroad depends both on US-Russia relations (particularly as these affect arrangements governing the flow of humanitarian aid to areas beyond regime control); and on whether, when, how and to what purpose, respectively, the United States and Iran re-engage.

Islamists

So long as Turkey is willing to use jihadist proxies as a means of preventing Kurds attaining territorial contiguity along its southern border, Islamist groups will remain reasonably secure, even as the United States manages to eliminate individual leaders of Islamic State and others deemed to pose a credible risk of engaging in terrorist attacks in the West. The main Islamist actor in Idlib, Hayat Tahrir al-Sham (HTS) is entrenched. It will continue to secure revenue through control of border crossings and taxing aid flows. With around 20,000 experienced fighters, and strong command and control systems, it is both militarily capable and politically astute enough to preserve its control. Its only challenge comes from fellow jihadist groups, notably Hurras al-Din, mostly with stronger, or at least more overt al-Qaida connections.

HTS is seeking acceptance as a body with whom western countries must deal, in effect, if humanitarian assistance is to be delivered to and through non-government bodies aiming to provide relief and protection to the most vulnerable. It seeks to reap the financial rewards of such dealings in order to control the province and defend against pressure from its Islamist rivals and the Assad regime—its relationship with Turkey and the military support it receives from Turkey are probably key to its interests in that respect.

Unlike Islamic State, HTS has no illusions about building a caliphate. It is a more pragmatic and sophisticated political operator than IS, at both the local and international level, pulling in recruits from jihadists evacuated from the south; inviting US officials to visit; adopting the guise of defender of civilians from the Assad regime and so on. It purports to have a localised agenda, and to have severed its links to al-Qaida (AQ), but it is unlikely to have done so for more than tactical reasons. It has a brutal internal security mechanism, and can draw on the well-founded fear of retribution by the Assad regime to sustain a degree of popular submission to its authority. The return to power in Afghanistan of the Taliban will provide it with an even stronger sense of its capacity to surmount external challenges.

In the medium term, HTS's capacity to embed itself in conservative Syrian society in Idlib province, and to build operational capability to match its ideological foundations should not be under-estimated. Speculation about the long-term effects of this situation has limited value, but where it exercises territorial control, we can expect HTS (as with Hezbollah and Hamas) to reshape already conservative societal attitudes through Salafist education, its judiciary, and violence, while presenting itself to external interlocutors as a fit party with whom to deal. On the other hand, since they do not pose a credible risk to any existing regime allied to the West, few western interlocutors would be likely to contemplate serious engagement with them.

Meanwhile, there is no willingness yet among any of the Syrian parties to seek political solutions, notwithstanding territorial gains and losses. Jihadists will be prepared to fight on at the expense of civilian populations. The regime, with Iranian and Russian support, will continue to clear, cleanse or kill its opponents where it can. Dissent anywhere will be crushed by whichever party has the means to do so. Beyond its coastal and urban areas Syria will be a wasteland for decades. Like Lebanon, the drivers of conflict will remain unresolved. For now, the momentum is with the regime, but its limited successes on the battlefield do not secure its future amidst economic collapse. This is a battle of wills rather than territory: sovereignty and political authority within Syria's borders will remain contested.

Lessons

Syria has highlighted the operational, tactical, humanitarian, ethical, political, diplomatic, narrative and strategic challenges of asymmetric warfare. Like the conflicts in Libya, Yemen and elsewhere, it raises significant questions about what sorts of military forces, skill sets, platforms and munitions are best fit for purpose in the changing Middle East operational and tactical environment. In the Middle East, and beyond, future conflict is likely to be characterised less by conventional warfare than by intra-state conflict and the use of technologies ranging from unmanned aerial vehicles to barrel bombs, as well as the deployment of expeditionary and mercenary forces.

The lessons to be drawn from the experience of Syria since 2011 are many and varied.[35] Despite the determination of Presidents Obama and Biden to avoid US entanglement in military conflict as part of the role the United States plans to play in the region going forward, the battles which displaced IS from Mosul in Iraq, and Raqqa in Syria, demonstrated that if jihadists become entrenched again in cities they won't be defeated without prolonged, substantial external kinetic, training, logistic, intelligence and other support. Inadequate support risks unsustainably high attrition rates among largely conscript armies (the attrition rate among well-trained elite forces in Mosul was 50–60%). All local actors, except Turkey, will have to rely on airpower support for both offensive and defensive purposes. Only external parties can supply—or deny—enough of it to shape the battle space effectively.

Other regional conflicts (Yemen; West and sub-Saharan Africa, especially Mali) will follow the Syrian pattern: multiple interconnected fights sharing the same space and time. Some (such as the north-south separatist contest in Yemen; and the al-Qaeda derivative in Mali exploiting farmer/herder tensions) won't be directly related to the struggle against the jihadists in Syria and Iraq. We should expect combinations of coercion, co-option and subversion; transactional, situation-specific alliances; vicious turf battles and unstable deals; and an absence of transitional justice.

Being an effective external actor in such conflicts requires more than the possession of kinetic capability. It requires

---

[35]These points are based on my article 'Seven Lessons from Syria', The Strategist, Australian Strategic Policy Institute (ASPI) 28 November, 2019.

language and cultural skills, and a sophisticated appreciation of micro-political dynamics, sensitivities, interests, personalities and ambitions at the local level. It demands flexibility, but it is not helped by mixed messages. It also demands levels of personal authenticity, credibility and skill in building a sense of solidarity of purpose. Those attributes are beyond the capacity of most external players. The US, Saudi and Qatari track record in in deciphering the political-military operating environment in Syria is haphazard, at best. It contrasts with the Russian approach, which is devoid of illusions about remaking the regime and the region, and backed by an intimate understanding of Syrian political culture and trends.

Significant new force deployments to the region are unlikely, and even more so following the collapse of the US-installed government which followed the US withdrawal from Afghanistan. Capable Western governments and political audiences are (correctly) risk-averse or (incorrectly) uninterested in Syria. Moreover, we are rarely likely to find there is a peace to keep, even when conflict abates, because of centre–periphery contests, regional dynamics, insurgency risks and, eventually, intra-regime contests over the division of spoils. UN Security Council legal frameworks to legitimise formal force deployments are also unlikely.

It remains to be seen what the legacy of the Jackson Pollock school of diplomacy, otherwise known as the Trump Administration, will produce in Syria and other broken states. But rhetoric aside, we are unlikely to see a return to values of the pre-Trump global order under Biden or his successors. Collective punishment, sieges, clear-felling of populated urban areas and the use of chemical weapons continued throughout the Syrian conflict because such practices work better at the tactical and regime-survival levels than high-intensity urban warfare. They have also proven to be almost cost-free for those who use them. And Syria has shown that all parties can become adept at ignoring or contesting the narratives surrounding blatant breaches of international humanitarian law.

Policy issues

The demonstrated failure of western countries to affect constructively the direction of events in Syria, including in respect of its human rights abuses are a sobering reflection, in the first instance of the agency of indigenous and regional forces inimical to western interests in the Middle East. It is also true that there are no innocent parties to the Syrian conflict: some of the key players are merely more guilty than others. But that does not absolve western countries from their responsibility to address their part in the imbroglio from which they would prefer to move on. It is also in their interests to do so.[36]

No western government should abide policy goals that are pursued through the collective punishment of the Syrian people. Falsely presented as a means of applying pressure to that odious regime, and perhaps for want of credible alternatives, the tacit acceptance of such collective punishment impacts almost entirely upon the Syrian population at large. It damages and degrades victims and perpetrators alike.

It is an approach which weakens the moral authority of western voices seeking to call others to account for their abuses of power. It weakens the moral foundations of the international order, damaging the interests of all but the most powerful countries benefitting from the predictability of that order. It does nothing to ease the predicament of 3.7 million Syrian refugees in Turkey, and those in Lebanon, Jordan and Europe. Nor does it alleviate the political pressures of refugee issues on the governments of

---

[36] 'Syria: The Consequences of Intellectual Failure and Moral Neglect', The Interpreter, Lowy Institute 12 August 2021. https://www.lowyinstitute.org/the-interpreter/syria-consequences-intellectual-failure-moral-neglect

those countries.

It is fundamentally immoral to deny shelter to children, whether it be by the Assad regime seeking to punish and coerce its opponents; or the Russians seeking to control access to areas outside regime control; or US politicians swayed by those who advocate such utterly futile policy approaches as a means of addressing their concerns about Iran.

Values are emphasised in foreign policy discourse for good reasons: if the goal is to save humanity from the scourge of war, the defence of ordinary people through the institutions created in the last century should shape policy objectives, development assistance and other advocacy. Syria should be no exception in that regard.

Earning respect for such values among an emerging generation of Arabs is in the interests of the western world. But it demands willingness on the part of governments to speak and act accordingly. And when increasing the vulnerability of children is accepted as a legitimate instrument of policy, and governments make no response to other abuses of the rights and dignity of ordinary people in the region, the message that is conveyed is that western rhetoric about values is hollow indeed.

Of course, even the notion of calibrating an easing of sanctions and a return to more normal dealing with the Syrian regime with an amelioration in its behavior toward its own citizens poses moral dilemmas. Who should judge how many people are to be spared from the gallows or torture (and for how long?) in return for an easing of restrictions on capital flows needed for reconstruction, fuel and food? Do political leaders really want to know if a deal with Damascus is being kept, especially if it enables them to enhance their domestic political fortunes through campaign promises to send Syrian asylum-seekers home?

Ultimately, however, Syria forces choices between bad and much, much worse. And even as the focus of international attention and the media cycle move elsewhere, western governments owe it to themselves, and their interests, and to Syrians, to be alert to the consequences of intellectual failure and moral neglect where Syria is concerned.

Australian policy

What, then, should be Australia's approach to Syria and the Assad regime?

To the dismay of some of my friends, I have advocated for a gradual, calibrated, conditional return to engagement with the Assad regime (I do not advocate for engagement with HTS), for want of any more appealing alternative. I appreciate that the main beneficiaries of attaching primacy to concern to uphold our values, and to relieve suffering, will not be those we would prefer to support. But the reality we must face is that humanitarian suffering has become weaponised, with considerable success, by parties to the conflict seeking political leverage to further their own objectives.

Our starting point has to be that Australia, like other western countries, has a deep and abiding interest in sustaining and strengthening respect for international law. Consistent with my views in regard to Israel and Palestine, my concern is that without respect for principles and institutions of international humanitarian law, and efforts to hold accountable those who breach them, predictable and constructive dealings between states, and the harnessing of human potential, are hardly possible. An absence of respect for those principles, both domestically and in dealings between states—and the weakening of political will to defend robustly the values of political liberalism and the moral authority of international norms and values—brings us closer to the scourge of wider war.

In the case of Syria, behind that self-evident truth are complex political and moral issues. Advocacy for human rights in the

Syrian context must be framed within a realistic acceptance that any return to effective political leadership to address human rights will have to come about within the existing Syrian power structure. And that poses an almost insurmountable problem: a leadership that has proven willing to see the death and displacement of so many of its own citizens—that would choose chemical weapons ahead of empowerment of its opponents—is not going to relinquish or genuinely share political power beyond its immediate base. If concerns exist at all in Damascus for the absence of accountability for brutality in the name of security, or for the opportunities for recruitment and indoctrination afforded by burgeoning prison environments, torture, and other abuses, they are seen as issues of a lower order than the immediate need to preserve the identity and essential character of the Syrian state itself.

Nevertheless, whether responsibility for the human tragedy of Syria rests mainly with the Syrian regime, other governments, Islamists or non-state actors, it is the Syrian poor, and the marginalised, who have been most demonised, dehumanised, and exploited. And the values that best protect Australia's interests at the global level have suffered, as respect for international law has been set aside by the parties to the conflict.

Our sense of identity and the values we claim to uphold should leave us no choice but to seek to relieve that humanitarian suffering. I want our values to be given concrete expression, and I believe it is in our interests overall to do so.

Conclusion

Words of sound and fury delivered in multilateral forums in Geneva and elsewhere aiming to resolve the conflict will make little difference in practice to Syrian behaviour. The challenge is to find an acceptable balance between upholding core principles of international humanitarian law in the Syrian context; and recognition that without a return to economic growth and security, those principles, however worthy we may consider them to be, will matter little to those Syrians who are most vulnerable. The application of economic sanctions to Syria—in practice, a manifestly inhumane, ineffective, and altogether despicable assault on the most vulnerable elements of Syrian society—add to the challenges ahead.

There is no chance of security or durable progress in Syria without economic advancement. The opportunity costs, in terms of wasted human potential, corruption, and human rights abuses associated with repression, insecurity, and conflict all weigh heavily against the likelihood of achieving levels of balanced economic performance that can restore infrastructure and human capital and combat Syria's growing ecological threats and food and water insecurity.

Looking ahead, the incremental advancement in Syria of empowerment, within the rule of law, at all levels, from the state to the society to the household, is as desirable and yet as remote a prospect for Syria as ending abuses of human rights. And remaking Syria—or Yemen or Libya—for the benefit of its citizens may not be possible without remaking the wider Middle East. History suggests that is something to which the rest of the world is unlikely to make a positive contribution. But history also demonstrates, very clearly, the cost of failure by western countries at least to strive in that direction.

Syria's future will continue to be affected by the often bewildering interplay on the ground of the interests and objectives of Turkey, Russia, Iran, the United States, the United Arab Emirates, the Kurds and Iraq. And it is in shaping that interaction that achieving at least the amelioration of suffering in Syria probably depends.

Syria, not unreasonably, also sees itself as deserving of international recognition as a country of substance and importance in the Arab and regional context. The ending of its isolation from the international community is important to it. For their part, Western governments will see their interests served best, not by ongoing insecurity and conflict and the imposition of collective punishment in Syria, but by the re-emergence, over time, of a Syria that is once again confident, economically dynamic, socially progressive, and respected within the region.

Calibrated, strategically planned US and European re-engagement with the Syrian regime, in consultation with Arab partners, offers the most likely path to seeing a Syria eventually emerge which may choose to benchmark its achievements, as an Arab state, against contemporary ideas among a younger generation, in Syria and within the wider Arab world, of what it means to be Arab and 'modern'. And it is among those ideas of what modernity looks like that the norms and institutions of international law are most likely to be respected.

It will need to be a cautious and conditional process. There must be some semblance of respect for the dignity and rights of its ordinary citizens if re-engagement with Western countries is to proceed. Assad himself has too much blood on his hands to be an acceptable interlocutor for most governments. Russian, Iranian, Israeli and Turkish sensitivities would need to be handled with particular care. But there is a strong case—humanitarian, diplomatic, and in recognition of the political and military realities on the ground—for further exploration of the limits to the possible.

The tragedy of Syria is also a symptom of much deeper concerns relating to governance and security, beyond the reach of external parties. Those concerns are likely to endure, long after the conflict subsides, or is contained, and the caliphs and the kings depart.

But if we wish our humanitarian, democratic and secular values to be respected among future generations of Syrians, and elsewhere in the region and beyond, we should be prepared to stand up for those values by using such political, diplomatic, and intellectual leverage as may be available to us. There will be costs, political and reputational, in doing so. But we should be prepared to take a long-term view of what is required.

Chapter 19

Egypt: where to from here?

In 2013, I remarked to an Egyptian friend that whereas it was increasingly rare but still not unusual to have a democratically-elected government replaced by a military one, it was quite novel to see a popular upheaval calling for the military to take power. 'Ah,' he replied, 'if you want a normal revolution, look for a normal country.'

Egypt is nobody's idea of a normal country. But since a quarter of the population of the Arab world is Egyptian, its future shapes the region. And, as the momentous events of 2011 and 2013 clearly demonstrate, Egypt faces a serious risk of failing to build strong and effective civil society institutions and a confident, progressive view of Arab modernity.

Egypt is yet to find a system of political and social authority whose legitimacy, authenticity and relevance to the expectations of contemporary Egyptian society is firmly established. Instead, the essential values of constitutionalism have been largely set aside, especially since the 2013 military coup, in favour of a reversion to authoritarianism and human rights abuses worse than any Egypt has seen in the modern era.

Egypt has also largely succeeded in obscuring these concerns from external attention. A few bombastic individuals aside (and even they have a degree of soft power value, especially those with world-class skills at selling themselves to American cable television networks) those in and around the Egyptian leadership display acumen and experience rarely matched elsewhere in the Arab world. Egyptians take diplomacy seriously, invest in it, and foster and demand professional excellence among its practitioners.

Meanwhile, however, aside from a handful of mostly secular, western-educated, very courageous liberal voices, Egyptians remain simultaneously fearful of their regime, and frightened of chaos. As Shadi Hamid has observed, we are seeing 'a collective loss of faith in politics, leading many to embrace, in panicked desperation, a violent absolutism.'[37] And, possibly in part because of those factors, most Egyptians remain more or less comfortable with the fundamentals of an authoritarian political order which is broadly consistent with (and perhaps a natural reflection of) authoritarian values at home, in education and in Egyptian society at large.

On their tenth anniversary, Hisham Melhem summed up the fate of the Arab uprisings with a metaphor particularly appropriate to Egypt. In his words,

> The uprisings faced not only entrenched ruling classes but also deep-rooted patriarchy and religious and cultural traditions that are not amenable to swift and significant social and cultural change. It appeared that decades happened in a few weeks in Tunisia and Egypt, and later in other countries when the tip of the ancient tyrannical pyramid was blown away. Ben Ali, Mubarak, and others have gone, but the pyramid — more broadly the political, economic, and security structure and the cultural superstructures that

---

[37]hadi Hamid, 'The End of Pluralism', The Atlantic, 23 July 2014.

supported these modern-day pharaohs and allowed them to torment their societies — is still intact.[38]

The tectonic plates of Egyptian society—the base of the pyramid—are shifting, albeit unevenly, through the impact of rising levels of education, literacy, nutrition, Web-based connectivity, wage-based employment of women, and many other, irreversible factors. But this is happening without achieving anything approaching consensus about the desirable direction of that change, or how it might be given concrete expression. Nor has the leadership of President al-Sisi shown the capacity to harness the intellectual energy of the middle class political audience and thereby to make durable progress in terms of human security and balanced economic development. Moreover, in addition to the fact that dissent anywhere in the Egyptian system is now brutally repressed, the year-long experience of a Muslim Brotherhood-led government under Morsi, and the fear that Egypt was embarking upon a political direction that would ultimately intrude into areas of personal lifestyle and behaviour have had a powerful and enduring impact.

For the West, there are limits to how far it may be possible to promote political and social reform. Clearly, ad hoc US counter terrorism support and military assistance provide an inadequate basis to build relationships capable of shaping the outlook for Egypt; but nor is there a durable domestic support base in Egypt for open-ended change.

In early 2011, like-minded reformist elements, both secular and Islamist, were able to draw upon experience from abroad and to share supportive imagery that gave them, for the first time, an empowered sense of self. The feeling that Mubarak had passed his use-by date was overwhelming. In practice, however,

---

[38]Hisham Melhem, 'The Tyranny Lingers On', Newlines Magazine, 25 January 2021 https://newlinesmag.com/first-person/the-tyranny-lingers-on/?fbclid=IwAR3prV4VVO7XvQYYbK1f9HZtkcPeKeweWiUOhdXxaPRDMfmAh1fPHZuTbYQ

emulation of western 'democracy' was not part of that process: like demands for bread, freedom and social justice, democracy as a slogan for mobilisation was fine, but it was a panacea, not a program for reform.

A decade on, there remains little evidence of popular support for tolerating views and values at odds with those of society at large, the core enabling values and practices that would make western-styled democracies attractive, if the regime were prepared to ease its control. It is even more difficult to assess with confidence the likely consequences, both intended and unintended, and the lag effects of any particular US or other western policy initiatives seeking to widen the space for political freedoms in Egypt and elsewhere in the Arab world.

Apart from seeking to protect their own citizens entangled in the Egyptian security and judicial systems, external players are not being asked to shape developments in that context directly. Unless handled with extraordinary care and sensitivity to local conditions, attempts on their part to become involved on behalf of the Egyptian and other Arab activists with whom they have worked in the past, or with whom they sympathise at present, are more likely than not to generate resentment and unanticipated outcomes.

Among academics and commentators, at least, there has perhaps been too much credence given to the promotion of democratic gains as an important objective of US policy under the Bush and Obama administrations. Despite stirring rhetoric, in reality Washington for its part always kept its appreciation of relations with countries such as Egypt broadly focussed. There was never going to be a choice between human rights agendas or strategic concerns, since both interests were important. Both enjoyed powerful US domestic constituencies. It was, and still is, rather, a question of how to keep those and several other interests and competing pressures in some sort of reasonable balance.

Mubarak and his entourage never took the Bush Administration's Freedom Agenda seriously in practice, nor did they see evidence of US rhetorical flourishes introducing any notion of accountability into the bilateral relationship between Washington and Cairo. In general, US pursuit of the issue of political freedom—or even protesting against the closure of major US-supported Non-Government Agencies by the regime—probably proved more useful to Mubarak in the domestic context as a means of discrediting critics of the regime than it posed a threat to his system. It would be surprising if, under a Biden Administration, the United States were to find a very different view on the part of President al-Sisi of how to manage such concerns.

The consequences of the failure of the Egyptian political class to seize the opportunity of the removal of Mubarak to adopt a more inclusive, progressive approach to Egyptian political life are impossible to quantify. It remains to be seen whether, in the future, there will be a further attempt in Egypt at political reform which proves more adept at achieving a reasonable and inclusive balance between progress and stability.

I expect that if it comes about at all, such reform will arise as part of a process of economic transformation which, if it is to achieve competitive results in the global marketplace, will have to attract and harness the abundant talents of educated young Egyptians who have experienced what it means to have a voice in corporate decision-making, who want peer-reviewed performance evaluation, and will not be content to leave modern corporate values and expectations behind when they leave the office in the evening. It is also important, however, to beware of assumptions based on values and expectations (including of political legitimacy and notions of linear progress) of outsiders which may not reflect how Egyptians might interpret their own priorities and circumstances.

For now, regrettably, the future is clouded. Experience and instinct suggest Egypt and Egyptians will find ways to survive, more or less on their own terms. But failing to protect the most basic freedoms of its own citizens will not secure Egypt's economic future, nor widen the space for intellectual creativity and social progress which were once the hallmarks of Egypt's contribution to the modern Arab world.

Chapter 20

The Arab Outlook: on the bridge of the Titanic, smelling ice[39]

In the Introduction to this book I referred to the differing perceptions at times of foreigners and Syrians—albeit in the particular case mentioned, in regard to the sale of underwear in Souk Hamidiyeh in Damascus—concerning their country. I recalled the comment of a Syrian that, "When foreigners look, they only see the mountain. Syrians see the volcano underneath."

Perhaps regimes across the Arab world have also failed to see their own volcanoes. With rare exceptions, the reluctance to cede power of authoritarian Arab leaders who inherited the institutions of the colonial period, initially while pursuing a nationalist vision and subsequently amidst the seductive and corrosive effects of power itself, effectively ensured stasis.

They manifestly failed to grasp how their interests would be affected by growing educational opportunities, evident in a rise in literacy from 18 per cent to 82 per cent since 1960. There was a thirty-fold increase in the number of Arabs online between 2000 and 2012, but regimes paid little attention to the

---

[39]This chapter is based on my articles 'Beware the Return of Hope' Inside Story 15 January 2016, https://insidestory.org.au/the-arab-outlook-beware-the-return-of-hope/ and 'Challenges Mount Up' The Interpreter, Lowy Institute 22 May 2018, updated to reflect subsequent developments.

impact of the internet and social media on alienated Muslims in Arab and Western societies. They welcomed foreign direct investment without appreciating that it also brought the values and disciplines of global business models and raised expectations of individual empowerment and altered gender relations. Most importantly, perhaps, they failed to recognise the significance of each of those factors in shaping inchoate desires within their societies to be modern, and Arab, and in many cases Muslim, in the twenty-first century.

Western policy-makers and officials, myself included, shared in that analytical failure. We were too close to, and too comfortable with, familiar Arab regimes. We wanted to believe their assurances about how they were reshaping their countries. Like all good diplomats and salespeople, they made us feel good about ourselves, and so we were inclined to discount our concerns about the real-time performance of ageing, sclerotic, parasitic leaderships. We anticipated that their time at the helm would pass, to be followed, surely, by a new generation more attuned to our vision of a globalising world.

In short, we didn't pay enough attention to the gaps between rhetoric and political and social reality. We underestimated the resilience of elites determined to protect their privileges and identities from encroachment by others. We conflated popular enthusiasm for elections with a coming triumph of democratic values. We hoped, assumed, or wished to believe, that leaderships would see the need for reform, and would act upon that pressure sufficiently to defuse and manage it constructively. And we failed, for want of understanding of the nature of power in the Arab world, to see that reform, when it came, could modify the functioning of systems, but not the values underpinning them.

With a handful of exceptions, we didn't see the uprisings of 2011 coming. We didn't think we had to look. We had missed the enthusiasm for change on public display. So when Mohamed

ElBaradei arrived at Cairo airport in early 2010, having completed his term as director-general of the International Atomic Energy Agency, to a tumultuous reception by Egyptians who saw him as a fresh political force, and then left again barely forty-eight hours later, we missed the point. We focused merely on what we saw as his political ineptitude, or on the capacity of the Mubarak regime to stare him down.

We also missed, and most Arab intellectuals dismissed, the significance of the re-joining of student and labour activism in Egypt from 2009 onwards, mostly because that initiative at first went nowhere. We did not appreciate how it could rebound, leveraged by the internet and social media, into a key factor in the unfolding events of 2011.

We should have been focused, in other words, both on the underlying factors making the turmoil of the Arab Uprisings a real possibility; and on the structural issues that pose serious challenges to achieving programmatic reform.

In 2002, under the sponsorship of the United Nations, Arab intellectuals had begun publishing a series of detailed analyses, known as the Arab Human Development Reports, identifying key regional social, economic and political deficits. Together with publications by Arab experts in other think tanks in the Western world, they warned that the Arab world was "richer than it was developed." We were placed on notice that reform was urgently required in areas ranging from gender empowerment to education if the gaps between the Arab world and other countries were to be closed.

Clearly written, evidence-based, intellectually cogent and devoid of self-pity and excuses, the analyses identified the causes of Arab ill-performance as arising mostly from institutions Arab governments had created but failed to reform. The political implications of the analyses were not clearly stated, but they were obvious enough. Within the Arab world, however, the analysts were mostly ignored, condemned or dismissed for their lack of political correctness. They had failed to pin responsibility, or even causality, elsewhere, and that was unacceptable.

As the twentieth anniversary of the first of those reports approaches, it is clear that none of the key concerns articulated by those Arab intellectuals have been addressed. Most Arab governments recognise the need for economic growth to absorb the aspirations of populations that are better educated, connected, demanding, and having greater potential for mobilisation than ever before. But significant gaps remain between urban and rural Arab populations, and between elites and others, not only in terms of literacy and numeracy but also in terms of their daily experience of dealing with instruments and agents of state authority, from police to bureaucrats and teachers.

Nor have the changes in the region during the past two decades made achieving the reforms they called for any easier. Instead, as mentioned earlier in regard to Egypt, the collapse of the Arab Uprisings has seen a reaffirmation of authoritarian values and practices. This has been reinforced by the abject failure of supposedly liberal Arab voices to rise above their political differences and defend a robust separation of powers.

No mainstream figure or political party (except perhaps in Tunisia, and even that is now headed in a decisively authoritarian direction) is insisting on respect for the values of inclusive politics and empowerment. Across the Arab world, political parties remain among the weakest elements in the search for reform, still resistant to transparency and the devolution of authority within their own ranks as well as in the wider society. Nor is there evidence that Arab governments have harnessed, mobilised and empowered creative middle class talent in business, politics or the arts.

Instead, perhaps as a result, in least in part, of a largely dysfunctional relationship between regimes and Arab civil society, we have witnessed a trend, including especially in politics and the academic realm, toward hermetically-sealed world views within Arab societies. Demonisation and vilification of those deemed to be bound by the shackles of colonial thinking, or considered to be inauthentic by virtue of their political views or religious orthodoxy, is all too common. The tendency to retreat into such political and intellectual bunkers may suggest a natural human reaction to feelings of disempowerment, and a desire to be respected and to find comfort within a like-minded peer group. But the fascist, retrogressive overtone to the discourse it generates has negative consequences for the prospects for achieving worthwhile, programmatic reform to institutions within the Arab world—and for protecting the most vulnerable within those countries.

Heroism and heroes—whether they are politicians, artists, business leaders, scientists or educators—shape visions of the possible. And among its many deficits, the deficit of heroes in the contemporary Arab world is alarming. Different as they are in almost all other respects, Nobel Peace Prize laureate ElBaradei—surely the sort of positive role model that is required if the Arab world is to realise its creative potential—and the late, unlamented Abu Bakr al-Baghdadi of Islamic State have in common that they inspired hope for an alternative future.

Radicalisation is fed by humiliation and despair, but Arab mobilisation is also driven by hope. We focus at our peril on the failures and shortcomings of Baghdadi and others like him, rather than on the groundswells—the volcanoes—into which they tap. In her magisterial analysis of the factors contributing to the outbreak of world war in 1914, Margaret MacMillan argued that popular mobilisation in Europe arose not as a result of despair and economic adversity, which was growing among the working classes, so much as in response to the promise, and excitement, of visions that proved to be catastrophic. The same can be said of the Arab world today.

Across the Arab Middle East, the counter-revolutionary impulse—a gadarene rush back to the familiar comforts of authoritarian rule at the expense of creativity, empowerment, human rights, accountability and transparency in government—can only succeed, even in the short term, with a strong, balanced economic performance. To be sustainable, it also requires a demonstrated sensitivity to popular expectations of dignity, in circumstances where interaction with the power of the state is unavoidable. Globally, the apparent success of repressive rule, from Turkey to China, may provide a measure of comfort to authoritarian Arab leaders determined to protect the status quo. But I remain convinced that, in the emerging Arab world, repression without justice is self-defeating. And it carries an opportunity cost that few governments can afford.

Accountable, constitutionally-based political leadership, not state-sponsored violence, is the key to meeting the challenges facing the Arab future. But such leadership is in short supply. Nor is there necessarily a political solution to be found to many of the most pressing challenges of the coming decade.

Meanwhile, across the Middle East, the demographic time bomb ticks on. A Middle East population of 83 million in 1950 will be almost 724 million by 2050.[40] Though still manageable, depending on oil prices, budget deficits in most countries are worsening. Graduate unemployment is at a record high: Egypt alone is graduating over 900,000 students annually from its universities.

Though now being addressed in most Arab countries, timorous responses over many decades to consumer demand for cheap energy and water, and the impact of global warming, poverty and

---

[40] UNICEF estimates 2021 in MENA Generation 2030. https://www.unicef.org/mena/media/4141/file/MENA-Gen2030.pdf. See also US Census Bureau estimates cited in Anthony H. Cordesman, 'The Need for Better Civil-Military Planning' in The Center for Strategic and International Studies (CSIS) Global Forecast 2015 pp. 53-56.

conflict on ill-equipped infrastructure have created increasingly obvious environmental problems. Temperatures have risen across the region faster than the world average. Precipitation is falling and droughts are expected to become more frequent and severe. The pressure on underground water aquifers in Jordan and the Persian Gulf states is unsustainable. Arab governments have begun to recognise the immensity of the problems ahead, but have been reluctant to make unpalatable choices in response to these and other challenges and financial pressures, for fear of the political and security consequences.

In 2020, some 69 per cent of the regional Arab population were under-nourished, according to the United Nations—a 91 per cent increase over the previous two decades.[41] Two-thirds of children in the region aged from five to fourteen were unable to read with proficiency even before the Covid-19 pandemic wiped out the possibility of normal schooling for two years. It is a calamity which, as my friend Rami Khouri observes,

> 'guarantees that several cohorts of undereducated Arab youth will not be able to contribute to their national economies beyond menial and manual labour in the informal economy. They will suffer lifetimes of poverty, vulnerability, and marginalisation, with problems of mental health, socialization, and low wellbeing and self-satisfaction.'[42]

The problem is as much social as political. Across the Arabic-speaking world repression comes naturally to regimes under threat—be they governments, patriarchs of families or other holders of privilege. Even beyond the realm of government and

---

[41]FAO. 2021. *Near East and North Africa – Regional Overview of Food Security and Nutrition 2021: Statistics and trends.* Cairo. https://doi.org/10.4060/cb7495en

---

[42]Rami Khouri, 'This past year was rough for the Arab world, the worst is yet to come', The New Arab, 24 December, 2021, https://english.alaraby.co.uk/opinion/worst-yet-come-arab-world

security apparatus—and most definitely among such circles—there is deep anxiety about the asking of open-ended questions about what it means to be young, Arab, Muslim and 'modern'; and where accountability for failures to meet aspirations begins and ends. But those questions will continue to be asked.

Among those who wish to see the existing Arab order replaced, notions of reality and purpose are apt to be shaped by lived experience of human rights abuse at the hands of government, and the politics of the prison yard, rather than abstract arguments about theology or democracy. Where states are weak, or complacent, the jihadist phenomenon has space to develop.

Where states are violent, but seen as unjust, the seductive imagery of a religiously-imbued higher purpose serves to legitimise acts of appalling violence, or ambitions to engage in such violence, at home and further abroad. Whereas political Islam is now in retreat, the sophistication, connectivity and lethality of jihadist forces increased dramatically during the past decade. Though in recent years they have lost physical control of territory they once dominated, they have not lost the will to fight. They are far from being defeated.

The fact that so far Arab regimes have risen to meet the Islamist challenge should not disguise the problem that they have done so at the expense of the creative potential of their citizens. Instead they have tended to consolidate webs of privilege, patronage networks and corruption. The secularism of "modernising" Arab regimes was always a phenomenon of the urban Arab elite, closely linked to issues of class and visceral rejection of the Islamist "other." But failing to capture the political imagination of the young middle class—which is by no means to be simply categorised as either secular or Islamist in its orientation—means regimes' sense of their own security, and therefore their commitment to genuine political, social and economic reform, will remain limited.

The vast majority of Arab populations are unlikely to experience a closing of the gaps between their economic and social circumstances and those that prevail in the rest of the developed world. State authority—a critical factor if programmatic reform is to be delivered rather than merely announced—is increasingly at risk when ordinary people feel little connection to national events and policies. In extreme cases, such as Syria, localised struggles for turf, or in some cases for survival, are privileging militias, traditional power-brokers and other regressive forms of rule.

On the other hand, grassroots empowerment, though essential in principle, is also open to exploitation by forces that are often, in practice, deeply disempowering and sectarian in their behaviour and beliefs. In the absence of political courage and leadership at the state level to balance those risks, the weakening of Arab states and the decentralisation of authority may yet prove to be the death knell of the progressive and creative elements within Arab society.

In summary, we should anticipate there will continue to be a surfeit of adversity across the Middle East, including ongoing population displacements, and economic malaise. The Arab world will emerge from the nightmares of the past decade into a world which is both different and, in some respects, unchanging. The rulers of the region will probably be even more fierce in their behaviour than before. They will do so, in part, because the defenders of privilege and predictability have found repression works—for them; and in part because the brief moment of popular mobilisation for change has been submerged, in almost all cases, by arguments that freedom is more likely to produce chaos and division rather than bread and social justice.

Governments in the region will struggle to find a sustainable balance between satisfying the expectations and sometimes contradictory demands of their political audiences, and meeting the imperatives of national survival in a globalised security environment. The human cost of conflicts, especially sectarian conflicts, will have corrosive social and political consequences enduring for generations to come. And the environment which may follow from the next chaotic contest between privilege, on the one hand, and unmet, scarcely-articulated aspirations on the other, has the potential to be deeply damaging, not only to the people and governments of the Middle East but also to the outlook for securing respect for values we believe to be of universal relevance.

It is too soon to know or to predict what the next wave of Arab political events might entail when, in due course, hope emerges for an alternative. The way forward demands a process, embedded in transparent, inclusive institutions, of establishing a new and broadly-accepted paradigm of Arab modernity in support of which the energy and resources of leaders, state and society can be directed.

Such a model may yet be found. It took the Titanic a long time to sink. But even if it is not found, the modern Arab world has no way to stop the drivers of change—which are generational and societal as well as political—that saw the uprisings begin a decade ago.

Chapter 21

The Arab World and the West

Success or failure for Arab countries of the Middle East seeking to surmount the pressures of demography and conflicting aspirations and values in a globalising world will be determined in large measure by the quality of the relationship between Arab society and world society. Unless states turn entirely inward (which would risk failure accordingly either to fulfil their potential or even to meet the demographic and other challenges they face) the Arab future is bound to be shaped by Arab interaction with the West. The dilemma, as Hisham Melhem once expressed it, is that:

> the West cannot save the Arabs from themselves, and the Arabs are unable or unwilling to exorcise their demons on their own.[42]

Conversely, Western interests are at stake in the outlook for the Arab world. Affirming and, wherever possible, actively upholding values shared with young, progressive-minded Arabs is necessary to remaining relevant to the aspirations of the sort of Middle East we may hope will emerge in coming decades.

---

[42]Hisham Melhem, 'The tyranny of the past, the uncertainty of the future', Al-Arabiya, 18 January, 2015.

Geographic links to the Mediterranean and Europe; sea and air lines of communication; oil and terrorism all bind the Arab world to a global network and therefore a place, albeit secondary for many, in the strategic calculations of major powers.

In *Beyond Peace*, I identified the need to understand the relationship between the domestic characteristics of states and regional security, in addition to more traditional concerns about state behaviour. Where once the Middle East International Relations discourse was focussed largely on states and structures, the academic ambition now is to incorporate into the discussion the shaping effects of globalization, mythologies, actors and political relationships. But the robustness of Arab authoritarianism and the conditions giving rise to it mean the relationship between actors and external parties remains multifaceted and rather ambiguous.

As a frustrated Russian diplomat once remarked, the Syrians 'take everything from us—except advice'. In Egypt, the interim military regime's repression of prominent US-sponsored civil society organizations, and the actions of the Egyptian military and General Sisi, when they seized power and crushed the Muslim Brotherhood and its supporters in July 2013 challenge the notion that leaderships are obliged to pay at least some heed to western values.

Like Mubarak, the Egyptian military's connections to the United States were long-standing, close and mutually-rewarding. They had actively courted American support throughout the 2011 crisis, and beyond, on the grounds that they were intent on 'saving democracy'. But they were not constrained by such rhetoric—or western expectations—when they deployed the violence of the state to suppress their opponents and critics in 2013 and since that time.

I usually began my graduate courses on Arab political, economic and social change (later re-labelled, in the hubris of the Arab uprisings, Revolution and Reform in the Arab World) by recalling an event in Sudan which took place on 24 November 1899. With the Mahdi (who had led the uprising against the British and killed General Gordon at Khartoum) having already died of dysentery, the remnants of his forces, commanded by Abdallahi ibn Mohammed, known as the Khalifa, were cornered at Umm Diwaykarat by Kitchener's Anglo-Egyptian expeditionary force under the command of Reginald Wingate. When he failed to rally his forces to do battle, the Khalifa and his senior officers sat on a cow hide to wait for their death.

The key fact of that episode was not its demonstration that British military technology and capability would prevail, but rather that the Sudanese would not surrender to a foreign force.

One can see that determination not to yield to pressure from any external party, let alone one with historical associations with colonial rule, underpinning Arab perceptions of their relationship with the United States to this day. When Gamal Abdel Nasser nationalised the Suez Canal in 1956 following the abrupt and discourteous withdrawal of the possibility of financial assistance from the United States and Britain, coupled with western press comments alleging Nasser was 'blackmailing' the United States and Britain and US comments denigrating Egypt's economic outlook, the popular acclaim he received at home and abroad reflected a sense that Nasser had chosen to defend the dignity of Egypt and Egyptians.

The absence (in contrast to the West) of popular regret across the Arab world at the fall of Anwar Sadat was linked to a sense that Egypt's dignity had been impugned following the conclusion of the Camp David Accords with Israel in 1978; his opening of the Egyptian economy to external investors (and the corruption that followed); and his cultivation of fawning relations with Washington (and vice versa). The rapturous response of Palestinians to Saddam Hussein's posturing against Israel prior to the invasion and subsequent liberation of Kuwait reflected a sense that here, at last, was an Arab leader willing to restore their dignity by pushing back militarily against the torment of their occupation.

Nor is the colonial period forgotten in the region: during the turmoil in Egypt in mid-2013 both supporters and opponents of the military government bitterly denounced the United States. Indeed, underlining the enduring power of the colonial metaphor, one leading Egyptian liberal commentator saw fit to describe the US ambassador as 'the American version of Lord Cromer', the British Controller-General and later Consul-General in Egypt from 1883 to 1907. And, as mentioned in regard to the response of Egyptians to the showing of *Rabbit-Proof Fence* in Cairo, there are powerful undercurrents of sympathy and empathy among Egyptians for those who are subject to foreign oppression.

Like most other nations, Arab societies are shaped by their own versions of history and of popular aversion, in many cases to near neighbours. The region has too much history, and not enough geography, to expect anything else. But memories and mythologies in which external players—primarily the United States—are cast in such negative terms have played a part in the fostering of Arab identities (both national and sectarian) framed by collective memories and mythologies of grievance where the West is concerned. And real and imagined memories and other social dynamics in the Arab context will continue to affect the capacity of Arab governments and societies to engage effectively with the West. As David Gardner aptly observed, there is a profound ambivalence towards the West, 'despised as predatory and corrupt at the same time as it is admired for its cultural, technical and military accomplishments'.[43]

The states and societies of the Middle East certainly have had more than their share of unequal and conflictual dealings with outside parties. Western policy-makers have also eroded our own

---

[43]David Gardner, Last Chance: The Middle East in the Balance (I.B. Tauris, London 2012) p. 50.

credibility by accommodating the corruption and human rights abuses of regimes—sometimes out of expediency, and sometimes for want of an alternative under the pressure of events. We have failed to apply the same moral standards to Israel as we apply to other parties in the Middle East. Our failures have damaged the standing of those in the region who respect our values and who sometimes pay heed to our advice.

Nor can the Arab outlook be separated from regional and global factors. Struggles for regional ascendancy between the conservative Arab states and Iran; competition between the United States and Russia; the role played by Turkey in regard to the Kurds, especially in the intricate ménage a trois with Iran and Russia that has aided and abetted the jihadist phenomenon in northern Syria; the unfolding of US policy toward Iran, and Israel; and the complex political future of the Gulf all increase the improbability of achieving a regional security architecture than can provide a basis for reasonably stable and predictable dealings within the region.

Most western countries would hope to see a conscious Arab political effort to build confidence in the prospect of achieving positive and constructive outcomes that engage Arab society with progressive, achievement-oriented world society. Part of the tragedy of much of the Arabic-speaking world however is that it is also all too easy, in the Arabic media, among the privileged, and even among some frustrated reformists, to fall back defensively on the familiar comforts of seeing external conspiracy as the root cause of Arab disunity and sedition against the popular will for stability, predictability and jobs.

At the same time, western governments will not easily find a durable balance between the pursuit of their strategic interests in the region, a task which hinges in large part upon the quality of dealings with regional governments, rather than societies; and the desire to uphold the values they regard as universal but which are not shared to the same degree at either the leadership or popular levels of Arab society. Moreover, there is an enormous gap between the removal of an authoritarian regime, such as those of Assad or Ghaddafi, and the creation of a viable, progressive alternative. The processes involved are different, and the consequences of regime change for what may follow are very difficult to predict.

The question of military intervention is especially problematic. History demonstrates that external military interventions in the Middle East can stabilise Arab regimes. In theory, adding to the capability of Middle East regimes to defend themselves may widen the space for reform. In practice, however, it will probably decrease their willingness and capacity to address underlying structural issues of state dysfunctionality (corruption, inequality of opportunity, human rights abuses, disempowerment) that lie at the core of legitimate opposition.

Those shortcomings also provide ongoing opportunities for non-state armed groups to recruit and grow, where circumstances allow, from West Africa to Yemen, from Afghanistan to Southeast Asia, and to attract support from the suburbs of Paris to Western Sydney. Such groups and actors are more ideologically rigid, and their dogma even less encumbered by normative considerations, than the regimes they oppose.

Interventions that served Western interests (for example, the UK/US intervention in Jordan and Lebanon in 1958; UK/Kuwait 1961; UK/Oman/PDRY in the 1970s; and US/UK/Kuwait 1990–91) had aims limited to securing the morale and capability of regimes seeking Western support and sharing or benefiting Western strategic interests. Most such interventions had a light military footprint. Some, such as Oman, had a special operations character. All had clear, limited political objectives directed towards supporting the *status quo*.

Interventions that arguably failed to serve Western interests

(Suez 1956; Iraq 2003; Libya 2011; US/Syria since 2011; Afghanistan) were aimed at, or evolved into, attempts at regime removal; or were undertaken in pursuit of illusionary goals, mostly driven or promoted by US or other western domestic political agendas. Some were also driven, initially, not by credible strategic analysis, but by political/principled concerns, such as not to witness a repeat of the massacre of Srebrenica in Benghazi.

The most important consideration among western countries should be to remain consistent in expressing their views on matters of principle; to act in accordance with those views where possible; and to do no harm to the voices within the Arab world that continue advocating political reform, inclusiveness and constitutionality as core values of Arab society. Balance and moderation in foreign policy choices, dialogue and continuing effort to address regional tensions can only work to the advantage of those advocating liberal democratic values within Arab society.

Ultimately, however, it is the capacity, and the will, of regimes to respond through mixtures of repression, coercion and co-optation to emerging threats, and the dynamics of military defection, that offer the best guide to the likelihood of regime change, at least in the Arab context. In most cases, rather than popular mobilisation, it is collapses of confidence in leaderships among elites and other key components of the deep state that are likely to determine the chances of regime survival, and the outlook for the interests of external parties engaged in the region.

Chapter 22

The United States, Iran, Israel and the Persian Gulf: Re-imagining the Middle East

The abandonment by the Trump Administration of the nuclear deal known as the Joint Comprehensive Plan of Action or JCPOA with which Iran was complying was an act of extraordinary strategic stupidity. However, while bounded by differences in values, and amidst wariness as to whether the Iranians may seek to develop a nuclear-weapon capability, there may still be some room for limited, but potentially important understandings to be reached between the United States and Iran in regard to their respective strategic interests.

The United States has thrown its weight behind efforts to develop strategic defence relationships between Israel and the Arab countries of the Persian Gulf to complement the normalisation of ties between them. Arab governments have welcomed opportunities to gain access to Israeli technology and tourism. Some may have recognised the importance to any future Republican President in Washington of being seen during the Trump era to have achieved a foreign policy success. Gulf Arab states are looking to address in particular their vulnerability to ballistic missile attacks, including by third parties such as the Houthis in Yemen or the Iranian Revolutionary Guards' Quds Force, acting in support of Iranian interests or in pursuit of their own agendas.

Less in the public gaze, but potentially of greater strategic importance, however, is the fact that a renewed attempt at engagement between Iran and the key Arab players of the Persian Gulf—Saudi Arabia, the UAE and Iraq—is also under way. Recent contacts, including most notably between Iran and Saudi Arabia, brokered especially by Iraq, appear to be moving from intelligence circles into the more formal realm of engagement between officials. Progress will be slow, and its goals and likely outcomes remain uncertain: relations between Saudi Arabia and Iran have been difficult since the Islamic Revolution in 1979, and diplomatic ties were severed in 2016.

No country can afford, however, to ignore the potential consequences of a nuclear-capable Iran for the regional security outlook, nor the risks attached to any pre-emptive strikes by Israel or the United States against Iranian nuclear facilities. And notwithstanding deep Arab suspicions of Iranian intentions, the key Arab players will all prefer to search, to varying degrees, for accommodation, not confrontation, with their Iranian neighbour.

Against that background, and with the impending failure of efforts to revive the nuclear deal between Iran and the major global powers and the IAEA, it is time for a recalibration of US strategy where Iran is concerned, and for absorbing lessons from the 'maximum pressure' debacle of the Trump era.

The obvious starting point for such a policy review is that while the US remains the most powerful military actor in the Middle East, the strategic environment is changing as a consequence of decades of events in the region, and policy choices beyond it.

The key, probably irreversible, feature of the emerging order in the region is the *perceived* absence of a credible US security umbrella. The perception arises, not for want of military capacity on the part of the United States to act, drawing on its assets in the region and beyond; but rather because of doubt among the Arab states of the Persian Gulf that, unless US interests are directly at stake, the United States would be prepared to engage in open-ended escalation of a conflict with Iran.

Certain circumstances may continue to justify the use of US military force, especially in response to immediate operational threats, and as a retaliatory measure. The US will not be humiliated, by Iran or its proxies, nor would it serve the interests of its friends for that to happen.

But as a different regional picture emerges, post-Afghanistan, military measures have limited value in shaping it for the better. Nor would they produce a more durable outcome than a process based around negotiation. Indeed, even in conjunction with a diplomatic process, military force is more likely to be counterproductive to creating a balanced, inclusive and predictable new architecture should regional countries choose to move in that direction.

Both the US and Iran can live without a nuclear deal. So can Israel, even if Iran is nuclear-capable. But it would be to Israel's advantage if, with US support and engagement in the process, the region moves towards a mature, wary but forward-looking relationship with the Iranians in which—and it is here that US diplomacy can especially play a constructive role—Israeli security concerns are regarded by all the protagonists as no less important than those of other regional countries.

It is in the emergence of such comprehensive security architecture that the solution to the Iranian nuclear issue resides. That may not be an agenda favoured in political circles by Washington, Riyadh and Jerusalem at present. But it is time for the United States to work with key Arab countries to persuade them that, in their dealings with Iran, their interests will be best served by urging the Iranians to pay serious attention to Israel's insecurities as well as their own; and at the same time leaving Israel in no doubt that it has to seek a place in a framework which is driven primarily, not by the United States, but by the agendas of the regional countries—including Iran—themselves.

Pivoting the US security posture towards protecting key interests and alliance partners in East Asia would not affect the US commitment to Israel's defence and security. Nor would a renewed US focus on Europe and the Atlantic alliance in the light of the Russian invasion of Ukraine. But especially since its own energy profile is changing towards self-sufficiency, US concern about energy security for the remainder of the world would now be unlikely to galvanize political support for sustained intensive US military action in the Gulf region unless Israel was directly threatened.

A strategic accommodation between the United States and Iran would be a conspiracy theorist's wet dream, and an Arab policy maker's nightmare. It won't happen.

Formal US acknowledgment to Iran of one highly sensitive regional reality—namely that Iranian influence, in a variety of forms, has always been and will remain part of the future in Iraq, Lebanon and even Syria—would open up for discussion the future security architecture of the Middle East. The United States engaging in a serious strategic dialogue with Iran on that basis would send political shock waves across the entire Middle East region.

For compelling historical, cultural and security-based reasons, the main Arab concern would be the sectarian aspects of a resurgence of Iranian influence across the region, and its capacity (perhaps more imagined than real) to stoke the embers of Shia resentment of their situation under authoritarian Sunni governments. At this juncture, such an outcome would leave the majority of Arab countries with a reinforced sense of betrayal. Many would also question, with good reason, the capacity of the United States to avoid being out-manoeuvred by the Iranians over the long term when it comes to power struggles on the ground, especially in Syria, Lebanon and Iraq. By contrast, among most Arab capitals, an absence of any amelioration in US-Iranian relations would be a relief.

A resumption (however unlikely) of Iranian charm offensives in New York and Geneva; the final departure of Donald Trump and, in due course, Ayatollah Khamenei, and some imaginative use of social media do not provide a genuine basis for turning the page in Iranian-US relations. The damage caused to US strategic interests by its sudden, ill-considered withdrawal from the JCPOA is obvious. The current and prospective leadership of Iran is deeply, and vehemently ill-disposed towards the United States.

Choosing not to explore the potential for a worthwhile strategic bargain between Washington and Tehran out of deference to the sensitivities of Arab countries and Israel, however, also leaves the United States with few worthwhile alternatives to the *status quo*. And that *status quo* is unlikely to be sustainable.

Looking ahead, the direction of US engagement with the region is being shaped by the cumulative effects of popular weariness in the United States with conflict, from the debacle of Afghanistan to the ongoing trauma of Iraq, and US budget pressures and domestic bickering over financial policy. Healing the divisions of the Trump era—assuming it is over, which is far from certain—will continue to absorb US political energy and attention. Few of those factors are likely to be reversed, at least in the foreseeable future. And whereas core US interests in the region (traditionally oil, Israel and the security of Arab allies) will remain largely unchanged, at least until world demand for Middle East oil falls considerably, US commitments in support of those interests seem certain to continue to face pressure to be adjusted downward.

Posturing aside, both Iran and Saudi Arabia would stand to gain, in theory, by building a much higher amount of credible and predictable, albeit adversarial, mutual dealing. The quality of the relationship on public view would be less important than achieving mutual reassurance in regard to the strategic behaviour and intent of the other party. In theory, the possibility cannot be ruled out of movement in that direction—potentially even encouraged by the United States, in the unlikely event a renewed deal on nuclear issues can be struck, or as a less bad option than seeing Saudi Arabia itself turn to development of a nuclear weapons capability.

In short, a viable, Gulf-centric, inclusive security architecture based on a degree of wary mutual accommodation between the Saudis and Iran, from which Israel could perhaps draw some comfort, with Saudi support, as far as its own security situation was concerned, cannot and should not be ruled out as an ultimate objective for US policy.

The reality at present looks very different. So far, at the strategic level the accommodation witnessed in 2019 between Israel, the United Arab Emirates and Saudi Arabia reflects little more than their separate concerns about Iran, and perhaps some uncertainty about the extent of support they may anticipate from the United States going forward. Although the relationship between Jerusalem and Riyadh is effectively open-ended, so long as the Saudis can contain the domestic political fallout, at this early stage, Saudi dealings with Israel at the strategic level are unlikely to progress beyond understandings at the highest level that neither side will threaten the other; and presumably some sharing of intelligence and security-related surveillance technology.

Where Iran is concerned, for their own respective reasons,

both Israel and Saudi Arabia wish to see the risks, both political and strategic, of an Iranian regional ascendancy contained. Of course, for Israel the challenges from Iran are real, whether Iran has a nuclear capability or not. But politics and propagandist references to wolves in sheep's clothing and mullahs with nukes aside, Israeli policy mostly reflects a clear-sighted appreciation of its strategic interests. Nervousness and rhetoric at the political level notwithstanding, it could be expected to calculate with care the potential costs and benefits of any putative realignment of the relationship between the United States and Iran, or between Iran and Saudi Arabia.

From an Israeli perspective, there is no reason to see Iranian repugnance towards Israel *as an idea* as having existential strategic ramifications, so long as the Iranians are believed to accept—however unwillingly—*Israel's durability* as a permanent feature of the region.

Moreover, if the Iranians would prefer to see a reduction or even the removal of most of the US military presence surrounding it, some form of US-backed but Gulf-centric regional security architecture acceptable to Israel would be essential. There are no attainable means by which Iran could expect to become part of a worthwhile regional cooperative security system of that kind—assuming they might wish to do so—without the active support of one, or both, of the Saudis and Israelis. Meanwhile, Israeli conventional military superiority as well as its nuclear and second-strike capability will continue to give it unsurpassed levels of security by regional standards.

Despite occasional frictions in the US-Israel relationship, Israeli diplomatic, political, informational and other influence on US policy approaches is certain to remain unsurpassed in the Middle East context. And it would have considerable capacity to press for US and Saudi guarantees that it would not be placed at risk by any movement toward accommodation between Washington and Tehran, or Tehran and Riyadh.

It must be stressed that the case against the emergence of a different dynamic between Iran and the United States is strong. The United States and Iran may well conclude, including for domestic political or ideological reasons, that achieving a stabilised, more interests-based relationship is illusory or undesirable. Both sides could demand concessions from the other that are unrealistic or undeliverable. Each is capable of over-playing their hand in pre-negotiation posturing.

It would require an enormous investment of US diplomatic and political resources—and a great deal of sheer good fortune—to place US approaches to Iran on a more durable and cost-effective basis, at a time when the primary concern of the US President is to deal with pressing domestic concerns, and other countries and issues such as China, Russia and climate change. The Iranians would need to provide credible assurances to sceptical US, Arab and other audiences about the limits to their strategic objectives in the region.

That is something that the complex, internally conflicted character of the Iranian system makes especially difficult to deliver, even if there may be those who advocate for such an approach. As Karim Sadjadpour has observed, the United States has tried, and failed, to engage a regime whose leadership does not want to be engaged, fearing the potential consequences of doing so; and to isolate a regime that arguably thrives on isolation.[44] There is a mountain of historical and legislative baggage between Washington and Tehran, some of which Biden could only begin to reduce with the support of Congress, where the very idea of concessions to the Iranians remains anathema.

It is also impossible to predict the approach (for example, with the Saudis, or without the Saudis?) toward achieving a more

---

[44] Karim Sadjadpour, 'What the US Gets Wrong about Iran', New York Times, 12 August 2022. https://www.nytimes.com/2022/08/12/opinion/iran-america-nuclear-policy.html?referringSource=articleShare

predictable relationship that Iran and the United States might choose to follow. A great deal might also depend on how the US and Iran addressed or dealt with the question of an ongoing US military presence in the region, with attendant US military facilities in almost all the Gulf Arab states.

Nevertheless, if one proceeds from the intellectual premise that changes in the power balances between states and dealings between them within regional systems, and tectonic shifts in societies, have the potential to generate shifts in strategy, then de-escalation with Iran and a broader-based US approach to Saudi Arabia and UAE would serve current and future US interests best. If mutual credibility and predictability thresholds can be met over an extended period; with the assistance of some departures from the political scene of key anti-American figures on the Iranian side; and especially if Saudi Arabia can be persuaded to rebuild its own relations with Iran as the conflict in Yemen subsides, US preparedness to engage more closely with Iran in pursuit of compatible US and Iranian interests is at least conceivable.

Perhaps the most interesting aspect of such a shift, if it were to eventuate, would be its political impact on Iran itself. The Iranian regime has drawn extensively on allegations of external malfeasance to rationalise its economic performance and its brutal quelling of internal dissent. If that pressure were eased, the regime would probably face renewed demands for an alternative model of successful economic development and social progress within an Islamic but more genuinely democratic framework.

Failure by Iran to provide greater opportunities for economic success and social freedoms as offered by Dubai and other Gulf emirates, in the absence of a credible external threat, would mean that the ideological basis of the Iranian system—and its willingness to set aside resources for defence, to accept the opportunity costs of negative relations with the United States and the Gulf Arab states, and its numbing effect on the talents and aspirations of ordinary Iranians—would wear even more thin. An already sclerotic and corrupt system would thus be at greater risk from the political demands of the globally-connected, cosmopolitan elements of the Iranian middle class, which continue to demonstrate extraordinary—and to its opponents, worrying—qualities of resilience.

As I have argued above, in Iran as in the Arab world, once hope is added to a picture of tectonic shifts, demands for change may prove irresistible.

Chapter 23

The Lessons of Menzies and Suez

When I had just turned 10, my parents took me with them to an open day at Talindert, the property of Sir Chester Manifold, at Camperdown in Victoria (my paternal great great grandfather, Dr Daniel Curdie, was a neighbour of the Manifold family in the mid-1800s). The Australian Prime Minister, Robert Menzies was there, a large man in a double-breasted suit, talking to some journalists. At my mother's insistence, I approached Menzies and asked for his autograph. He ignored me. I asked again, with the same result. When I asked for a third time, the journalists asked Menzies to give me an autograph, probably just to be rid of me. Menzies did so. I immediately lost it. I realised two things, however—Menzies didn't like me, and I didn't like him.

It was wryly amusing, therefore, some 60 years later, to have spent much of the decade from 2011 onwards pursuing a research project for the Department of Foreign Affairs and Trade on the part played by Australia, under the Menzies Government, in the Suez Crisis of 1956.

Seven Cabinet submissions, and more than 20 Cabinet decisions made Suez the key Middle East policy issue of the 1950s for Australia. But my introductory analysis of the documentary record became so extensive that the Department decided it warranted publication in 2019 as a separate monograph, *Australia, Menzies and Suez: Australian Policymaking on the Middle East Before, During and After the Suez Crisis* (Australia in the World: The Foreign Affairs and Trade Files, No. 6) to highlight key issues and provide a guide to the material in its companion volume of edited documents. The edited volume published in 2021 on Australia and Suez was co-edited with the erudite and insightful Departmental historian, Matthew Jordan.

Though not trained as a historian, I found the subject of Suez a fascinating source of insights into two important, timeless concerns of diplomacy. One was the interaction between advice and policy-making—especially the management of the grey space between analysis and advice on the one hand, and the politics of policy-making on the other. It is the upper level battle space in which senior officials must operate, and it is under-studied.

The second question arising from Suez was how to approach relationships with allies when the global relativities of national power are changing. It is a question that involves notions of identity and values, as well as strategic, economic and political concerns. For Australia, ultimately, Suez was not about Menzies, or Nasser, or the Canal. It was, essentially, about the dilemmas of identity politics, and adapting to changing realities of national power. And because it went to the heart of what drives alliances, it raised questions for Australia in the present era.

Australia had joined the UK in seeking to reverse the nationalization by Egypt of the Suez Canal Company in July 1956 following the abrupt withdrawal of the possibility of securing US and British funding for the construction of the Aswan High Dam, the centrepiece of Nasser's plans for modernisation of the Egyptian economy. At the request of the United States and Britain, Menzies led a delegation to Cairo seeking, without success, to persuade Nasser to relinquish control of the Canal.

Menzies was at pains to show his was not a 'negotiation' with Nasser but rather a presentation and explanation of the proposals arising from the London conference of Canal user countries. He was keen to attribute some blame to Eisenhower for the outcome, but he was hardly bothered by it: he had gained a measure of international prominence and positive political focus within Australia for playing a part, and it stood him in good stead with Eden and others whose approval he desired.

From British and French perspectives, Nasser's refusal was an outcome they welcomed, as part of 'clearing the deck' for attempting to fulfil their undeclared ambition of Nasser's removal from power. From Dulles' perspective, the mission, like the Suez Canal Users Association fiasco that came in its wake, was a means of buying time for tempers (hopefully) to cool in London. In that limited sense, Dulles also was at least somewhat successful. Although it probably mattered little to the personal and political calculus of either man, Menzies' discussions with Nasser were not acrimonious most of the time—although Nasser rose to the theatrical possibilities of the occasion by threatening to walk out when Menzies rather clumsily told him there would not be a problem unless Nasser failed to agree.

Although later negotiations under UN auspices showed signs of resolving the dispute, Anglo-French forces invaded Egypt in early November 1956, supposedly to protect the Suez Canal from fighting between Egypt and Israel. In fact, the attack, launched initially by Israel in late October, was part of a plan conceived by France and Israel, and coordinated with the United Kingdom, seeking to achieve the overthrow of Nasser through the humiliation of a major military defeat.

At the direction of Menzies, who had the enthusiastic backing of almost all of his Cabinet except the foreign minister, Richard Casey, Australia gave strong support to the actions of Britain and France. It did so in the UN Security Council, where it was a member at the time, in very limited company. However, the outcome—a cease-fire followed by withdrawal imposed on the UK and France by Eisenhower, the humiliation of Eden and the UK Government, and the end of Eden's political career—was as inevitable as it was predictable. Australia's diplomatic relations with Egypt were severed by the Egyptians on 6 November 1956 and were not restored until late 1959. Australia became part of the UK imperial twilight in the Middle East.

Most historians point to ideological blinkering and systemic weaknesses under Menzies in the formulation of foreign policy where Britain was concerned. Moreover, my research assistant Miguel Galsim found that Menzies was in possession of correspondence between Eden and Eisenhower, highlighting Eisenhower's rejection of Eden's arguments for the use of force, which he withheld from his Cabinet colleagues. And although there is no report in the Australian Archives of his meeting with Eisenhower on 3 August 1956, we know from an American summary that Menzies was told by Eisenhower that he hoped the UK and France would exercise restraint.

But it would probably have made little difference if Menzies had shared that advice. Throughout the crisis, the intellectual quality of debate within the Menzies Cabinet regarding Suez was abysmal. And when the conflict broke out, Cabinet's determination to support the UK was based entirely on political grounds, unencumbered by strategic analysis, willingness to question UK motives, consideration of possible consequences for US-Australia relations, or even any assessment of Eden's prospects for success. There was a general feeling in Cabinet of condescension toward the United States, including references to the need to 'tone up' the US approach to align with that of the UK. Analysis of regional political realities was entirely absent. Casey counselled restraint, but Casey's unsolicited advice went unheeded.

Throughout the crisis, those External Affairs officials regarded by Menzies as 'Casey's men', including the Secretary of External Affairs, Arthur Tange, were marginalised. Tange was excluded from the meetings between Menzies and Nasser. Later, when Eisenhower insisted on the withdrawal of UK and French forces, Tange tried to dissuade Menzies from criticism of the US role. He failed. In the complex nexus between politics, personalities and foreign policy advice, romanticised notions of a British Australian identity — Tina Turner's 'sweet, old-fashioned notion'—impacted powerfully upon Australia's policy choices on Suez. And they did so despite obvious shifts in the relativities of national power in the post-World War II Middle East.

Officials skirted the question of whether, as the US insisted, Suez was being used by the UK merely as a pretext for a reassertion of British power against Nasser and revisionist tendencies sweeping the Middle East. External Affairs never examined and offered advice whether the overthrow of Nasser (as distinct from military pressure to leverage diplomacy) served Australia's interests—including whether it was appropriate, feasible and sustainable.

Most surprisingly, it did not highlight the potential for damage to Australia's relations with Washington that could arise from too close an association with Eden over the issue. In practice, Australia directed its diplomatic energy toward goals that were beyond reach, such as the restoration of international control of the Canal; or the question of freedom of navigation through the Canal, whose disruption was perhaps a 'disconcerting possibility', as a Cabinet submission put it, but was far from an actual or unmanageable threat.

Meanwhile, British flattery of Menzies spoke to mythologies about a shared British identity, and nobility of purpose, that were largely immune from Casey's concerns and arguments. Menzies, the Anglophile Australian nationalist, wanted Eden to throw him the ball. Eden was happy to oblige by waving him off to Cairo to deal with Nasser. Menzies repaid the favour by giving Eden the strongest possible personal and political support as events unfolded and the British position deteriorated, maintaining direct contact with Eden throughout the crisis, mainly through the UK High Commission in Canberra and only very rarely through the Australian diplomatic communications network. There is no evidence of inputs by External Affairs to his correspondence with Eden.

My monograph also provided an opportunity to describe one of the most remarkable, but almost unknown, moments in Australian diplomacy.[45] Some 11 days after President Eisenhower had imposed his will on the British and broken Eden's career as Prime Minister, Menzies took it upon himself (with Eden's enthusiastic support) to write to Eisenhower castigating him for the US stance. The idea of interjecting unsolicited advice into the spat between Eden and Eisenhower should, as Banjo Paterson would have said, made even the boldest hold their breath. But Menzies waved his proverbial stockwhip and told Eisenhower that the British role—furiously rejected by Eisenhower—had been proper and correct.

Menzies said that the United States had failed to understand the British position, that the US handling of the issue in the United Nations had been inopportune, and had left the British and French 'not only rebuked but humiliated', to the benefit of the Russians and Nasser. He warned Eisenhower that unless the UN peacekeeping force being assembled as the Anglo-French forces withdrew was 'cohesive, powerful and effective enough' to settle the 'great issues' (that is, as Menzies put it elsewhere, to prevent Nasser from remaining 'in possession of the spoils') then 'quick consideration may conceivably be given to resuming military operations …'.

---

[45]See my *Australia, Menzies and Suez*, pp. 80-83.

It fell to Casey, who was in New York, to deliver the message to Eisenhower in Washington. Fortunately for Casey, Eisenhower did not want to see him. While he waited for an appointment, Casey and his senior accompanying External Affairs official, James Plimsoll shared the Menzies message with their British counterparts and came up with what Casey described as a 'summary of its main points', which they handed over, together with the Menzies letter, to the Acting US Secretary of State, Herbert Hoover Jnr. The 'summary' (which Casey wisely did not send back to Canberra until after his meeting) and the record of the discussion with Hoover excluded the condescending language employed by Menzies, and the inflammatory reference to possibly resuming the conflict, in favour of some gracious comments about US strength and prestige, and the importance of the United States and Britain resolving their differences. Eisenhower provided a cool but courteous response to Menzies a week later, and the exchange of letters between the heads of government sank without trace.

There is no doubt that the finest diplomacy exercised by Australia during the Suez Crisis was the part played by Casey and Plimsoll between Menzies and Eisenhower.

I have outlined the history of Australia's role during the Suez Crisis here in some detail because, as noted earlier, it raises questions about contemporary challenges facing Australian foreign policy, when a rebalancing of the global order is in progress.

Suez posed, or perhaps in retrospect should have posed, fundamental questions for Australia about the decline of an empire to which, in many respects, Australia and most Australians still wished to belong. For Menzies, and his senior political figures, there was a deep reluctance to acknowledge the irreversible changes that had taken place in the Middle East region and in Britain's standing globally, including in relation to the United States. Cabinet discussions—and inputs from External Affairs—were almost entirely devoid of discussion of what those changes meant for Australia's interests. Australia's determination to back Britain was driven primarily by political instincts and identity politics, not strategic calculation. And the political position hardened over time.

In the cauldron of human and political chemistry of Cabinet, there was unwillingness to breathe the rarefied air of uncertainty posed by the declining global position of Britain in the post-colonial era. Casey therefore had few supporters in his opposition to the use of force against Nasser. At no stage at the political level was the Suez crisis the subject of fundamental questioning about the values Australia was seeking to uphold by extending unadulterated support to the United Kingdom.

Therein lies a contemporary dilemma for Australia as it confronts change in the relativities of power in the Asia-Pacific. The dictum about having no permanent friends, only permanent interests, is only partially correct. Suez showed that the perception of interests is not easily separated from notions of identity. Where Britain was concerned, Menzies and his cohort were unwilling—personally, politically, ideologically and intellectually—to confront the challenge of change consequent upon Britain's post-war decline. Suez demonstrated that the loyalty we may feel toward a relationship, which in the case of the United States is also a relationship which for excellent reasons we seek constantly to cultivate, may contribute to failure at the political level to pay sufficient attention to tectonic changes affecting our future.

By the standards and expectations of the time he served, mostly after the Second World War, Robert Menzies was a fine Prime Minister. It would be unfair to judge him by his Anglophile pretensions, or his lamentable performance over Suez. His government reshaped the focus and direction of Australia's foreign policy toward the Asia-Pacific. At home, he brought a progressive vision of Australia to fruition. He was an exceptionally gifted politician, who towered above his contemporaries on all sides of politics. Even Menzies' role in regard to Suez has some utility, in retrospect, insofar as it reminds us of the perils of political leadership that seeks to function within an echo chamber of assumptions and perceptions of national interest. It is a clear warning against setting notions of identity ahead of inclusive and constructive debate about strategic perils and possibilities.

Alongside the failures of the Menzies government at the leadership and Cabinet levels over Suez, in the 1950s External Affairs similarly lacked a forward-looking, objective, policy analysis mechanism that could connect the Suez crisis to a much larger picture, correctly interpret British motivations and US intentions, and invite attention to the policy questions the decline of Britain in the post-war era posed for Australia. Instead, insurmountable political and bureaucratic odds faced those officials who might otherwise have urged and facilitated greater clarity of thinking from ministers about Australia's policy objectives, and the means of achieving them in a changing global and regional context.

The importance of having such a mechanism examining and recommending policy to ministers is at least as important now as it was then.

More than six decades have passed since the Suez crisis. We have seen the unfolding of a very different Middle East, and a very different Australia. But Suez still provides a wealth of evidence and insight to those who seek to understand the factors that may shape outcomes arising from the complex relationship between, on the one hand, the demands of providing policy advice to government, and on the other hand the shaping of policy outcomes at the political level. And it reminds us that when questions of identity become entangled with shifts in the relativities of power, and sober, balanced advice is ignored, or worse still, not offered at critical moments, Suez still has cautionary lessons for us all.

Chapter 24

Australia and the Middle East

Although some countries may be more exposed than Australia, no country is immune from the consequences of what unfolds in the Middle East. A secure Middle East protects and promotes Australian interests. Moreover, history suggests that if western countries choose to turn their backs on the region, it can bite them on the bum. Despite the rise of other urgent concerns in our economic and security environment, it deserves to remain a major focus for Australian diplomacy and policy makers.

For all the reasons outlined in earlier chapters, it is a region in transition whose economic and political trajectory is uncertain. That uncertainty is set to continue, fostered by uneven economic performance, security and political challenges to the authority of governments, deep-seated rivalries between leading regional governments, and the entrenchment of sectarian divisions untempered by balanced economic growth. Developments in the region affect the interests of the major global powers, pose serious challenges to multilateral institutions and alliance relationships important to Australia, and command the attention of significant audiences in Australia and elsewhere.

Because of the political and strategic importance accorded to the region in Washington, Australian policy toward the Middle

East will continue to be shaped to a large extent by concern for the anticipated consequences of policy decisions for the effective management of the ANZUS alliance and Australian influence in Washington. However, Australia's increasingly close relations with the Arab states of the Persian Gulf mean that perceptions on their part of the role played by the United States should also matter to us.

Like the United States, and most other western countries, Australia has a direct stake in the stability of the Persian Gulf. There is, of course, a substantial overlap between Australian and US interests in addressing the challenges of terrorism and jihadist ideology directed against western institutions. We have developed worthwhile defence and intelligence links with several Arab countries of the region, initially because of the need to ensure the protection of Australian forces deployed in conjunction with the US presence. Those networks, which rely upon personal trust and familiarity, should continue to be fostered.

It is an important, but highly competitive, market for Australian primary products and a growing source of support for Australian tertiary industry, including the education and tourism sectors. Global economic security and Australia's economic well-being depend to some extent on Middle East energy (both oil and gas) being readily available to major consumers of our raw materials. We would prefer to see governments in the region that are accountable, stable and progressive in the values they promote. We have a lightly-staffed but comprehensive and competent diplomatic presence across the region.

Australia is not an important or consequential interlocutor on the major security and political questions shaping the regional outlook, but Australian firms, individuals and embassies have sustained an enviable reputation for Australia in the Arab world, and Iran, over many decades. In large part, that situation arises because in the eyes of the region we remain without historical baggage. As I discussed, in relation to my experience in Egypt and Jordan, few of those with whom we deal resent, or are even aware of our long history of military activity in the region. We are seen as honest and reliable interlocutors from a country devoid of self-seeking political agendas where the region is concerned. We should be content for that limited profile to remain the case.

In the multilateral domain, however, our ability to command respect and to secure regional support on tangible matters, especially for Australian candidacies, will be made easier if our overall public policy positions are broadly in step with other western countries regarding issues of particular sensitivity. Prominent among those issues will be western responses to Israeli settlement activity, the status of Jerusalem, the rights of minorities, and dealings with Iran and Syria.

The problem here is that these issues are rarely addressed in Canberra on their foreign policy merits: they are primarily issues of domestic political policy in which the views of those who are strongly supportive of Israeli views and concerns vastly outweigh all others. Politics and propaganda in speech-making aside, I have rarely found that ministers are positively disposed in private toward the behaviour of Israel toward the Palestinians. Most display a sophisticated appreciation of, and interest in, the political and other complexities of the region. The foreign ministers and others to whom I worked (and who, in some cases, continued to seek my views after I left the Public Service) consistently welcomed objective assessments of regional developments and their likely implications for Australia.

Policy toward the Middle East, however, is the prerogative and usually a particular interest of the Prime Minister of the day. And in that tight-knit policy circle, the comfort and political instincts of enjoying the favour of Israel's supporters, sometimes combined with superficial or untested assumptions about supporting alliance relationships, and the cold reality of political calculation, electorate by electorate, all but exclude the likelihood of Australia taking a public stance critical of Israel. If anything, there is a tendency—which I deplore—to wear isolation from the positions taken by other western countries where Israel is concerned, on issues ranging from Jerusalem to Jewish settlements, as a badge of honour, probably with potential to be converted to political currency in the domestic context.

Notwithstanding that particular political reality (and despite my demonstrated inability to affect it) I believe it remains in Australia's interest to see the successful promulgation of values we believe to be of universal application in the Middle East.

This is a moment of perilous opportunity for the region, unlike any it has seen since the end of the Second World War. As I discussed earlier, generational changes, graduate unemployment, global connectivity and debate over what it means to be Arab or Iranian, Muslim and 'modern' are reshaping Arab and Iranian society. Attitudes in the Arab world toward authority, and gender, are changing. Demographic and environmental pressures will pose enormous social challenges in most countries of the region in the coming decade, particularly if economic growth remains inadequate to allow remaking of traditional or familiar, but increasingly dysfunctional, authoritarian political and economic systems.

Assisting those who genuinely support the values we would wish to be respected among coming generations in the Arab world is among the most sensitive and difficult of all policy questions. I suggested earlier that Arab values will only be rebooted by those societies themselves. Unless pursued with great care and sensitivity, external ambitions to affect that process directly are likely to produce unintended consequences, mostly to the disadvantage of those reformists we would wish to see succeed.

For Australia, the more productive approach over coming decades would be to seek opportunities for advancing people to people and institution to institution cooperation through which we may expose others to our own example and experience, and in doing so demonstrate indirectly the values and methods that others may (or may not) see as relevant to the needs of their region.

Such an approach obviously will apply especially in areas where Australia's reputation for providing expertise relevant to regional countries' needs is highest. Food security concerns, for example, loom large for the region, and Australia has almost unique skills and experience to share in that regard. The termination of Australian government assistance to dryland farming research in the region through the International Centre for Agriculture Research in Dry Areas (ICARDA) was especially unfortunate: not only was ICARDA an institution that highlighted Australian skills and technology, but the end of Australian support limited the contact between Australian and Arab researchers and research programs to our mutual disadvantage. We should also, however, look beyond agriculture and seek more such opportunities for capacity building using Australian expertise—including in such non-traditional areas as regulatory reform, taxation, curriculum development, mining regulation and environment law.

At the same time, we should remain consistent in affirming the core values underpinning our foreign policy in regard to multilateral cooperation, including the role of United Nations agencies, notably UNRWA, and the UN Security Council. We are a substantial player on the international stage, often exercising on the ground a degree of quiet and constructive influence in multilateral settings larger than many Australians might expect. And in the Middle East context, as elsewhere, multilateral approaches to building peace and security, while imperfect, nevertheless serve Australian interests better than any departure from the obligations upon state actors and the moral authority arising from international law.

We should focus on lending practical support to programs to strengthen the observance of human rights in the region, rather than taking a higher profile than other western countries on concerns about the record of individual countries. But we should not disassociate ourselves from criticism of Israel, Iran, Turkey, Syria and others—including both state and non-state actors—where their actions impact upon Australian interest in the emergence of a stable, secure and progressive region, and challenge respect for international humanitarian law.

Looking beyond our multilateral interests—and as I alluded to in regard to the lessons of the 1956 Suez Crisis for Australia—in the Middle East context, as elsewhere, securing Australia's interests within the ANZUS alliance framework requires continued calibration of the nature and timing of Australian commitments and stances, based on careful evaluation of where the balance of Australian interests may lie. Responses to the needs of the US alliance can take a variety of forms, and any future calls for Australian military involvement in the Middle East, in particular, need to be weighed against clear-sighted evaluation of the goals, objectives, achievability and sustainability of US approaches.

As was the case regarding Iraq in 2003, we will have to manage adroitly the policy outcomes that political instincts and judgments determine, seeking to harmonise those policy directions with such capabilities as may exist at any given time. But beyond such operational and planning concerns, it is important to be forthright in conveying to government the risks—strategic, reputational and other—that ultimately we cannot entirely control.

The capacity to make such judgements and offer advice accordingly will hinge upon having the expertise independently to evaluate regional conditions, and to assess the potential risks and benefits of possible Australian actions. The area skills, including language skills, relevant to the region, and the networks developed since 1973 in the Middle East among regional defence and security circles need actively to be maintained within DFAT and the Australian Defence Force.

There is also a need to build area skills in other Australian government agencies contributing their expertise to policy deliberations. Ministerial visits to the region, both federal and state, are essential for the networking opportunities they provide. Investment of resources in the capacity of embassies in the region and in Washington to keep Canberra abreast of US policy thinking in regard to the Middle East will be vital to the protection of Australian interests in an environment—both in the United States and in the Middle East—which promises to be less predictable than before.

Finally, we should recognise, as I suggested earlier, that we face the further possibility that after decades of unfulfilled promises, hope will be offered, possibly to increasingly radicalised audiences, by those whose views and values are deeply antagonistic to our own.

We may well succeed over time in degrading the potency of the vision offered by Islamic State, al-Qaeda and other jihadist groups, partly through military measures to reverse their momentum. We can, and should, highlight their cynicism, debunk their narratives, castigate their brutality and condemn those governments who travel with them. We should be consistent in upholding and defending our own values while we do so. The rules of war must be respected on our side, even when those we fight, and some of those who fight for us, choose to ignore them.

But if we fail to support hope among the peoples of the region for a future consistent with the values we would like to see emerge there, we will not have secured our future, or helped them to secure theirs.

Chapter 25

Australian Archaeologists in the Middle East

I could not conclude this memoir without making at least a brief reference to the importance to me personally, and to Australia's interests in the Middle East, of the part played by Australian archaeologists. Diplomacy and archeology are a rewarding mixture, even though at first glance there may not appear to be much in common between them.

The most important tasks of diplomacy are to ensure your views are understood, and your national interests are advanced. Diplomats deal with contemporary history, living personalities, unfolding issues and politics whose nuances may not be obvious to researchers one hundred, or fifty or even twenty years later. Diplomacy demands an acute awareness of the human condition: the key to one's effectiveness lies in understanding the person with whom you are dealing; his or her hopes and fears, beliefs and perceptions, and in still getting your message across.

After a thousand years, with the added difficulty of altered contemporary perceptions, a great deal of context inevitably will be lost. Archaeologists may have physical evidence to assist them, if they are fortunate; and historians may have records and narratives to assist them. I doubt, however, that many archaeologists or historians could bring to bear the sort of intimate understanding in real time of what makes people tick, and what makes events happen, that diplomats bring to their work.

Working environments aside, where diplomats and archaeologists may differ most of all is that unlike archaeologists, the past fills most diplomats with misgiving. Our instincts usually are averse to touching it. In almost any circumstances references to the past can have unpredictable consequences; and there are few things diplomats loathe more than unpredictability.

We seek to manage problems, and preferably resolve them. In the search for constructive approaches, we generally leave it to poets and intellectuals to seize hold of old wounds. It is not for diplomats to squeeze them until the pus flows.

To the lay person, archeology conjures a different range of professional skills to those demanded by diplomacy. It is a profession which demands exact science; practical precision, often despite working under physically demanding conditions; and an inordinate amount of time spent in recording and destroying in order to record some more. Archaeologists interpret material and publish by utilising insights from an extraordinary range of professional skills, backgrounds and experience. I cannot identify an academic area that requires higher levels, simultaneously, of intellectual ability and physical endurance than archeology.

Archaeologists are more familiar than most diplomats with the roots from which we have developed. They live among the trials we have endured as societies, and evidence of the frailty of human achievements. They know, literally, where skeletons are buried; how long they have been there and sometimes who put them there. They even keep records of which way they were heading when they were found.

Archaeologists also delight in uncovering enigmas: the late Bill

Jobling found an inscription in Wadi Rum which said "Romans always conquer". Conquer what? If a Roman wrote it (as it was in Greek, that would seem likely) was he a conqueror? Who was he trying to impress? Did the people he conquered read Greek? If not, was his next step to teach them? As the Roman takeover of the Nabatean kingdom in AD106 was a political arrangement, rather than the result of a major conquest, could the graffiti have been written by a subtle Nabatean asking why his tribe could not be as clever as these Romans?

Could he have been taking a gentle dig at those terribly competent and earnest but arguably less than imaginative Romans, with their urge to conquer everything in sight, even when it didn't amount to much? If there is a basis for observing contemporary reality as a step toward understanding the past, guile would surely then as now have been part of local realities. Could there have been, beside the inscription, a wayside stall dispensing drinks (at locally-adjusted prices) to lonely, weary, dusty legionnaires, far removed from Dalmatia or wherever, who needed to feel welcome somewhere? Would it have been worth investing in the time required to learn a little Greek, just for the sake of the family business?

Walking with Basil Hennessy, Alan Walmsley, John Tidmarsh, Pam Watson and Chris Browne around Pella, seeing the ways in which societies continued to function despite natural and man-made disasters, and understanding the processes and drivers of change, as well as the changes themselves, helped me to bring the modern Middle East into perspective. That is not to suggest that there is anything cyclical about Middle East history—to do so would be a political minefield well beyond this book—but rather to acknowledge that the human element of history, and its capacity to rebuild, is its most enduring aspect.

Australian archaeologists also have a remarkable ability to bring civilizations to life. To see Ben Churcher creating a

Natufian society from a semicircle of stones; to wonder with Richard Wright at the emergence of lithic assemblages around the globe within a rather short period; to watch Basil Hennessy transform a piece of chocolate-on-white ware into a short history of the development of human creativity; to see Maggie O'Hea reconstructing the context of a shackled human sacrifice; or Jodie Benton searching for the library at Pella but turning up instead a Bronze Age toilet were wonderful experiences.

So too was accompanying Phil Edwards and Phil Macumber at a site south of the Dead Sea perhaps as ancient as the Olduvai Gorge. Coming around a bend in the creek bed, I was confronted for a memorable moment by the sight of a short, dark, hairy slightly bow-legged hominid gazing at a pebble tool. The hominid in question was only connected to the twentieth century by the fact he was wearing jeans and an Akubra.

Australian archaeologists working in the Middle East have academic reputations of the highest quality: I recall vividly the impression made upon the Crown Prince of Jordan when, at Prince Hassan's request, and without any prior warning, Alan Walmsley provided, without obvious effort, a superb ten-minute oral synopsis of the outcomes of a three day academic conference held at Yarmouk University.

But Australian archaeologists bring more than purely academic achievement with them. They have also earned widespread respect because of their reputation for sensitivity towards the rights and prerogatives of their hosts, and for probity and decent dealing. Naguib Kanawati in Egypt, Basil Hennessy and Tony McNicol in Jordan, Dan Potts in the United Arab Emirates, Ina Kehrberg-Ostraz and her Polish husband Antik at Jerash, and a great many others earned pre-eminence among their peers, and among informed circles in the region, for precisely those reasons. The pursuit of permissions to dig, and the division of the finds between Australian teams and their national hosts have invariably been managed with sensitivity and mutual respect. And, on my postings around the region, Australian teams from Luxor to Pella were extraordinarily generous with their time and patience as they welcomed visitors, both foreign and local, to see their work.

In short, the tasks for our embassies in building networks and pursuing Australian interests would be far more difficult without our archaeologists. In Jordan, the friendship between Basil Hennessy and Crown Prince Hassan undoubtedly shaped the tenor of the bilateral relationship. And, after Stephen Bourke escorted the ever-enthusiastic Barry Jones and the then Jordanian Minister for Antiquities (and later Prime Minister) Abdul Karim Kabariti around a series of goat trails at Pella, an event calculated to bring on cabinet reshuffles at any moment in both countries, Kabariti decided he had a particular affection for Australians.

There is usually a diplomat in the soul of the successful archaeologist. Some of my closest friends and respected colleagues during my career in DFAT—such as Ian Biggs, Ross Burns and Robert Merrillees—successfully combined the intellectual training and academic discipline of archaeology with their profession as diplomats. And if one could go back in time, and Ramses the Second had felt the need for some diplomatic advice before taking on the Hittites at Qadesh, or Mut-ba'alu had wanted some help with his correspondence with the Pharaoh Akhenaten, I have no doubt there would have been Australian archaeologists who could have risen to the occasion.

Chapter 26

On Turning Away

I would fain go back to the old grey river,
To the old bush days when our hearts were light,
But alas! those days they have fled for ever,
They are like the swans that have swept from sight.
And I know full well that the strangers' faces
Would meet us now in our dearest places;
For our day is dead and has left no traces
But the thoughts that live in my mind to-night.
A.B. (Banjo) Paterson, Black Swans (1893)

I decided to write these professional memoirs, and to commit to paper my views on several of the issues with which I engaged during my career, for two reasons. First, it had become clear when I reached my early 70s that age was catching up with my body. My old friend Ian Haig once told me that if I wanted to survive in the Middle East more than a few years, I should stick to mutton chops and whisky. It was well-meaning advice I never took. But I recognise that the opportunity to write on those matters, for anyone who might be interested, could one day be lost, possibly without warning. I have also reached a stage in life where I have time to look back, and reflect. Retirement has its charms in that respect.

The second reason for writing is that I no longer have the degree of connection to current events in the Middle East that I once enjoyed. After the end of my posting to Cairo in 2008 until early 2016 I continued to have close engagement with Egypt, mainly because of my work as a non-executive director on the board of Centamin. But since that time I have made few visits to Cairo, or elsewhere in the Middle East. My last visit to Iran was in 2016, to Jordan and Saudi Arabia 2012 and to Syria in 2010. Most of those with whom I interacted in those countries and elsewhere in the region are now either retired from public life, or dead.

In Canberra, although I continue to publish with Lowy and other think tanks, mainly on Syria, much of the past three years was devoted to completing my research on Australia and the Suez crisis, working from home and in the Australian National Archives. My last academic book on the contemporary Middle East, Egypt and the Politics of Change in the Arab Middle East, was published in 2013 and sank without trace. Although I still assist with supervision of some PhD candidates and give guest lectures on Palestinian refugees my adjunct appointments at the Australian National University were not able to be extended beyond 2019. I maintain cordial relations with those with whom I served in the Department of Foreign Affairs and Trade, but they too are retiring and passing away. I have provided some support to the Diplomatic Academy at DFAT, but I have almost no contact with those officers in the Department who work currently on the Middle East.

The nature of the domestic environment within which Australian diplomats must function has also changed, and not for the better. Ministerial attention spans will always vary according to personality and workloads, but there is a shift within the Department toward giving priority to dealing with trade and consular crisis management ahead of the research and intellectual effort that underpins effective foreign policy planning and advocacy. Of course Ministers will determine their own portfolio priorities and work methods, and consular and trade issues can have real-world human consequences that justify the allocation of time and scarce departmental resources. But the effectiveness of our foreign policy machinery depends on more than our capacity to respond positively and constructively to trade and consular challenges, or enhancing passport availability, or helping to meet the pressures and demands upon ministers of the news cycle.

I am not privy to the policy planning and policy advice being undertaken by DFAT in recent years, but my impression is that policy, increasingly, is created in ministerial offices, with DFAT seen more as an implementing agency for those outcomes. That is a deeply problematic direction for any government, or government department, to take.

The most impressive heads of mission for whom I worked, such as the cerebral John Rowland, and other notable practitioners of diplomacy whom I admired, such as George Kennan, and many of the colleagues of my generation in Canberra were individuals of the highest intellectual calibre. They wrote with courage, clarity and profound insight on policy issues arising from changing circumstances. I am sure the intellectual standard of departmental officers remains of a similar order to that of previous generations—the Department now also draws on a wider range of talent, irrespective of gender, in its recruitment and promotion practices—but whereas it was once the case that senior officers were expected to develop and test their ideas, insights and experience in the form of despatches and cables, including on policy issues, the final decade or two of my time in the Department saw a shift to reporting by cable that was prone to be concise rather than nuanced. It was directed in its brevity toward immediate briefing needs, rather than the evaluation of trends and their consequences for Australian interests.

I became a better analyst for having to defend my views, including in debates with colleagues in Canberra and other posts. The capacity of the Department to provide policy advice in Canberra probably improved as well through the forthright exchanges in which posts engaged from time to time. But under the Howard Government, despatches became a thing of the past. Although I wrote a series of valedictory cables from Cairo, which were despatches in all but name, by the time I retired it had become almost unthinkable to reflect on broader issues, let alone to challenge policy settings, in cable traffic.

Finally, I sense I am once again at a familiar stage of the cycle, through which all of those who work on the Middle East usually pass, of weariness with the passions and the seemingly insoluble political problems the region presents. I am also tired of the incessant back-biting and intemperate attitudes of far too many of those who share the cyber space reserved for Middle East issues. The antidote to that weariness is usually to be found through personal contact with friends in the region: their resilience, calm humour and determination to survive have always had a restorative effect; but now with limited opportunity to travel, I no longer have that privilege.

The cumulative effect of these matters is that I feel my insight into current events, my capacity and even my concern to explain and inform wider audiences on them is declining. It does not prevent me from continuing a certain amount of academic activity, mainly directed toward introducing students to the complexity of the political and moral questions posed by the region. However I now do so with a growing sense that I have very little to say that is new, important or interesting.

In short, I am an ageing Middle East war horse, now turned

out to pasture. And that is not necessarily an appropriate position from which to comment on the contemporary Middle East.

Understanding Arab history and Arab cultures, and acquiring familiarity with key actors and events of the recent past as seen through Arab eyes, will remain key to interpreting the region. But much has changed in Arab society in the past five decades, under the cumulative influence of education, literacy, nutrition, internet connectivity, access to technologies enabling new forms of both mobilisation and repression, and exposure to external models of business practice, gender empowerment and other values unknown to the region a generation or two ago. The search for a post-oil economic future for most Arab countries, amidst a demographic explosion and, at the time of writing, a pandemic, is far removed from the issues confronting someone who began his career in the Arab world during the oil boom of the early 1970s.

Unlike during the Cold War era, in the contemporary Middle East it frankly makes next to no difference on the ground what outsiders think or say. The challenges facing the region are now driven primarily by the countries of the region themselves, rather than, as was once sometimes the case, the outcome to varying degrees of strategic competition between outside parties. There has also been a blurring between what is local, regional and global among the forces shaping its future.

Understanding the region and its potential, for good or ill, is best undertaken by those who have experienced those changes themselves. I regret the waste of human potential I have seen in recent years. I will continue to argue that we should both speak, and act, according to our values because we want those values to be respected. It is in our interests for the international system to be strengthened by observation of those values.

But our primary responsibility should be to listen, and to respond, where we can, to those who carry the burdens and opportunities of a changing Middle East. It is Arabs, and Iranians, who must reboot their institutions according to their own sense of what it means to be Arab, or Iranian, in this century.

The children on my 70th birthday: Sam (an academic authority on Islamic art), Karmen (beside me), Kim and Tabitha (R).

I look back at my professional involvement in the Middle East with a sense of satisfaction in some areas, mixed with frustration in others. Frustration arose mainly when I witnessed policy choices being made under intense political pressure, or by people simply responding to their instincts, emotions and predispositions without sufficient knowledge and understanding of the region. Rarely, if ever, have I seen informed reflection, in the grey space between policy advice and policy outcomes, on the likely consequences of particular decisions when domestic political considerations are involved.

But I also accept three realities about working on the region.

First, Middle East policy is not a morality play. I have argued that upholding our values protects our interests. But it is in the nature of things that expediency, whether political or alliance-related, sometimes shapes decisions. The logic of strategy is not always consistent with the logic of politics. As those Australian Cabinet deliberations with which I am broadly familiar clearly demonstrate, on issues ranging from Suez to Iraq, the greater the strategic import of a particular decision, the more likely it is to be based primarily on political judgements, visceral emotions and inclinations.

Second, it pays to be wary of assumptions based on one's own values and expectations, including in regard to political legitimacy, in dealing with the region. It is important to beware, especially, of narratives from urbane, English-speaking interlocutors that suit, by chance or by design, our own political leanings and values while all but erasing the voices and views that do not fit into such narratives. We have a professional, intellectual and moral duty to grapple with the complexity of Arab society. We must accept that views, interests, and values within Arab societies are more than likely to differ from our own: any apparent synchronicity of views should be cause for caution, as well as celebration.

Anyone who has worked on the region knows that both the assessment and the communication of strategic intent are especially challenging. Interpretations of past events and future trends are bound to be contested on both empirical and intellectual grounds. In the Arab world, messages about values and priorities matter; and when it comes to conveying the intent behind policy choices, the reception accorded to such messages will be shaped, if not driven, by demons of history, personalities, and collective memories and narratives.

Nor, because the region itself is far from static, do those factors shaping perceptions remain constant. As I have outlined earlier, experiencing the unstoppable forces of education, connectivity, demography, gender-based and other aspirations for empowerment, opportunity and dignity, the Middle East remains, as my Egyptian friends would say, pregnant with possibilities.

Third, and finally, I have learnt that it is in the nature of the Middle East for problems to linger, and grow more complex, if not increasingly intractable. It is fine to be an academic or commentator on the bridge of the Middle East Titanic, alternating between expressing hope and smelling ice. It is rewarding as an academic to present students with the complexity and the quandaries presented by Middle East issues, and to encourage them to reflect on their own values in debating them. But some sympathy is warranted for those who seek to deal constructively with those problems, and the ambiguities and moral and practical conundrums they usually entail, rather than merely admiring the issues from afar.

The Middle East is a diabolically complex region to understand. It is a potential policy and career graveyard for those who choose to enter it. Presenting, as an official, arguments in favour of one policy option over another is a professional responsibility which tests one's values, intellectual honesty, and often one's endurance.

The choices available to policy makers may sometimes be presented as being between principles—especially a supposed search for order (amidst incipient violence and the mutual demonisation of regimes and their critics and opponents) versus somewhat ill-defined notions of justice. Whatever their appeal to western audiences, within the Middle East the latter notions may appear, all too frequently, to pose existential identity and other concerns, thereby rendering compromise impossible.

In practice—whether it be responding to Mongols advancing from Baghdad to Aleppo in the thirteenth century, or seeking ways of persuading or applying pressure to the behaviour of recalcitrant regimes in the modern era—the decisions we have to live with, and the region has to live with, are usually, and probably have always been, policy choices between bad and much worse.

For my part, I would like to be remembered as someone who, in struggling with those issues throughout his career, loved his wife and family—and was loved by them—without reservation; who took personal and professional responsibility seriously, and who refused to compromise his integrity and his sense of what was right. Even as my career took me into some improbable places and challenging experiences, occasionally with more than a little adrenalin involved, I remained at heart a country boy with a sense of humour. I hope I never lost the honesty and directness that I inherited from my parents.

I made mistakes. I was not always a great communicator. I did not always recognise the possibility, and the risks, that others would see issues differently. Brought up to be self-reliant, I never became a networker, either as an official or as an academic. My judgement of people and situational requirements was sometimes wrong. Occasionally, based on very little more than instinct born of historical experience and hard-earned personal insight; and with a tendency to focus intently, even single-mindedly, on the pursuit of key outcomes, I assumed, erroneously, that others understood and shared the reasoning behind my views and behaviour. Whereas I was capable of being articulate on policy issues, and in the media, I was never comfortable or adept at self-promotion.

When I look back at the key moments that shaped my career, or sometimes the series of small events and incidents that had that effect, my usual concern is to ask myself whether I did the right thing. What was right, of course, is open to debate, and one's views can change according to many factors. But it still comes down to a question of whether, at the time, I acted according to some sense of principle.

A few such moments stand out. I went down in flames on

the policy question of Palestinian self-determination when the Howard government came to power in 1996. Few others are aware of what had happened at the time, including the battles I fought within DFAT over the issue, only to be trumped by the Prime Minister. But I have never regretted doing so, despite the strain on me and the burden that placed on Jenny, and the fact that it led me to leave DFAT for a few years to work for UNRWA. Whereas a more career-minded and astute public servant might have gone with the flow, I tried to protect values that I believed mattered, both to Australia and to me personally.

None of those decisions on my part were taken lightly. They had considerable personal costs. But they forced me to think about what mattered most to me, and in doing so they helped to define who I am. I do not regard my approaches as a model for others. It would be perfectly understandable to attach a higher priority to other concerns, or to see such challenges in different ways and requiring different responses. But I would hope that in my case I thought through challenges by having regard to how I could live with, and explain the reasons, for any decision that I made.

If I made a positive difference, it was when I did my best to support others and demonstrate leadership, especially in Jordan during the Gulf war 1990/91; in responding to the Cairo bus crash, and helping to secure the release of George Forbes in South Sudan. And, where I encountered adversity in various forms I will always be grateful that I managed, with the help of my loving partner, family, close friends and colleagues, to keep those matters in perspective and to move on.

In doing these things I tried to convey my enthusiasm for the Middle East, in all its complexity. I supported those who chose to pursue their interests along that path. And, despite almost 50 years of exposure to the Arab world, I remained free of tribal delusions, except where Collingwood is concerned.

With Jenny Bowker, on the Darling River, 2020. (Photo credit: Liz Aitken)

Bibliography

Published books by the author are as follows:

Beyond Peace: the Search for Security in the Middle East (Lynne Rienner, 1996)

Palestinian Refugees: Mythology, Identity and the Search for Peace (Lynne Rienner, 2003)

Egypt and the Politics of Change in the Arab Middle East (Edward Elgar, 2010)

Australia, Menzies and Suez: Australian Policy Making on the Middle East Before, During and After the Suez Crisis (Australia in the World Series, Department of Foreign Affairs and Trade, 2019)

Australia and the Suez Crisis 1950-1957 (co-edited with Matthew Jordan) (Documents in Australian Foreign Policy Series, Department of Foreign Affairs and Trade, UNSW Press, April 2021).

Research papers, and articles relevant to this book include the following:

'Egypt: Diplomacy and Change', *Middle East Journal*, 67 (4) June 2013.

Ending Sykes-Picot: The Arab World and the West after 2011, (Durham University, September 2013).

'Playing second fiddle in a dysfunctional orchestra: Australia, Britain and the Suez Canal 1950-56', *Global Change, Peace and Security* 25, 2013, pp. 325-37.

'Beware the Return of Hope' *Inside Story* 15 January 2016.

'Challenges Mount Up' *The Interpreter,* Lowy Institute 22 May 2018.

'Syria: Is it Time to Talk with Assad?', *The Interpreter,* Lowy Institute 19 September 2019.

'Seven Lessons from Syria', *The Strategist,* Australian Strategic Policy Institute (ASPI) 28 November 2019.

'The Piano Stool: Israel, Palestine and the Arc of History', *Pearls and Irritations/EA Worldview,* 20 May 2020.

'Syria: The Consequences of Intellectual Failure and Moral Neglect', *The Interpreter,* Lowy Institute 12 August 2021.

Other works cited in this book are as follows:

Fouad Ajami, *The Dream Palace of the Arabs: A Generation's Odyssey* (Vintage Books, 1998)

Amnesty International, Israel's Apartheid Against Palestinians: A Look into Decades of Oppression and Domination, https://www.amnesty.org/en/latest/campaigns/2022/02/israels-system-of-apartheid/

Anthony H. Cordesman, 'The Need for Better Civil-Military Planning' in The Center for Strategic and International Studies (CSIS) *Global Forecast 2015* pp. 53-56.

Nur Arafeh, 'Which Jerusalem: Israel's Little-Known Master Plans', *Al-Shabaka,* 31 May 2016 https://al-shabaka.org/briefs/jerusalem-israels-little-known-master-plans/

Fabrice Balanche, 'The Assad Regime has Failed to Restore Full Sovereignty Over Syria', *PolicyWatch* 3433, Washington Institute for Near East Policy, 10 February 2021. https://www.washingtoninstitute.org/policy-analysis/assad-regime-has-failed-restore-full-sovereignty-over-syria

Julie-Anne Davies, 'Out of Africa' *The Bulletin,* 19 June 2007

Khaled Elgindy, 'Washington Has Enabled Israeli Extremism', *Foreign Policy,* 6 May 2021,

David Gardner, *Last Chance: The Middle East in the Balance* (I.B. Tauris, London 2012).

Shadi Hamid, 'The End of Pluralism', *The Atlantic*, 23 July 2014.

Yara Hawari, 'The Revival of People-to-People Projects: Relinquishing Israeli Accountability' *al-Shabaka*, 6 April 2021, https://al-shabaka.org/briefs/the-revival-of-people-to-people-projects-relinquishing-israeli-accountability/

Human Rights Watch, *A Threshold Crossed: Israeli Authorities and the Crimes of Apartheid and Persecution*, April 2021

Dylan Kassin and David Pollock, *'Arab Public Opinion on Arab-Israeli Normalization and Abraham Accords'* Washington Institute for Near East Policy, 15 July 2022, https://www.washingtoninstitute.org/policy-analysis/arab-public-opinion-arab-israeli-normalization-and-abraham-accords

Kennan, George F., *Memoirs: 1925-1950* (Little, Brown and Co., 1967)

Rami Khouri, 'This past year was rough for the Arab world, the worst is yet to come', *The New Arab*, 24 December, 2021, https://english.alaraby.co.uk/opinion/worst-yet-come-arab-world

Michael Lipka, *'Among Israeli Arabs and Jews, limited optimism about a two-state solution'*, Pew Research Center, 9 March 2016

Aron Lund, *'The Politics of Memory: Ten Years of War in Syria'*, *The Century Foundation*, 15 March 2021, https://tcf.org/content/commentary/politics-memory-ten-years-war-syria/

Hisham Melhem, 'The tyranny of the past, the uncertainty of the future', *Al-Arabiya*, 18 January, 2015.

Hisham Melhem, 'The Tyranny Lingers On', *Newlines Magazine*, 25 January 2021

Marwan Muasher, 'After the Two-State Solution: New Israel-Palestine Peace Efforts Must Focus on Equality',

Foreign Affairs, 27 April, 2021 https://www.foreignaffairs.com/articles/israel/2021-04-27/after-two-state-solution .

Caroline Rose and Alexander Soderholm, *The Captagon Threat: A Profile of Illicit Trade, Consumption and Regional Realities,* Newlines Institute for Strategy and Policy, 5 April 2022. https://newlinesinstitute.org/terrorism/the-captagon-threat-a-profile-of-illicit-trade-consumption-and-regional-realities/

Karim Sadjadpour, 'What the US Gets Wrong about Iran', *New York Times,* 12 August 2022. https://www.nytimes.com/2022/08/12/opinion/iran-america-nuclear-policy.html?referringSource=articleShare

Anne B. Shlay and Gillard Rosen, *Jerusalem: The Spatial Politics of a Divided Metropolis,* Polity, May 2015.

David Shipler, *Arab and Jew: Wounded Spirits in a Promised Land* (London: Bloomsbury, 1987)

Cameron Stuart, 'Our Man in Sudan', *The Weekend Australian Magazine,* September 15-16, 2007.

Nathan Thrall, 'A Day in the Life of Abed Salama', *The New York Review,* 19 March 2021.

Elsina Wainwright, *Building the Peace: Australia and the Future of Iraq,* Australian Strategic Policy Institute (ASPI), May 2003.

Shawline Publishing Group Pty Ltd
www.shawlinepublishing.com.au